Writing Prejudices

*The Psychoanalysis and Pedagogy of Discrimination
from Shakespeare to Toni Morrison*

Robert Samuels

STATE UNIVERSITY OF NEW YORK PRESS

Published by
State University of New York Press, Albany

Printed in the United States of America

For information, address State University of New York Press,
90 State Street, Suite 700, Albany, NY, 12207

Production by Cathleen Collins
Marketing by Anne M. Valentine

Library of Congress Cataloging in Publication Data

Samuels, Robert, 1961–
  Writing prejudices : the psychoanalysis and pedagogy of discrimination from
Shakespeare to Toni Morrison / Robert Samuels.
      p. cm.—(SUNY series in psychoanalysis and culture)
  Includes bibliographical references and index.
  ISBN 0-7914-4875-4 (alk. paper)—ISBN 0-7914-4876-2 (pbk. : alk. paper)
  1. English literature—History and criticism—Theory, etc. 2. Morrison, Toni—
Criticism and interpretation. 3. Psychoanalysis and literature—England.
4. Psychoanalysis and literature—United States. 5. Homophobia in literature.
6. Racism in literature. 7. Prejudices in literature. 8. Discrimination in literature.
I. Title. II. Series.
PR408.P8 S26 2001
820.9'353—dc21
                                                                                00-039479

10 9 8 7 6 5 4 3 2 1

WRITING PREJUDICES

SUNY series in Psychoanalysis and Culture
Edited by Henry Sussman

*For Benjamin, Isaac, Gabriel,
Mikah, and Remy*

CONTENTS

ACKNOWLEDGMENTS

I would like to thank Mark Bracher for all of his help on this project. I am also indebted to Marshall Alcorn, Elisabeth Young-Bruehl, Slavoj Žižek, James Peltz, Henry Sussman, Ronald Corthell, Jean Wyatt, Marcia Ian, and Steve Brown. This book would not have been possible without the support of my family and friends.

CHAPTER ONE

Introduction

Writing Prejudices argues that recent critical attempts to undermine prejudice through education in general, and literary studies in particular, have often failed because they have not taken into account: (1) the different forms of prejudice; (2) the role played by homophobia in racism and sexism; (3) the structure of what Lacan calls symbolic castration; and (4) the unconscious foundations of cultural formations.[1] In order to address these deficiencies, I will examine manifestations of racism, sexism, ethnocentrism, and homophobia in literary works from three different periods. After I develop a differential model of prejudices, I will then show how distinct modes of oppression feed off each other and the diverse ways that cultural critics can work to undermine these systems of oppression.

The fundamental cycle of prejudices that I will examine is based on the homophobic rejection of same-sex desires, which often results in the racist projection of unwanted libidinal impulses onto culturally debased Others. Within this structure, the dominant social order equates homosexual desire with a loss of linguistic control and a breakdown of the symbolic structure of sexual difference. In order to overcome this sense of symbolic confusion, subjects force others to submit to a sexist form of symbolic castration.

For Lacan, linguistic castration is defined by the fact that human subjects must submit themselves and their desires to a symbolic discourse that alienates them from their natural bodies and perceptions.[2] This fundamental form of alienation is unconsciously experienced as a subjective state of enslavement in which one's body is mediated and transformed by the desire of the social Other. Furthermore, I will argue throughout this study that one way subjects attempt to escape feelings of linguistic, social, and political submission is by subjecting others to their will and by projecting their repressed desires onto debased Others.[3]

Many forms of prejudice are structured by this double movement of the projection of repressed sexuality onto a cultural Other that is followed by

1

the attempt to force the Other to submit to the symbolic law of castration. In perverse forms of racism and sexism, women and minorities are first attacked for being hypersexual and linguistically inadequate, and then they are punished and compelled to subject their desires to the dominant social order. Perverse subjects thus link sexual transgression to discourse and punishment in an attempt to master the trauma of linguistic loss and lack by repeating the scene of castration in erotic symbolic scenarios.[4] These subjects use symbolic representation as a way of translating and displacing the initial trauma of language onto different social relations by producing a debased and devalorized object. We shall see how this displacement and projection of linguistic loss plays an essential role in many forms of prejudice.[5]

LACANIAN PSYCHOCULTURAL STRUCTURES

In order to trace the ways that same-sex desires and linguistic castration are repressed and projected onto debased cultural Others, I will be returning to Lacan's theory of subjectivity as it is represented in his schema L (*Ecrits* 193–196):

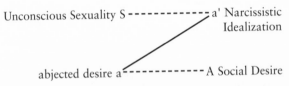

Following Freud, Lacan posits that the initial state of being for every subject (S) involves an unmediated access to the real of bodily enjoyment and a freedom from any form of social regulation.[6] In the second stage of this structure, this original mode of polymorphous desire is replaced by an ideal image of pleasure (a') that supports the subject's desire for unity and identity. In order to explain this narcissistic structure of imaginary identity, Lacan posits that the subject first gains a sense of being a unified and separate self by seeing the unified and complete body of the other. By looking into a mirror or at a similar person, subjects gain access to an imaginary representation of their own body. The third phase of this logic designates the fact that all modes of desire are transformed and mediated by the symbolic discourse of law and language (A). By claiming that "the desire of the subject is the desire of the Other," Lacan posits that human sexuality is determined by this level of social reality and symbolic castration.[7] Finally, the object (a) designates the refusal of desire to be completely regulated by either imaginary narcissism or symbolic sexual difference. This object (a) represents all of the forms of sexuality and identity that the dominant social order abjects and excludes.

This model of subjectivity can be used to develop a psychosexual cultural schema of interrelated prejudices:

Homophobia S- - - - - - - -a' Homosocial
                                 Ethnocentrism

Racism a'- - - - - - - -A Patriarchal Sexism

In the movement of this structure, the cultural rejection of same-sex desire (S) is supported by the production of an imaginary mode of homosocial male bonding (a'). Due to the fact that homosexual desires can be experienced as an intrusion of an uncontrollable form of unconscious and illicit sexual enjoyment, homosocial relationships create a sense of imaginary identity through the idealization of the same gender and ethnicity. This ethnocentric idealization of the bonds between men is, in turn, anchored in a sexist form of patriarchy (A) that uses women as the receptacles for men's repressed desire for other men. However, since there is always a residue of homosexual desire (a) that persists in every subject's unconscious, this desire is projected onto other cultures and people who have been socially placed in positions of abjection and amorality (a). What in part defines this racist abjection of the out-group is that they are considered to be the polar opposite of the idealized homosocial group.[8]

In the literary texts that I will be examining, we will continually encounter this psychocultural structure of prejudice. A paradigmatic example of this cycle of prejudice can be found in the literature and history of exploration. In a wide array of texts documenting the first encounters between sailing Europeans and native populations, we find that the men who take a voyage together in order to explore or colonize another culture are often forced to deal with their desires for each other. In order to fight against these same-sex desires, these men perform a series of hypermasculine rituals. However, once they land on the island that they are sailing to, they project their own repressed desires onto the natives, which not only frees the explorers of their own troubling desires, but also helps to justify the subjection of the "dark Other." I will posit that this movement from homophobic homosociality to a racist form of projected sexuality is inherent in the very structure of Western culture.

PSYCHOANALYTIC STRUCTURES OF PREJUDICE

My understanding of the psychoanalytic structures of prejudice have been greatly influenced by Elisabeth Young-Bruehl's account of racism, sexism, homophobia, and anti-Semitism. In *The Anatomy of Prejudice,* Young-Bruehl observes that most theorists of prejudice have employed a single explanatory model to describe such diverse phenomena as anti-Semitism, racism, sexism, and homophobia.[9] In order to counter this theoretical flaw, Young-Bruehl identifies three different forms of prejudice, which she labels hysterical racism, obsessional anti-Semitism, and narcissistic sexism. I will employ this psychoanalytic structure of prejudice, but I will modify it by connecting it to the Freudian distinction between psychosis, neurosis, and perversion.

Through this theory, I will argue that hysterical racism is most often based on a psychotic foreclosure of same-sex desire, while narcissistic sexism can be best explained as a perverse attempt at forcing all sexual desire and linguistic castration into a symbolic sadomasochistic structure. I will also argue that Young-Bruehl's conception of obsessional anti-Semitism can be applied to a neurotic form of homosocial ethnocentrism. One of the central, defining distinctions between these different modes of prejudice is their respective primary modes of defense—projection (psychosis), repression (neurosis), or denial (perversion)—against the threatening aspects of sexual enjoyment and the loss of linguistic control.

In racism, as Young-Bruehl explains, one finds a hysterical projection of unwanted desires onto a debased out-group:

> When they are prejudiced ... they have projected their desires onto the objects of prejudice, [and] the others have become the image of their forbidden or frustrated desires. But this means that the others, while classified as forbidden, are also alluring. (229)

In this structure, the hysterical racist projects his or her own unconscious fears and desires onto an abjected cultural Other. The result of this process is that this Other becomes a symbol of hypersexuality and aggression.[10]

According to Young-Bruehl, in order for hysterical subjects to control and contain their projected unconscious, they need to enforce strict rules concerning marriage, social hierarchy, and political power. The domestic Other or outsider must be contained in a fixed location or position within the house or nation.[11] Young-Bruehl adds that the ultimate threat to this form of social control is intermarriage, where an outsider becomes associated with an insider:

> The quintessential act of transgression is intermarriage between the higher and the lower. Marriage represents equality for the partner and thus destroys the main theme of the hysterical character's prejudice—"They have a place and they must stay in it." (224)

This fear of intermarriage is therefore in part determined by the desire to maintain social inequality and the need to keep the Other in the role of the repository of projected desires.

One limitation of Young-Bruehl's theory of hysterical racism is that it does not take into account more severe forms of pathology. Taken to its logical extreme, hysterical racism can result in a psychotic form of prejudice that depends on the delusional projection of unconscious desires onto a debased Other. Thus, Freud's fundamental hypothesis concerning psychosis is that the paranoid subject rejects his own (homosexual) desires and projects those feelings onto an external Other:

> The most striking characteristic of symptom-formation in paranoia is the process which deserves the name of projection. An internal perception is suppressed, and instead, its content, after undergoing a certain degree of distortion, enters consciousness in the form of an external perception. ("Psychoanalytic Notes" 169)

This psychotic model is thus based on the confusion between rejected sexual desires and the perception of the desire of the Other. For psychotic subjects, the Other represents in the real their own unconscious wishes and fears.[12]

Moreover, Freud centers this theory of psychotic projection on a homophobic foreclosure of same-sex desires. In Freud's model, all forms of psychosis are related to the projection and transformation of the proposition "I (a man) love him." In the case of the delusion of persecution, this fundamental phrase is transformed into: "I do not love him—I hate him" ("Notes" 165). This second phrase is then inverted through the process of projection: "He hates (persecutes) me" (166). This same process of rejection and projection is evident in erotomania, where Freud posits that the gender of the love-object is switched and the statement "I do not love him—I love her" is transformed into the phrase: "I notice that she loves me" (166). Likewise, in delusional jealousy, the declaration of same-sex desire is inverted and reversed through a changing of the gender of the speaker: "It is not I who love the man—she loves him" (167). According to Freud, every form of paranoia is thus based on a fundamental rejection of same-sex desire.

What determines psychotic racism and homophobia is the way that the rejection of same-sex desire is linked to the foreclosure of the symbolic regulation of sexuality and subjectivity. As Lacan argues, the psychotic subject forecloses the social mediation of desire (Name-of-the-Father) and the complex of castration, and the result of this foreclosure or radical rejection is a return in the real of the rejected symbolic Other.[13] Lacan thus downplays the homosexual grounding of this structure in order to emphasize the heterosexual role of the paternal metaphor (the superego) and the resolution of the Oedipus complex. In other terms, since the social control of desire within a patriarchal system (Name-of-the-Father) is dependent on the cultural rejection of homosexuality, same-sex desire is perceived to represent a threat to the dominant social order.[14]

Linked to this primary form of prejudice, we find the structure of what Young-Bruehl calls obsessional anti-Semitism. In this mode of prejudice, a subjective stress on assimilation and conformity results in a fear of losing control to authority figures and the penetrating Other. For obsessional anti-Semites, "the Jew" represents the scum and dirt that they are trying to clean away. However, since for the obsessional subject, everything is always the Other's fault, the Other comes to symbolize both the powerless poor and the powerful rich (215). Thus, National Socialists believed both that the Jews controlled all the banks and that they were no different from animals and dirt (215).

Young-Bruehl argues that the fundamental fear of these obsessional anti-Semites is being passive in front of an all-powerful Other (218–219). This fear of passivity is centered on the double threat posed by castration and by the Other's enjoyment. For both the eruption of uncontrollable sexual enjoyment *(jouissance)* and castration threaten the obsessional subject's sense of bodily and mental control. For Lacan, the obsessional subject sacrifices his or her own sexual enjoyment in order to perform and work for a powerful Other, but he or she can receive sexual pleasure only by transgressing the law of the Other.[15] For this subject, it is always the Other who is having all of the enjoyment and pleasure.

According to Jacques-Alain Miller, this question of the enjoyment of the Other is essential to the understanding of all forms of prejudice:

> Why does the Other remain Other? What is the cause of our hatred for him, for our hatred of him in his very being? It is hatred of the enjoyment of the Other.
>
> This would be the most general formula of the modern racism that we are witnessing today: a hatred of the particular way the Other enjoys . . . It is located on the level of the tolerance and intolerance toward the enjoyment of the Other, the Other as he who essentially steals my own enjoyment.[16]

Miller's argument here allows us to see the connection between prejudice and sexual enjoyment; however, this theory fails to distinguish between the hysterical projection of one's own rejected sexual enjoyment and the obsessional fear that the Other is stealing our sexual pleasure.

I will expand Young-Bruehl's theory of obsessional anti-Semitism by equating it with the general structure of ethnocentrism, for central to the celebration of ethnic sameness and the debasement of cultural difference is an obsessional investment in imaginary forms of social homogeneity and national unity. In this structure, the presence of foreigners in one's home culture represents a threat to bodily unity and a menace of bodily penetration.

In order to ward off these feelings of vulnerability, obsessional ethnocentrists develop homosocial bonds of racial and sexual sameness.[17]

One way that this ethnocentric desire for cultural unity and sameness can manifest itself is in the final form of prejudice that Young-Bruehl discusses: sexism. In the narcissistic structure of sexism, the prejudiced subject's fear of internal disintegration and loss of identity causes a desire for sameness and a rejection of all forms of difference (230–38). For the narcissistic male sexist, all inferior subjects are feminine or feminized, and in order to work against sexual and cultural difference, the narcissist forms peer groups or gangs that turn the "I" into a "we" (235). In this structure, homosocial male bonding protects against the recognition of sexual difference.

I will argue that narcissistic sexism is most often structured by a perverse form of subjectivity rather than a neurotic mode. This distinction is crucial because one cannot examine or treat perverse and neurotic subjects in the same way.[18] In perverse sado-masochism, as defined by Freud, the essential features include the unconscious denial of sexual difference, the formation of a fetish, the rigid distinction between active masculinity and passive femininity, and the negation of castration.[19] Lacan adds that perverse subjects seek to force all of their sexual enjoyment into the Symbolic Other in order to find an absolute law of desire (*Four Concepts* 183). Thus, in order to fully symbolize their sexuality, perverse subjects need to wear uniforms, play out social scenarios, depict social roles, and transgress the various forms of political authority and law. Lacan posits that in these perverse scenes, subjects are attempting to master their subjection to language and culture by transforming symbolic castration into an erotic relationship. Moreover, by sexualizing symbolic castration and different forms of masochistic subjection, the subject is able to transform the threatening aspects of sexuality into a symbolic binary code. From this viewpoint, cross-dressing, hypermasculinity, and hyperfemininity can be seen as perverse attempts to symbolize sexual trauma and difference. While these modes of gender transformation may appear to subvert different forms of sexism, Lacan's account of perversion ultimately shows that these types of sexual masquerade and mimicry repeat and reinforce the strict symbolic codes that they ostensibly try to undermine.

In the last section of this work, I will examine the ways that this perverse form of prejudice dominates in our current postmodern culture. Both postmodern and perverse modes of subjectivity are determined by a stress on the commodification of desire, subjective division, the social construction of gender and the body, symbolic role-playing, and the intense fear of bodily fragmentation. By examining two novels by Toni Morrison, we will see how the postmodern idealization of whiteness is not only an aesthetic or a racial formation but also has clear sexual and economic roots. Through her descriptions of advertising, children's toys, and literature, Morrison ties postmodern capitalism to the circulation of desire in a color-coded structure. Furthermore, we learn in Morrison's text that postmodern capitalism not only works by producing new desires and new objects for consumption, it also serves to produce these desires within a racist and ethnocentric order.

The "beauty industry" is the prime example of the way that global capitalism has linked itself to a cycle of prejudices. In this postmodern structure, the homosocial and ethnocentric celebration of whiteness and heterosexuality is tied to a mass-mediated form of racial desire. Morrison shows that all modes of representation (books, toys, movies, billboards, stores, magazines, newspapers, etc.) in our current culture tend to idealize the desire for whiteness and devalue the presence of blackness. Her text thus relates the internalization of racism to the power of postmodern capitalism in the shaping of unconscious subjective desires and fears.

In the final chapter, I will use this model of prejudices to examine the ways that literary texts both facilitate and challenge diverse modes of oppression. While I will connect these different forms of prejudice together, I will also stress the importance of understanding their differences. These theoretical distinctions are crucial to the work against prejudice because different forms of discrimination require different types of remedies. For example, the perverse form of sexism cannot be undermined by educational strategies that merely stress the need to correct the wrong ideas that these men have about women. Such a technique will fail because perverse subjects will take any new knowledge, no matter how enlightened, and submit it to their binary way of thinking. Similarly, educational strategies opposing hysterical racism often do not work because they do not push subjects to examine their unconscious fears and desires. Thus the link between homophobia and racism requires that any attempt to fight against hysterical racism must also address questions of cultural and personal homophobia. Furthermore, since hysterical racism plays on class and ethnic hierarchies, the unconscious desire for social inequality should be addressed along with a quest for greater social and economic justice.

The question of economic inequality also plays a crucial role in the work against obsessional anti-Semitism and homosocial ethnocentrism. The obsessional subject's demonization of the Other is often motivated out of a double fear of bodily penetration and a loss of social and economic status. These subjective fears and desires must be explored and addressed in order to undermine the obsessional need for male bonding and racial narcissism.

LITERARY MODELS OF PREJUDICE

In order to examine how this cycle of prejudice has been circulated from one generation to the next, *Writing Prejudices* will look at three different Western literary periods. By highlighting the continuities and discontinuities in these written texts, I hope to show how the theme of prejudice has been a central motif throughout the history of Western literature. However, I also want to argue that the structures and forms of prejudices change as we move from the Early Modern to the Modern and Postmodern literary periods. By starting with a consideration of three texts by Shakespeare, I will lay the foundations for our own culture of prejudices in the Early Modern Period.

This exploration of Early Modern prejudices begins with chapter 2, where I interpret Shakespeare's *Othello* in order to articulate the differences and connections among racism, sexism, homophobia, and ethnocentrism. One of my central arguments will be that Iago gets Othello to hate himself (internalized racism) and his wife (narcissistic sexism) by conjuring up a strong sense of same-sex desire and homophobia. As in Freud's classic theory on homosexuality, paranoia, and jealousy, Othello represses his own same-sex desires and projects them onto Desdemona, who becomes a symbol of sexual excess. Homophobia thus fuels the other modes of prejudice in the play.

In chapter 3, the relationship among homophobia, sexism, racism, and ethnocentrism are explored in Shakespeare's *Sonnets*. Through the homosocial celebration of white beauty, the poet of these sonnets attempts to hide his same-sex desires and to debase his dark female Other in a sexist and racist way. The poet not only seeks to reject his homosexuality but also tries to project linguistic loss and lack onto his "dark Other." These sonnets thus become essential in our examination of the role played by linguistic castration in diverse forms of prejudice.

In chapter 4, I complete this study of early modern prejudice by examining *The Tempest* as a text of ideological colonization. I posit that in many voyages of discovery, there is a rejection of same-sex desires that are then projected onto the native population. In this play, Caliban becomes the object of Prospero's culture's repressed homosexuality. In order for men to fend off the feelings that they have for each other in this culture, they not only develop this form of racial homophobia, but they also seek to celebrate an idealized mode of heterosexuality and homosociality. By tying the cycle of prejudices to acts of colonial exploitation, I will display some of the political and historical consequences of our cultural homophobia and racism.

After this examination of early modern prejudices, I turn my attention to the nineteenth-century literature of colonialization. In chapter 5, I interpret

Mary Shelley's *Frankenstein* as a veiled critique of slavery that links together homophobia, racism, sexism, and homosociality within a colonial context. For Victor Frankenstein, the monster becomes the depository of all of his repressed same-sex desires and cultural fears. Moreover, the monster presents himself as a victim of prejudice who seeks out a color-blind society. Shelley's text helps us to connect the structure of prejudice to the psychology of both the victim and victimizer of oppression.

In chapter 6, I conclude this analysis of nineteenth-century colonialist prejudices by reading Joseph Conrad's *Heart of Darkness* as an example of an obsessional form of homophobia. Conrad's homophobic panic and obsessional discourse is centered on a rhetorical use of irony and other distancing techniques that serve to give the reader and the writer a sense of ego mastery by repressing all forms of sexual and cultural Otherness. This mode of discourse is also connected to the dominant types of literary criticism that project onto cultural texts diverse social and cultural problems that serve to divorce personal responsibility from cultural analysis.

In the last section of this work, I examine two African-American texts in order to discuss the ways that victims of prejudice resist or internalize the forms of oppression that they are subjected to. In Chapter 7, I read Toni Morrison's *The Bluest Eye* to articulate the cycle of prejudices within an African-American context. Morrison's text also allows us to formulate the relationship between class structure and distinct forms of subjective prejudice.

In the final chapter, I interpret Morrison's *Beloved* as a postmodern slave narrative that asks all Americans to deal with the parts of our past that we continue to repress. By developing Žižek's theory of the national unconscious, I articulate a psychoanalytic theory of communal healing. This psychoanalytic cultural criticism allows us to determine ways to overcome the different forms of prejudice that I will be analyzing.

PSYCHOANALYTIC CULTURAL CRITICISM

Throughout this work, I will be stressing a psychoanalytic form of cultural criticism that links subjective modes of prejudice to larger cultural forces. One of the major issues that I will be addressing is the reason subjects may masochistically enjoy the social and ideological forces that oppress them. Slavoj Žižek's theory of ideological enjoyment will be employed in order to analyze this enjoyment of subjection and the many ways that subjective desires serve to reinforce dominant social ideologies (*Sublime* 30–53).

For Žižek, a subject's fantasy life and unconscious desire are often ideologically determined. In fact, one of the most powerful means of containing and controlling subjectivity and desire is the production of socially deter-mined private lives. According to Žižek, society uses the subject's irrational and incomprehensible desire in order to get him or her to submit to an irra-tional and incomprehensible social order. Instead of opposing the moralistic superego to the amoral id, Žižek insists that the two often work together:

> This regressive, blind, 'automatic' behavior, which bears all the signs of the Id, far from liberating us from the pressures of the ex-isting social order, adheres perfectly to the demands of the Superego, and is therefore already enlisted in the service of the so-cial order. (*Tarrying* 16)

In other terms, society controls subjects by containing and producing their irrational desires and enjoyments. This theory of masochistic ideological en-joyment helps us to understand why victims of prejudice and oppression may unconsciously accept their states of subjection.

Following Althusser, Žižek claims that ideological enjoyment is realized through externalized actions and not internalized convictions: "The illusion is not on the side of knowledge, it is already on the side of reality itself, of what people are doing. What they do not know is that their social reality it-self, their activity, is guided by an illusion" (*Sublime* 32). Žižek's argument here is that social reality and ideology are structured by a series of fictions and deceptions that people blindly follow in their everyday actions.

This conception of the fictional nature of social reality undermines most attempts to counter forms of prejudice by simply pointing to the distortions on which they are based. As Žižek posits, a social system that is founded on deception cannot be transformed by truth, because every subject in that sys-tem has decided to accept deception over truth. Thus, in the famous story of "The Emperor's New Clothes," all of the citizens feel more comfortable ac-cepting the lie that the emperor is dressed than acknowledging the truth that he is naked. Due to this general acceptance of cultural lies, one cannot sim-ply undermine prejudices by pointing to their false grounds, because the prejudiced subject can easily respond by stating: "I know that I am a racist and that racism is wrong. But, still racial stereotypes are the way that we structure our social reality." In other terms, the postmodern subject accepts the fictional nature of all ideological constructions and thus refuses to give up prejudices just because they are based on fictions.

In order to fight against the forces of racism, sexism, and homophobia, we need to take into account on a national and social level the repressed de-sires and fears that support our own society. In *Writing Prejudices*, I will provide a pedagogical method for undermining naturalized racist metaphors and exposing the perverse eroticization of power relations. This mode of teaching is predicated on a form of psychoanalytic criticism that is not content with just interpreting texts but that seeks to motivate real social change. One of the ways that this form of change can occur is through the recognition of social and psychological patterns of subjection. By examining the masochistic aspects of internalized prejudices, we can help to undermine the power of diverse forms of oppression. This work entails the development of a communal form of psychoanalysis that explores the dialectic between the national unconscious and diverse forms of subjectivity.

Throughout *Writing Prejudices*, I will outline a series of pedagogical interventions that can help teachers and students to go beyond the simple detection of prejudices. This process includes:

1. Helping students to acknowledge and express their own repressed desires, fears, and anxieties;
2. Connecting the cultural to the personal by constantly linking literary texts to current social contexts;
3. Discussing alternative modes of identity and identification that do not require the debasement of a devalorized Other;
4. Exploring the defenses and resistances that prevent the detection of the underlying psychological roots of prejudice;
5. Connecting the formation of prejudices to economic and political forces;
6. Exploring the social construction of homophobia and the way that it produces other modes of prejudice;
7. Educating in a way that allows students and teachers to express their own divided subjectivities;
8. Insisting that students and teachers formulate possible solutions to social problems.

Many of these suggestions involve making the educational process more personal and relevant for our current students. For some critics and scholars, these strategies may seem like a naive attempt to do away with historical differences. However, I would like to affirm that history only becomes important if it is related to the present and the future. Like art for art's sake, history for history's sake only serves to reinforce the destructive cycle of prejudice that still functions today.

PART ONE

Early Modern Prejudice

CHAPTER TWO

Racism, Sexism, and Homophobia in *Othello*

In this chapter, I will develop a psychoanalytic form of cultural criticism that provides a theoretical framework for the analysis of a diverse range of prejudices. One of the goals of this work is to explore the unconscious desires and fears that lead to socially destructive modes of behavior. While this project stresses the role played by unconscious and subjective aspects of prejudice, it does not concentrate on a purely individual or character-based form of analysis; rather, it emphasizes the way that all unconscious and subjective formations are shaped by larger social forces.[1]

An example of how subjectivity and prejudices are determined by cultural structures can be found in the fundamental role that homophobia plays in other forms of discrimination. Homophobia is never a purely subjective or personal experience; the rejection of same-sex desire is always tied to a cultural intolerance of a form of sexuality that threatens the foundations of a society based on male bonding and patriarchal heterosexuality. This means that when particular people or literary characters express their homophobia, they are manifesting an ideology of oppression that has deep structural and cultural roots. Moreover, the general acceptance and internalization of homophobia helps to clear the way for other forms of prejudice that feed off of the rejection and projection of repressed homoerotic desires.

We can find an explanation for the link between homophobia and other forms of prejudice in Freud's "Some Neurotic Mechanisms in Jealousy, Paranoia, and Homosexuality." In this essay, Freud reiterates his argument that all social formations are derived from a sublimation of homosexual desire (208). Moreover, he posits that in order for men to overcome an intense sense of competition and desire for each other, they must transform their homosexual and hostile impulses into idealized homosocial activities. According to Freud, paranoia represents an exaggeration of a normal social process: "In both processes there is first the presence of jealous and hostile impulses which cannot achieve satisfaction; and both the affectionate and

15

the social feelings of identification arise as reactive formations against the repressed aggressive impulses" (207). Freud's argument is based on a central
opposition between the social structure and same-sex desire. From this perspective, society can only function if homosexual desire is repressed into the
unconscious.[2] However, this repression is never complete, and thus there is a
constant threat of the return of these repressed homosexual impulses.

Freud uses this theory of sublimated homosexual desire in order to account for the paranoid's sense of jealousy. In certain cases of paranoia, the
repressed homosexual experiences a feeling of jealousy after every satisfaction of a heterosexual nature. Freud's idea is that heterosexual intercourse
can only work if the homosexual component is split off. Yet this split-off desire always returns in the distorted form of a jealous accusation: "After every
satisfaction of the heterosexual libido the homosexual component, likewise
stimulated by the act, forced an outlet for itself in the attack of jealousy"
(200). I will argue throughout this work that it is this split-off repressed desire that is a fundamental source of diverse forms of prejudice.

Freud's theory of jealousy allows us to posit a structural relationship between patriarchal heterosexuality and a paranoid form of homophobia. In
order for heterosexuality to become the norm of desire, homosexuality has
to be constantly repressed and debased. However, no form of desire can be
completely repressed, thus there is a constant threat of the return of same-
sex desire. Moreover, one can posit that this threat of homosexual desire
often prevents the analysis of homophobia in literary and cultural texts.

HOMOPHOBIA RECONSIDERED

In *The Anatomy of Prejudices,* Elisabeth Young-Bruehl posits that the study
of homophobia has been blocked by the insistence that homophobia is only
a type of sexism:

> Those psychologists who have focused their attention on male
> prejudice against male homosexuals are almost unanimous in see-
> ing this prejudice as a particular sort of sexism. They view it as a
> male's denigration of the femaleness and femininity in other men
> and in himself. (148)

Young-Bruehl does not argue that this mode of sexist homophobia does not
exist; rather, she insists that there are several different forms of homophobia.[3] In her study of different ideal character types, Young-Bruehl posits that
there are narcissistic, obsessional, and hysterical modes of prejudice (152).

Linked to this problem of defining homophobia is the similar difficulty
in categorizing homosexuality: "The homosexual is a kind of fiction,

because homosexual behavior occurs along a continuum, ranging from entertaining homoerotic fantasies to having a single experience or period of experience of exclusive preference" (142). This hinderance in defining homosexuality is in part due to the invisibility of its existence for most people: it is often obvious who is a female and who is a person of color, but it is often difficult to determine what or who is homosexual (141).

Due to the difficulty in defining homosexuality, homophobic people are able to label any act or person that they want to debase with this term: "Homophobia is an assertion of control over the category 'homosexual.' Homophobes try to seize the power of definition" (143). This connection between the instability of the terms homosexuality and homophobia pushes Young-Bruehl to posit that this form of prejudice is a "category accusation" that is aimed at specific acts and not at a particular cultural or subjective identity: "Homophobia is mainly a category accusation because it is primarily directed at acts and what acts represent in fantasy, and only secondarily at the people who commit those acts" (143). As the recent example of "gays in the military" has shown, homosexuality is often tolerated if it remains invisible and unspoken.[4]

These problems in seeing and defining homosexuality and homophobia point to the multiple threats that this form of sexuality can represent for the dominant social order. The mere presence of same-sex desire threatens to undermine many of the binary oppositions that we use to structure our social reality. If men can love men and women can love women, the rigid sexual difference of the patriarchal order is called into question. Furthermore, if a man can act like a woman and a woman can act like a man, subjective modes of identity and gender identification are rendered problematic. Homoerotism thus represents a cultural crisis of social definitions and categories.[5]

In turning to Shakespeare's *Othello,* we shall see how homophobia is linked to obsessional ethnocentrism, hysterical racism, and perverse sexism.[6] My central hypothesis is that Iago gets Othello to be jealous of his wife by first cultivating and then displacing a traumatic form of same-sex desire. Throughout the play, Iago controls different characters by playing on their homophobic fears and by threatening them with anal penetration.[7] In fact, the hysterical racism and the perverse sexism that are expressed in this work are fueled by this production and repression of same-sex desires. We can outline this displacement of prejudices with the following model:

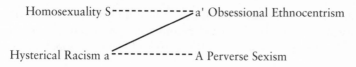

Homosexuality S------------a' Obsessional Ethnocentrism

Hysterical Racism a------------ A Perverse Sexism

This structure posits that the initial form of unconscious homosexuality is repressed by every subject (S) in the play. This repression is utilized by Iago in his obsessional idealization of subjective and cultural sameness (a'). In turn, Iago displaces his own homophobia and fear of cultural difference onto Brabantio, who takes on a hysterical form of racism. Finally, Othello himself internalizes both Brabantio's racism and Iago's homophobia in a perverse form of sexism that serves to demonize Desdemona.[8]

IAGO'S OBESSIONAL HOMOPHOBIA

Within the structure of Shakespeare's play, Iago can be considered an obsessional homophobe who equates all threats to his social status with a menace of anal penetration. As Young-Bruehl has shown, obsessional subjects often blame their own social and economic instability on out-groups or foreign people who are seen as parasitic forces that have entered the national body and are penetrating it from behind (215). For Iago, Othello embodies this external enemy that has made its way into the home culture and now threatens everyone from within. Iago plays on this penetrating threat when he declares, "I do suspect the lusty Moor / Hath leaped into my seat; the thought whereof / Doth, like a poisonous mineral, gnaw my inwards" (2.1.289– 91). Not only does Othello threaten Iago inside of his body: this act of leaping into his seat plays on a threat both of losing his social position and of anal penetration.[9]

The paranoid fear that Iago develops over his concern that Othello has penetrated both his nation and his body points to the obsessional nature of his homophobic ethnocentrism. Since the obsessional subject equates his or her own imagined bodily unity to the unity of his or her nation and social order, all threats to social and ethnic identity are displaced onto cultural Others. Young-Bruehl connects this threat of social and bodily integrity in her discussion of obsessional anti-Semitism:

> Obsessionals construe their enemies as enormously aggressive—
> they invest them with their own aggression—both physically and
> mentally; their enemies are physically intrusive and mentally insin-
> uating—they get inside in every way possible, they are parasites in
> the bodies and minds of the prejudiced. (215–16)

This displacement of aggression onto the cultural Other occurs not only in anti-Semitism but also in ethnocentrism and homophobia. In all three forms of prejudice, outsiders are seen as a threat to bodily and national integrity.[10]

For Freud, the obsessional subject is defined by a subjective stress on economic and bodily control.[11] Young-Bruehl has cataloged some of the traits of the obsessional subject in the following manner:

> People with obsessional traits or characters are regular or rigid in routines, well organized and dedicated to devices of organizations . . . usually neat, aversive to dirt, and efficient. (210)

For the obsessional subject, bodily cleanliness and order are equated with social organization and unity.[12] Iago's constant concern over his place in the Venetian military can be related to his obsession with social order and organization.[13] In order to maintain the unity and idealization of his own self, Iago will seek out a homosocial form of ethnocentrism that celebrates all forms of cultural sameness and debases all modes of sexual and ethnic Otherness.

Iago's obsessional discourse is marked by his desire to control every level of discourse and social circulation in the play. One way of reading his famous "put money in your purse" speech would be as a combination of an early Puritan work ethic and a displaced form of anal eroticism. In the very first lines of this work, Roderigo complains: "I take it much unkindly / That thou, Iago, who has had my purse / As if the strings were thine" (1.1.1–3). Here, "purse" represents not only Roderigo's mind and free will that are controlled by Iago but also a container of money, a holder of thoughts, and a bodily orifice. All of these meanings point to the obsessional need to save, control, and retain. Of course, the flip side of this anal retention is the fear of being penetrating by the Other from behind.

Connected to this threat of penetration, obsessional subjects have a great need to displace their sense of shame concerning their own bodies onto other subjects. "Their pleasure often focuses on humiliations they are able to bring about in the domain of their anal fixations. They relish making their victims feel shame over their bodily needs" (Young-Bruehl 214). Iago displays his desire to shame and humiliate others by starting his speech to Brabantio concerning his daughter's rebellion with the following remark: "For shame, put on your gown" (1.1.86–87). In this scene, Iago displaces the shame that he feels about his anal desires onto Brabantio and his concerns over his daughter and his own body.

With this neurotic form of prejudice, what we find is that the subject's desires and fears are shaped by his or her anal economy and the precarious nature of his or her social or class position. Iago's need for control is based on his fear of losing his position to both the debased and the exalted Other. What he projects onto this Other is not his same-sex desire but rather his own sense of shame and his fear of anal penetration. In this structure, homophobia appears to be the starting point for the elaboration of prejudice.

BRABANTIO'S HYSTERICAL RACISM

In the continuation of Iago's speech to Brabantio, this obsessional form of homophobia is used in order to connect Desdemona's elopement to a threat of bestiality:

> Your heart is burst; you have lost half your soul.
> Even now, now, very now, an old black ram
> Is tupping your white ewe. Arise, arise!
> Awake the snorting citizens with the bell,
> Or else the devil will make a grandsire out of you.
>
> (1.1.87–91)

In the structure of this passage, Iago first ties the loss of Desdemona to the loss of an internal part of Brabantio's own self.[14] He then plays on the racist equation of Moors with animals, and he ends by once again internalizing this threat of the outsider's penetration. In the phrase "white ewe," we can hear the words "white you" that indicate that Brabantio is the actual target of Othello's sodomitical penetration.

Iago thus gets Brabantio to play the role of the hysterical racist by connecting his daughter's interracial marriage to a part of Brabantio's own split-off self ("you have lost half your soul").[15] In fact, Brabantio tells Iago that he already anticipated this marriage in his unconscious: "This accident is not unlike my dream. / Belief of it oppresses me already" (1.1.141–42). From a psychoanalytic viewpoint, one can posit that the transgressive marriage between Othello and Desdemona is in part determined by Brabantio's repressed desire. After all, it is Brabantio who often invited Othello into his house: "Her father loved me, oft invited me" (1.3.128), Othello reports. By inviting Othello into his home and allowing him to seduce his daughter, Brabantio plays the role of the hysterical racist who fears what he desires and desires what he fears.

As an internalized outsider, Othello becomes the symbol of the repressed desire of Venetian society.[16] His marriage to Desdemona, like the cultivation of same-sex desire, serves to threaten all of the hierarchies that regulate this culture and the dominant patriarchal society. When Brabantio begins to believe that his daughter is really with the Moor, he declares: "O heaven! How got she out? O treason of the blood! / Fathers, from hence trust not your daughter's minds" (1.1.168–69). Desdemona's rebellion is experienced by her father as a general rebellion of daughters against patriarchal authority. Once again, in this passage, Shakespeare stresses the cultural and ideological foundations of subjective fear and desire: Brabantio's fear and horror is a personal reaction that is formed out of the dominant ideological systems of patriarchy and racial purity.

Like the hysterical racists that Young-Bruehl discusses, Brabantio's prejudices are linked to the closeness between his desires and his fears. One of the things that horrifies him about his daughter's relationship with the Moor is that she has chosen to desire exactly what she should reject: "Whether a maid so tender, fair, and happy . . . Would ever have, t'incur a general mock, / Run from her guardage to the sooty bosom, / of such a thing as thou—to fear, not to delight" (1.2.66–72). Desdemona's transgression thus not only challenges Brabantio's patriarchal control but also threatens to undermine his culture's hysterical desire for racial purity and the rigid separation between what is considered to be delightful and what is fearful. Brabantio's hysterical rage reaches its climactic point when he declares that Desdemona's interracial marriage threatens to undermine the very basis of his own culture and religion:

> The Duke himself,
> Or any of my brothers of the state,
> Cannot but feel this wrong as 'twere their own;
> For if such actions may have passage free,
> Bondslaves and pagans shall our statesmen be.

> (1.2.98–99)

Brabantio's panic must be read within the context of his culture's hysterical need to maintain rigid hierarchies of racial, sexual, and economic difference. In this sense, Othello's and Desdemona's expressed desires threaten to subvert the careful separation of the high and the low that is so essential in Shakespeare's society.[17]

This form of hysterical racism that is expressed through Brabantio's character is based on his rejection and projection of his culture's deepest desires and fears. On the one hand, Brabantio is attracted to Othello because of his military prowess and his adventurous stories; yet on the other hand, Brabantio still desires to support his society's rigid gender and ethnic hierarchies. His continuous stress on his daughter's fairness and purity, and on Othello's blackness and evilness, represents in part his own hysterical splitting between a good self and a bad self. For Young-Bruehl, this subjective division is the essential aspect of all forms of hysterical prejudice: "People of this type often live some form of double life . . . ; they may have a good side and a bad side, a chaste side and a lascivious side" (220–221). This division of the subject is doubled by the strict dichotomy between good objects and bad objects. In Brabantio's case, Desdemona represents, at first, the good, pure, white female, while Othello is a symbol of the evil, dark, foreign male. If Desdemona represents the good white part of Brabantio's self and Othello stands for the bad black part, their marriage together threatens to break down all of the divisions that are so necessary for his hysterical personality.

In relating Shakespeare's play to Young-Bruehl's theory, we see how subjective forms of pathology and prejudice are often influenced by larger ideological and cultural divisions. When Brabantio expresses a hysterical mode of racism, the particular form taken by his emotional panic is determined in part by his culture's need to maintain racial and sexual hierarchies. From this perspective, we can affirm Lacan's claim that "the unconscious is the discourse of the Other" and Slavoj Žižek's stress on the ideological nature of private fantasies and desires. Just as Brabantio's fear of interracial marriage is socially determined, his repressed and projected desire to be sexually assaulted by Othello is a product of his own culture's most forbidden desires. This theory of the socially motivated unconscious implies that in order to work against subjective aspects of prejudice, one needs to explore the ways that larger social ideologies help to shape individual desires and fears. Likewise, social prejudices and ideological structures must be connected to the subjective pathologies that support and shape them. Even the most pathological forms of subjectivity can help us learn a great deal about our own culture and society.

HOMOPHOBIA AS A MEDIATING LINK

In this social analysis of psychoanalytic structures, I have been arguing that what links Iago's obsessional discourse to Brabantio's hysterical racism is the circulation of a cultural form of homophobia. Moreover, Brabantio is the one who is first seduced by Othello, and in this sense, we can interpret Othello's desire for Desdemona as a displacement of the desire between Othello and Brabantio. Homosociality thus mediates and supports heterosexuality by repressing and displacing homosexual desire. However, this system of displaced desire breaks down once Iago connects Othello's heterosexual marriage to a racist threat of homosexuality. In this structure, Brabantio's fear of bestial penetration pushes him to accept the racist discourses that surround him. Homophobia is thus connected here to the generation of hysterical racism.

This association between homophobia and hysterical racism points to a cultural structure of displaced desire. In Shakespeare's tragedy, Iago is able to manipulate the different male characters in the play because he plays on his own society's stress on male bonding and repressed same-sex desire. Iago's use of homophobia, homosociality, and the threat of anal penetration is presented in the opening scene of the play, when he tells Roderigo: "Many a duteous and knee-crooking knave, / That doting on his own obsequious bondage, / Wears out his time, much like his master's ass" (1.1.45–47). In this passage, Iago is warning Roderigo not to be a slave to his master and not to let himself become as worn out as his master's ass. Here, ass refers to both the donkey and the backside of his master. The underlying threat that Iago uses here is to compare slavery and servitude to a forced form of anal penetration; the dutiful servant is someone who is constantly servicing his master's ass.[18]

In order to rebel against this form of bondage and sexual submission, Iago later declares that he will abuse Othello by playing on the Moor's naïveté: "The Moor is of a free and open nature / That thinks men honest that but seem to be so; / And will as tenderly be led by th'nose / as Asses are" (1.3.393–96). Once again in this phrase, the ass is the place of masculine vulnerability and control. Thus, for Iago not to be his master's ass, he must make an ass out of his master.

This process of turning Othello into an ass is linked to Iago's desire to render his master paranoid and jealous: "Make the Moor thank me, love me, and reward me / for making him egregiously an ass / and practicing upon his peace and quiet / Even to madness" (2.1.302–305). Iago here undermines Othello's sanity by using him like an ass and threatening him with a constant fear of homoerotic anal penetration.

OTHELLO'S INTERNALIZED RACISM

As many commentators have pointed out, one of the underlying themes of this play is the way that Iago gets Othello to become jealous of his wife in a paranoid and sexist fashion. Coupled with Othello's increased jealousy, we also find a development of his own internalized racism. The climactic point of this structure is when Othello declares that Desdemona's name "that was as fresh / As Dian's visage, is now begrimmed and black / As mine own face" (3.3.386–88). In the structure of these lines, Othello identifies with Desdemona at the same time that he accepts the dominant culture's racist attitudes toward his own blackness.[19] By equating blackness with his own skin color and sexual immorality, Othello reiterates the connection between hysterical racism and sexism. In both forms of prejudice, darkness is attached to the rejection of the subject's own repressed desires.

What I believe most critics have missed in the development of Othello's psychopathology and internalized racism is the way that Iago manifests and then displaces his own culture's homophobia and same-sex desires. The central instance of this cultivation of homosexuality occurs when Iago tells Othello about Cassio talking in his sleep:

> In sleep, I heard him say, 'Sweet Desdemona,
> Let us be wary, let us hide our loves!'

And then, sir, would he gripe and wring my hand,
Cry out 'Sweet creature!' and then kiss me hard.

(3.3.419–22)

My argument is that Iago gets Othello to be jealous of Cassio (whose name contains the word ass) by first conjuring up a strong feeling of homosexual desire between Cassio and Iago that Othello then projects onto Desdemona with a reversal of objects. Othello unconsciously states, "Cassio, a man, loves Iago." This statement is then transformed into "It is not Cassio who loves men—Desdemona loves them." In this theory, cultural homophobia becomes one of the essential forces behind projected sexism and racism. In other terms, Othello's fear of same-sex desire motivates him to kill Desdemona and to demonize his own blackness. Othello's paranoid racism can be thus traced back to his acceptance and internalization of his culture's homophobia.

Tied to the development of Othello's homophobia and internalized racism, we find his constant attempt to fashion his self through the ideology of the Other. This form of social mimicry locks him into a purely symbolic construction of his own subjectivity; since he can not speak for himself, he lets the racist discourse of Others speak through him.[20] Othello expresses this aspect of his internalized racism when he declares:

I will a round unvarnished tale deliver
Of my whole course of love—what drugs, what charms
What conjuration, and what mighty magic
(For such preceding am I charged withal)
I won his daughter.

(1.3.90–93)

What is significant in this speech is the way that Othello is playing on several of the stereotypes regarding his race and reputed powers of magic, charms, and drugs. He is thus constructing his own story by mimicking what other people think about him.

The essential moment of Othello's self-fashioning through the discourse of the Other occurs in his explanation of how he really seduced Desdemona.[21] He begins this speech by indicating that it was Brabantio who first invited him to their house and asked him to tell the story of his life (1.3.128–29). There is thus a homosocial bonding that is first established before Desdemona enters into the discourse, and in many ways, we can read this first part of Othello's speech as an attempt to seduce Brabantio by telling him what he expects to hear in a traveler's history. Othello remarks along these lines:

It was my hint to speak—such was the process;
And of the Cannibals that each other eat

The anthropophagi, and men whose heads
Do grow beneath their shoulders.

(1.3.142–45)

What is this "process" that Othello is referring to, and how is it linked to the narrative about cannibals? On one level, we can call this process the ritual of courting. Yet it is still unclear who is courting whom.

One way of approaching Othello's seduction of Desdemona and Brabantio is to emphasize the way that the Moor presents himself as a subject without any true content. In order to fit into Venetian society, this colonized black man has been forced to wear a series of white and black masks that serve to hide his real identity and desires. In other terms, Othello has to deny his own same-sex desires and his own sexuality in order to distance himself from the racist equation between blackness and hypersexuality. The result of this denial of desire is the production of a disembodied sense of self. Accordingly, Joel Fineman interprets Othello's mention of cannibals and men with their heads beneath their shoulders as "an illustration of the way that this kind of materialized absence of self to itself might be imagined" (*Shakespeare's Perjured* 149–50). In this strange act of self-fashioning, Othello presents himself to Brabantio as a subject without a self or head. He thus seduces the Venetian society by declaring himself to be nothing but the discourse of the Other. Furthermore, this aspect of Othello's lack of a true self becomes apparent when he declares that Desdemona responded to his story by thanking him and saying that "if I had a friend that loved her, / I should but teach him how to tell my story, / And that would woo her" (1.3.164–66). It is clear from this passage that Othello's story and his value can be detached from his real presence and attached to another person. In Othello's mind, Desdemona loves him for the pre-scripted discourse that he or someone else can deliver. As a victim of racism, Othello becomes a disembodied subject who is void of any internal desires. In many ways, he has accepted the dominant culture's projection of subjective loss and lack onto his dark body.

FROM RACISM TO SEXISM

Another way that Othello attempts to construct himself out of the ideology of the Other is through his heterosexual relationship with Desdemona. The power of Desdemona to ground Othello's sense of self becomes obvious once he begins to believe that she has been unfaithful, and he declares, "When I love thee not, / Chaos is come again" (3.3.91–92). Othello's fear of chaos can be connected to Young-Bruehl's theory that the narcissistic sexist experiences women and other forms of Otherness as a threat of self-disintegration:

Narcissism . . . is expressed as a strong anxiety about bodily intact-
ness or mental integrity, a strong fear of bodily injury or maiming.
. . . The others, the objects of prejudice, then seem like agents of
destruction, not of penetration and persecutory pollution in the
obsessional manner, but of disintegration or castration. (236)

Othello's sexism is thus based on a need to deny castration and the power of
feminine sexuality.[22] In many ways, Desdemona represents for Othello the
loss of the self that he has been trying so hard to construct and fashion.
Moreover, by constructing himself out of the discourse of the Other, Othello
has identified himself with the barred subject of the symbolic order. This
sense of being barred or effaced is then projected onto Desdemona, and she
becomes the cause of Othello's self-disintegration.

Othello's sexism is thus motivated out of his own internalized racism
and his rejection of same-sex desires. In this sense, his narcissistic horror of
the feminine can be equated to a general cultural horror of the loss of self
and civilized behavior. Othello's fear of feminine sexuality can help to explain one of the central mysteries of the play: the question of the consumma-
tion of their marriage. Although we do not know how long this couple has
been married, we do receive several indications that they never had sex before they get together in Cyprus. We learn about this delay in the consum-
mation of their marriage when the Herald declares:

It is Othello's pleasure, our noble and valiant general, that, . . .
each man to what his sport and revels his addictions lead him. For
besides these beneficial news, it is the celebration of his nuptial. So
much was this pleasure should be proclaimed. All offices are open,
and there is full liberty of feasting. (2.2.1–9)

We can read this passage as indicating that Othello's encounter with feminine sexuality is dependent on a breaking down of all of the civilized forms
of repression that have turned him into a dutiful servant. In order for him to
open up sexually, he has to allow everyone else to participate in a homosocial carnival of sexuality and drinking. Furthermore, just as he must face
open orifices, he declares that all offices are open and everyone is free to pursue their pleasure. The encounter with feminine sexuality is thus attached to
a complete loss of self and cultural control.

This play is in part determined by the feminine subject's transition from
being the ideal representation of stability and stasis to being the symbol of
the threatening tempest that undermines the social order. Roderigo points to
this sexist logic when he tells Brabantio:

Your daughter, if you have not given her leave,
I say again, hath made a gross revolt,

Tying her duty, beauty, wit and fortunes
To an extravagant and wheeling stranger.

(1.1.132–35)

This passage is structured by the cultural opposition between the romantic courtly ideals of "duty, beauty, wit and fortunes" and the sexually tinged description of Othello as being an "extravagant" and "wheeling stranger."[23] In the binary logic of narcissistic and perverse sexism, women can either be the pure and faithful Madonna-figure or a threatening sexual whore.[24]

Just as same-sex desire and foreign sexuality are presented in the play as threatening forces, feminine sexuality is equated with rebellion and violence. Desdemona stresses the strong nature of her passion when she begins to defend her love for Othello: "That I did love the Moor to live with him, / My downright violence, and storm of fortunes, / May trumpet to the world" (1.3.248–50). In these lines, Desdemona identifies herself with the tempest and the violent nature of sexual desire at the same time that she announces to her father the fact that she is living with Othello. Of course it is precisely this stormy form of sexuality and desire that Othello seeks to avoid through his marriage to Desdemona. When he first sees her on Cyprus, after escaping a storm and battle, Othello exclaims: "O my soul's joy! / If after every tempest come such calms" (2.1.182–83). As we know from Desdemona's previous self-disclosure, she is anything but this state of calmness that Othello desires her to be. This discrepancy between Othello's ideal representation of his beloved and her real way of being helps to open up the gap that Iago will exploit.

On a certain level, Iago convinces different characters of Desdemona's ability to be unfaithful by highlighting her strong desires and independence. In order to egg Roderigo on, Iago states:

> Mark me with what violence she first loved the Moor. . . . Her eye
> must be fed; and what delight shall she have to look on the devil?
> When the blood is made dull with the act of sport, there should be,
> again to inflame it and to satiety a fresh appetite, loveliness in
> favor, sympathy in years, manner and beauties; all which the Moor
> is defective in. (2.1.220–26)

Iago's strategy works here by linking the initial violence of Desdemona's desire to Othello's ethnic and sexual difference. Othello is no longer being represented as the "genital Moor"; rather, he has become a symbol of impotency and demonic defectiveness.[25] Feminine sexuality has thus rendered the powerful male figure impotent in its quest for a new love object. Faced with this excessive and uncontrollable aspect of feminine desire, Othello is forced to turn toward a violent act in order to transform his storm into a stable white surface.[26] In other words, this black subject seeks to establish a sense of stable white identity by killing off his own desire.

When he first enters Desdemona's bedroom to perform this act, Othello highlights his desire to maintain her on the level of fair pureness: "Yet I'll not shed her blood, / Nor scar the whiter skin of hers than snow, / And smooth as monumental alabaster" (5.2.3–5). These lines clearly show that Othello worships an ideal state of feminine and ethnic whiteness. Moreover, this ideal of purity is so important to him that he would rather love a dead white corpse than a black or foul living woman. His necrophilic desire becomes apparent when he declares "Be thus when thou art dead, and I will kill thee, / And love thee after" (5.2.18–19). At this point, Shakespeare has taken the whole Petrarchan tradition of courtly love to its ultimate extreme. The dead female lover is the ultimate object of desire because she is nothing but a blank surface onto which men can project all of their desires and fears. By having Othello kill and then love Desdemona, we are shown the way the masculine structure of desire is founded on the need to strip women of all subjectivity and independence.[27]

This form of sexism is thus based on a combination of homosocial bonding and the fear of the feminine. By subjecting Desdemona to the symbolic death drive, Othello is able to overcome his own fear of castration and subjective disintegration. In many ways, Othello represents the postmodern subject who has submitted himself and his love object to a socially constructed identity that results in a profound sense of subjective fragmentation.[28] This sense of self-construction and disintegration is presented in Othello's final speech:

> When you shall these unlucky deeds relate,
> Speak of me as I am . . . of one whose hand,
> Like the base Judean, threw a pearl away
> Richer than all his tribe; of one whose subdued eyes,
> Albeit unused to the melting mood,
> Drop tears as fast as the Arabian trees . . .
> And say besides that in Aleppo once,
> Where a malignant and turbaned Turk
> Beat a Venetian and traduced the state.

> (5.2.341–54)

Before he kills himself, Othello thus asks for an accurate historical account of his life but he once again transforms himself into the discourse of the Other. However, this Other is no longer only representing the dominant ideology and social group; rather, Othello presents himself as a Venetian, a Jew, and an Arab. He has therefore affirmed his multicultural status as a marginalized and debased subject, and yet this moment of self-revelation is coupled with his own suicide.[29]

We can equate Othello's final submission to the symbolic order to his horror of same-sex desire and his idealization of homosocial relations. He is a subject without any depth or center because he has rejected his own connection to feminine desire and castration. Furthermore, Othello's narcissistic denial of same-sex desires prevents him from seeing how Iago manipulates everyone by playing on their homophobic fears.

As I argued in the Introduction, Young-Bruehl's theory of narcissistic sexism can be better understood through Lacan's notion of perversion. What defines a perverse subject like Othello is a denial of castration, a stress on symbolic role-playing, an effacement of subjective intentionality, and a rigid division of the world into sexual oppositions. Othello is forced into this perverse form of subjectivity because his status of being a black man in a white world pushes him to define himself in an alien symbolic discourse. In order to escape from the Venetian culture's hatred of his racial identity, Othello affirms a postmodern discourse of constructed Otherness.

We therefore learn in *Othello* that one of the unifying forces in Western culture is a form of homophobia that serves to support a diverse range of prejudices. This relation among homophobia, racism, sexism, and ethnocentrism entails that in order to work effectively against these destructive forces in our culture, we must first examine the ways that we reject and project our own same-sex desires and the ways that social order is often centered on a fear of anal penetration. Moreover, just as we should differentiate between these different forms of prejudice in order to work against them, we must also see how they are related to each other.

In the following chapters, I will use this model of interrelated prejudices to examine the ways that literary texts circulate and challenge diverse modes of oppression. In the next chapter, I will suggest that Shakespeare's *Sonnets* represent a reversal of the structure of *Othello*. For these poems concentrate on the relationship between two fair (white) men and a dark (black) female, and thus they allow us to see the other side of the black man/white woman couple. Moreover, the homoerotic relation between the poet and his fair young male lover forces the readers of the *Sonnets* to address their own cultural homophobia.

CHAPTER THREE

The Cycle of Prejudice in Shakespeare's Miscegenating *Sonnets*

In recent years, many cultural critics and literary theorists have concentrated on the discovery and exposure of racism, sexism, and homophobia in literary texts, yet most of these cultural workers have not questioned the social value of merely exposing these diverse forms of prejudice. Critics have often assumed that if one reveals the presence of prejudice in cultural texts, one has contributed to the fight for social justice and the undermining of different forms of social oppression. I will argue that this assumption is misguided.

The idea that revelation means resolution is in part derived from a misreading of the psychotherapeutic process that stresses the confessional mode of discourse and neglects the unconscious and affective foundations of diverse social phenomena. Simply put, the idea has emerged in the human sciences that if one linguistically exposes and condemns a cultural form of oppression, that mode of injustice will disappear. However, we learn from Freud's work on negation that the verbal or written avowal of repressed desires and fears often acts to strengthen these unconscious elements by splitting off their unconscious affective investment from their intellectual content:

> Negation is a way of taking into account of what is repressed; indeed, it is actually a removal of the repression, though not, of course, an acceptance of what is repressed. It is to be seen how the intellectual function is here distinct from the affective process. ("Negation" 214)

Through this theory of negation, Freud highlights the way that a subject can be split between an intellectual declaration and an unconscious affective desire.[1] The intellectual and discursive critique of prejudice may thus only serve to displace and heighten certain fears and desires that underwrite the diverse structures of racism, sexism, and homophobia.

To work against this form of intellectual displacement, cultural critics need to examine the ways that readers are affected by texts in a transferential relationship. This form of psychoanalytic criticism entails a detailed assessment of the precise psychological transactions that occur between texts and readers. In particular, cultural critics must examine the ways that readers are interpellated into texts through the processes of idealization, identification, masochistic submission, and the production of a variety of unconscious desires and fears that the reader can project onto the realm of the textual Other.[2]

By examining Shakespeare's *Sonnets,* we will see how the reader of these poems is asked to identify with the poet's desire to celebrate a narcissistic form of male bonding. In other words, the act of reading itself is considered to be a homosocial process that serves to unite the writer with a masculine-oriented audience. The *Sonnets* summons their readers to identify with the cultural values, desires, and fears of the writer/poet/narrator.[3] This level of identification is predicated on a mode of male bonding and ethnocentric narcissism that celebrates white male poetry through the idealization of the "fair young man" and the initial devalorization of the "dark lady."[4] However, this sexist and ethnocentric form of white racism is constantly being undermined by the poet's awareness of his own repressed same-sex desires. From this perspective, we can argue that the destabilizing expression of homosexuality in these sonnets solicits the reader's own unconscious desire to break away from the dominant social order's circulation of cultural prejudices. Yet, this potentially transformative aspect of same-sex desire can also serve as a cultural safety valve for the purely textual deconstruction of values. In other words, readers may use texts in order release the desires and fears that they cannot act on in their own lives. In this structure, the act of reading is determined by the negation described by Freud: the reader comes into contact with his or her prejudices on a textual level, but this intellectual avowal is coupled with the unconscious insistence of the desires and fears that produce these forms of discrimination.[5]

To work against this mode of textual negation, cultural critics need to attach the discovery of prejudices in texts to the prejudices that dominate our own culture and subjectivity. By taking a nonhistorical approach to the study of literature and history, critics can motivate readers to encounter their own unconscious fears and desires, and thus they can help to undermine the subjective foundations of prejudice.[6]

THE CYCLE OF PREJUDICE IN THE *SONNETS*

In analyzing the psychosexual dynamics of the *Sonnets,* I will articulate a fundamental logic of Western culture that is still at work today. This logic serves to construct a cycle of prejudices that is based on the homophobic rejection of same-sex desires, the ethnocentric celebration of male-bonding, and a patriarchal form of white racism. In this foundational structure, white men bond together in order to prove their masculinity and to defend against the desires that they have for each other. In order to distance their homosocial activities from the specter of homosexual desire, these men turn to the idealization of women within a strict sexist logic. In other terms, Western culture, as many have argued, is dominated by the masculine need to repress same-sex desires and to express a strong commitment to heterosexual love.[7] One of the results of this process is that men project their own rejected desires onto other races, and in turn, see the "dark Other" as a hypersexual demon or animal.

This psychosexual logic constantly returns in our culture and is based on the dual stress on male bonding and racial purity.[8] We can more effectively explain this structure by referring to the following schema of interrelated prejudices:

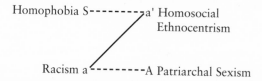

Homophobia S - - - - - - - a' Homosocial
                              Ethnocentrism

Racism a - - - - - - - A Patriarchal Sexism

In the movement of this structure, the rejection of same-sex desire (S) produces and supports homosocial male-bonding (a'). This idealization of the bonds between men is anchored in a sexist form of patriarchy (A) that uses women as the displaced symbols of masculine desire. In other terms, instead of men expressing their desire for each other directly, they displace their shared interests onto women. However, since there is always a residue of homosexual desire that persists in every subject's unconscious, this desire is often transformed and projected onto other cultures and people who have been socially placed in positions of abjection (a) and amorality.

What in part defines this abjection of the out-group is that they are considered to be the polar opposite of the idealized homosocial group. For example, a group of white men sit at a bar and they simultaneously reduce the women around them to sexual objects while they make racist remarks about anyone who appears to be different from themselves. From a structural perspective, we can argue that these men are trying to prove their virility to each other by eroticizing women and by clearly showing that their friendliness is heterosexually oriented. This form of male bonding only works if threats of homosexuality and racial difference are policed and rejected.[9]

Consider a typical men's basketball game from this structural perspective. On one level, there are the home team, usually dressed in white, and the visiting team, often wearing a dark uniform. On another level, there are the provocatively dressed female cheerleaders who serve to celebrate the home team and debase the enemy team. Separated from the game, we find the viewing subjects who are exercising their natural functions (eating, drinking, screaming, and using the rest room):

Polymorphous Audience S-------- a' Idealized Home Team

Debased Away Team a-------- A Sexualized Cheerleaders

On the one hand, the men who are playing together, and who are constantly touching each other, display their idealized homosocial bodies and actions. On the other hand, the women who are cheering them on represent the patriarchal division between masculine activity and feminine passivity. Moreover, these women are used to represent the desire for the men and the objects that the men desire. In other terms, the female cheerleaders act as the point of social recognition for the proof of masculinity and the embodiment of the heterosexual couple. While this model appears to be based solely on an economy of sexual desire, it also feeds into a racist logic of celebrated sameness and abjected Otherness. Not only do these teams wear different colors, but each team's sense of group identity is reinforced by their debasement of the Other team.

While these examples may seem to be marginal, they help us to link literary models of prejudice to current social and cultural formations. In reading Shakespeare's *Sonnets,* I will use this model to account for the circulation of desire through four basic forms of prejudice.[10] On its most elementary level, this structure shows how homophobia leads to homosociality and a sexist form of patriarchy that is then ethnocentrically reinforced through racism. While many theorists have recognized the presence of these forms of prejudice, they have not recognized how these diverse modes of oppression are linked to each other.

In Shakespeare's *Sonnets,* we find a clear illustration of this model. On the most manifest level, these poems tell the story of a male poet's quest to convince a fair young man to have a son, so that the young man's name and fame will live on. This sonnet sequence thus begins with a homosocial relationship between the fair young man and the poet that is directed toward motivating the young man to enter into a heterosexual relationship in order to procreate. However, the young man's relationship with a woman soon causes the poet to become jealous of both his former young lover and another rival poet. The poet's intense sense of erotic jealousy and paranoia is also fed by his repression and expression of same-sex desires toward the young man. This series of displaced desires is indicative of a general cultural psychosexual structure in which homosocial bonding leads to a heterosexual union, which in turn results in an intensification of same-sex desire and the production of a paranoid form of erotic jealousy.[11] In these poems, the not-so-repressed homosexual desires and fears of the poet are projected onto the dark lady who becomes a symbol of cultural and sexual difference. From this perspective, internalized homophobia leads to a racist depiction of (hetero)sexual difference.

In opposition to this narrative structure of the *Sonnets,* Shakespeare also presents a latent discourse that refuses to repress same-sex desires in the service of a heterosexual union. On what we may call the unconscious and affective level of his text, the poet allows for the return of repressed forms of bisexual and biracial desire.[12] By analyzing these poems, we will discover that the reader's unconscious desires and fears concerning sexuality and race are called into play by the writer's own repressed desire. Transference in the reading relationship is therefore constituted when the unconscious of the reader resonates with the unconscious of the writer in their mutual resistance to the dominant symbolic orders.[13] Since the unconscious is determined by the rejection of the social norms that govern sexuality and diverse forms of expression, repressed desire constantly challenges the prevailing cultural order.[14] However, the continual repression of these unconscious forces prevents subjects from realizing that their real desire is always countercultural. We shall see how Shakespeare's *Sonnets* are dominated by the continuous expression and repression of destabilizing forms of desire.

IDEALIZED WHITE MALES AND THE DEBASED DARK LADY

Matching the dialectical use of same-sex desire in these poems, we also find an alternation between the idealization of whiteness and the debasement of all forms of darkness. As Joel Fineman argues, the first subsequence of sonnets is dominated by the traditional visual and spectral tropes of metaphor and mimesis that result in a poetic idealization of the poet, the beloved, and the language of poetry itself.[15] This poetry of praise is determined by a narcissistic relation between the poet and his "fair, kind, and true" young other. In contrast, the dark lady sonnets are dominated by the de-idealizing verbal symbolic language of heterosexual dissimulation. These later verses play off of the poet's quest for narcissistic sameness and identity by highlighting the difference and heterogeneity of the Other. This relationship between ethnocentric narcissism and heterosexual racism can be mapped on a modified version of Lacan's schema L:

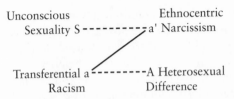

Unconscious   Ethnocentric
Sexuality S ----------- a' Narcissism

Transferential a --------A Heterosexual
Racism   Difference

In this structure, the relation between the debased object (a) of desire and the idealized object (a') of visual narcissistic pleasure is placed in opposition to the heterosexual and linguistic relationship between the subject (S) and the dark lady (A). Furthermore, the displaced racism of this structure is determined by the opposition between the object (a') of white idealization and the black object (a) of debased desire.[16] These four terms can be restated in the following structure:

Man -------- Fair

Dark -------- Lady

On the one hand, in the context of white ethnocentrism, fairness is equated with the idealization of narcissistic male bonding, while darkness is connected to the racist de-idealization of desire and vision.[17] On the other hand, the heterosexist celebration of the Lady is opposed by the repressed aspects of homosexual desire. This psychosexual formation of the *Sonnets* points to the way that different forms of prejudice feed off of each other. In Western culture, white ethnocentrism and racism are often determined by the visual and narcissistic economy of homosocial male-bonding. The celebration of the fair young man is in this sense connected to the debasement of the dark lady. Likewise, the positing of a sexist form of heterosexual love is linked to the homophobic rejection of same-sex desire.[18]

In the *Sonnets,* we find that the first subsequence of poems attempts to establish an ethnocentric poetry of likeness and self-reflection that fits in well with the classic metaphors, themes, and images of Petrarchan verse and the call for a narcissistic celebration of white men's poetry. The opening lines of the first sonnet proclaim: "From fairest creatures we desire increase, / That thereby beauty's rose might never die" (1.1–2). This call for the increase of white fairness and beauty is tied to the literal and figurative reproduction of masculine desire and form. The poet only desires an increase of beautiful fair young men. However, as Fineman notes, from the very beginning of these sonnets, Shakespeare attaches this inherited language to a sense of temporal loss and distance: "But as the riper should by time decrease, / His tender heir might bear his memory" (1.3–4). We shall see how the poet throughout these poems appears to be in a quest to fight off not only his own aging process but also the aging of the white Petrarchan and patriarchal tradition. In other words, his narcissistic idealization of the fair young man is based on his own fear of death and lost idealization.[19]

By adding a temporal dimension to the structure of idealization, Shakespeare is able to show how the narcissistic subject needs to constantly reinforce his or her imaginary sense of unity and completeness. In this context of the imaginary idealization of whiteness and youth, we see why the obsessional ethnocentric subject must continually reaffirm his or her whiteness and debase the darkness of the Other.[20]

One way that this fight against time and lost white idealization is enacted is through the poet's admiration of the youth and beauty of the fair young man: "My glass shall not persuade me I am old / So long as youth and thou are of one date" (22.1–2). If the poet can fully identify himself in a mirror relation with this younger and brighter version of his own self, he can fight off the deadening effects of time and thus give birth to a new poetic subjectivity and language. However, since the young man is also a bachelor who is wrapped up in his own narcissism, he must be persuaded to find a woman and have a son, so that his own "sun" does not burn out. Sonnet 7 directly connects the movements of the sun to the production of the fair young man's son: "So thou, thyself outgoing in thy noon, / Unlooked on diest unless thou get a son" (7.13–14). I submit that this continuous stress on fairness and the light of illumination in these early sonnets represents in part a quest to maintain a certain dominance of white culture over a growing population of ethnic and cultural difference.[21]

At the same time that the poet/narrator obsessionally struggles to defend the whiteness and fairness of himself, his beloved, and his culture, he is also faced with the contradiction between his desire for a form of homosocial male bonding that precludes procreation and the need for his male-dominated culture to reproduce itself. The constant demand by the poet that his lover/double create a son forces the seemingly homosexual eroticism of the first subsequence to take on a decidedly homosocial signification. Sonnet 10 depicts this interaction between same-sex desire, homosocial bonding, and heterosexual procreation: "Make thee another self for love of me, / That beauty still may live in thine or thee" (10.13–14). These lines argue that in order for the young man's beauty and fairness to be reproduced, he must follow the advice of his loving male friend and find himself a woman to procreate with.[22]

In order to maintain the social dominance of both men and whites, cultural workers have to produce a form of sexual representation that uses same-sex bonding in order to circulate heterosexual object-choices. In this structure, male poets write to other males about their sexuality and desire for women. On a certain level, women are used in this structure only as symbols that reflect the displaced desire that men have for each other. This stress on the cultural reproduction of male bonding and displaced same-sex desire is still dominant in our current mass media.[23] In fact, the very notion of "mass media" implies that our desires are mediated by the symbolic forces that are still mainly controlled by white, heterosexual males.

Shakespeare's poems expose the contradiction that result from our own social structure's use of homosociality to induce heterosexuality for narcissistic reasons by revealing the latent homosexual nature of this form of cultural discourse. In the first sonnet-sequence, Shakespeare expresses what is normally repressed by presenting a male love-object instead of the traditional female love-object. In turn, he grounds this type of homosociality in an antisocial form of narcissism that precludes any possibility of procreation and thus cultural reproduction. When the poet tells the fair young man to "Look in thy glass, and tell the face thou viewest / Now is the time that face should form another" (3.1–2), he is trying to motivate the young man to give up his narcissism in favor of an encounter with sexual Otherness.[24] The subtle moral of this structure is that a culture that celebrates only homosocial sameness will soon stagnate and become nothing but a hall of impotent mirroring. These poems thus make the strong claim that for a culture to reproduce itself it needs difference and an encounter with the Other.

From the very start of the first sonnet subsequence, Shakespeare connects this narcissistic and obsessional reproduction of the same to an awareness of the limits of both vision and idealization. When at the end of the third sonnet, the poet exclaims, "Die single, and thine image dies with thee," poetic death is tied to the death of the imaginary order and the failure of procreation. This potential loss of the image represents a threat to the entire tradition of mimetic narcissism. In fact, the first sonnet already indicates that the imaginary realm of idealization is not only "self-substantial" but also self-consuming. This is due to the fact that in the structure of narcissism, the subject is completely alienated in the image of the other and therefore experiences his or her own self as a pure state of nothingness.[25] Lines 5–7 highlight this dialectical opposition between the illumination of the other and the darkness of the subject: "But thou, contracted to thine own bright eyes, / Feed'st thy light's flame with self-substantial fuel, / Making a famine where abundance lies" (1). One could paraphrase these lines as saying that the fair young man hordes all light and energy for himself and leaves nothing but famine for the poet.

In this lack and famine of light, we are very far from a poetry of praise that equally idealizes the poet, the beloved, and mimetic language. The great celebration of poetic light and whiteness that we have grown to expect from this type of sonneteering is radically called into question by Shakespeare's keen awareness that the flip side of narcissism is total self-negation. For if one defines oneself completely by the reflected image of the other, one has no internal substance. In a certain sense, the poet tries to hide his existential knowledge concerning this radical state of nothingness and the failures of mimetic brightness by blaming the decaying effects of time for the potential loss of the ideal. This defensive strategy is at the heart of the argument of the second sonnet where time digs "deep trenches" into the young man's brow and forces all of his past lusts and treasures to be buried in his "deep-sunken eyes." The temporal eating away at the vision and beauty of the young man is based on the idea that he has now become the old poet himself. Through age, the fair young man loses his own beauty and light and thus he can no longer be the object of idealization and praise. The only way that the old-young man can retain his beauty is through a succession where his son becomes the repetitive symbol of his past illumination.[26]

Linked to this failure of narcissistic ethnocentric idealization, we find an eruption of bisexual desire and the emergence of a crossing of gender boundaries. In a strange twist that is rarely highlighted, the third sonnet tells the young man not only to look into the mirror and see another but it also urges him to change his sex and become a mother: "Thou art thy mother's glass, and shee in thee / Calls back the lovely April of her prime." If the beloved has now become a mirror for his mother, he is also a mirror for the poet, and thus we can assume that either the mirror holds the image of both the poet and the mother or that the poet and the mother are the same person. Through this self-reflecting structure, we can begin to see how Shakespeare can become the mother of his own son and sonnet and how the role of the mother has become appropriated by the male poet and beloved.

THE READER IN THE *SONNETS*

The poet's appropriation of the female role in procreation serves to highlight the way that all heterosexual relations in these poems are dictated by a masculine homosocial form of desire. Moreover, this creation of a mirroring and male-bonding relationship between the poet and his beloved helps to shape the potential relationship between Shakespeare's poetry and his future readers. Throughout these poems it is always possible to interpret the "thous" and "thys" as addressed to the reader. In this sense, the poet of praise seduces his audience by telling them that in the windows of his poetry, they can find their own "golden time" (3). Within this structure, the brightness and fairness of the text makes the reader feel bright and fair him- or herself.

The poet, then, not only seeks to construct his own subjectivity but also attempts to create his own audience or Other. This argument helps us to understand the generalized "eye" and "I" that are apparent in sonnet 5: "Those hours that with gentle work did frame / The lovely gaze where every eye doth dwell / Will play the tyrants to the very same." These lines indicate that all readers are en-framed in the poems that they read—their vision is always already contained in the text that functions, at the same time, as a window and as a mirror.

When we read these sonnets, and other texts, we search for some representation of ourselves as if we are looking into a mirror. Yet, at the same time, we look into these poems as if they are a window that will allow us to see more clearly our world and the world of Others.[27] Shakespeare plays on this connection between the window-mirror and the sonnet by urging all of our eyes to follow the idealizing movements of the sun/son/sonnet:

> Lo, in the orient when the gracious light
> Lifts up his burning head, each under eye
> Doth homage to his new-appearing sight,
> Serving with looks his sacred majesty.
>
> (7.1–4)

In these lines, the poet does not address a single person or object but seeks to establish a universal metaphor to which we all can relate. It is indeed a warm feeling to think that every time we look at the sun we are being graced by some type of majestic illumination, just as it is rewarding to get the same effect by reading one of Shakespeare's sonnets.

We can approach the development of this narcissistic and ethnocentric form of cultural submission by examining Aristotle's theory of aesthetics. In an essay entitled "White Mythology: Metaphor in the Text of Philosophy," Jacques Derrida traces this connection between the pleasure of the reader, metaphorical structures, and the sun back to Aristotle's *Poetics* and *Rhetoric*. Already in the Greek tradition, the sun represents a figure of both physical and mental illumination, and for Aristotle there is an explicit connection between the sun that flames forth light and visibility and the son that is a result of procreation and dissemination. Derrida argues that in the *Poetics*:

> There is only one sun whose referent has the originality of always being original, unique, and irreplaceable, at least in the representation that we give of it. There is only one sun in this system. . . . Everything turns around it, everything turns towards it. (qtd. in Derrida 243)

The power of this metaphor is that it is both physical and psychological; almost everyone has seen or felt the sun and everyone is affected by its power.

Furthermore, the pleasure of the solar metaphor is derived from the pleasure that the sun/son gives us. In the first book of his *Rhetoric,* Aristotle connects the quest for personal pleasure to the beauty of the aesthetic form:

Everything like and akin to oneself is pleasant . . . And because we are all fond of ourselves, it follows that what is our own is pleasant to all of us, as for instance our own deeds. That is why we are usually fond of our flatterers, and honour; also of our children, for our children are our own work. (qtd. in Derrida 239)

In this pleasure principle of aesthetic judgment, Aristotle directly ties the narcissistic contemplation of art to the act of having a child. This theory gives even more credence to our reading of Shakespeare's coaxing of us to have a son. For the narcissistic pleasure that we take in reading a text is equivalent to the pleasure that we take in procreating. In both relations, the subject is concerned with reproducing a cultural and subjective form of sameness.

These poetics of the same and of narcissistic mirroring are given a psychological foundation by Aristotle. One takes pleasure in one's own repetition and imitation, just as one enjoys basking in the sun of a solar poetics. Yet, the problem with this linking of the sun and the son to the mimetic power of language is that the sun always sets and darkness is always just a matter of time: "So thou, thyself outgoing in thy noon, / Unlooked on diest unless thou get a son" (7). In these lines, the poet warns the beloved that just as the sun must always die, the beloved is also threatened with extinction. The only way to prevent his own death is thus for the young man to replace his metaphorical sun with a physical son. This desire to turn figurative language into physical objects represents a constant theme in Shakespeare's work. It is not enough for this poet to merely contemplate his metaphorical sun; he also desires to have his own poetry read by an actual son.

This metaphorical production of the son of the illumination and the pleasure of the same can help us to understand some of the deeper psychological motives that are behind white racism and ethnocentrism. The pleasure of repetition and sameness calls for the obsessional reproduction of the white male ego. Not only does the poet fall in love with an ideal white representation of his own fair self, he also seeks to interpellate the reader into this same idealized state. This structure is centered on the imaginary form of obsessional ethnocentrism and narcissism, where subjects only love and find pleasure in other people who appear to be the same.

In sonnet 98, this quest for the narcissistic repetition of whiteness is connected to the way that nature imitates the fairness of the young man:

Nor did I wonder at the lily's white,
Nor praise the deep vermillion in the rose.
They were but sweet, but figures of delight
Drawn after you, you pattern of all those.

(98.9–12)

In a reversal of the traditional metaphorical structure where nature is copied by the human artist, this sonnet argues that nature itself imitates the perfect image of the fair young man.

In this imaginary structure, the fair young man re-presents the imaginary "white" ego that can only conceive of its own self in the image of a past perfection that is anticipated in the future. This temporal dialectic is at the heart of Lacan's concept of the mirror stage: the subject anticipates in the image of the other his or her own illusionary conception of an ideal past sense of wholeness and totality (Lacan, *Ecrits* 1–7). This imaginary quest for a perfection that never was is characteristic not only of the psychology of the self but also of the history of literature.[28]

BLACK IS BEAUTIFUL

In opposition to these poems that stress the idealization of whiteness and the fair young man, the second subsequence of sonnets is centered on the poet's relation to the dark lady. This encounter with cultural and sexual Otherness presents a form of difference that the fair young man sonnets appear to exclude. In many ways, these later poems reemploy a classical metaphorics of racial difference. While whiteness is attached to being "fair," "true," and "kind" through an idealization of vision, light, and illumination, blackness is associated with the negative attributes of being "unfair," "unkind," and "untrue."[29]

One of the central inverting and subverting themes of these sonnets is the attempt to make black "fair" and beautiful. Just as his lady's eyes are nothing like the sun (130), Shakespeare introduces into his text a totally new form of Otherness that transforms the classical tradition of solar poetics and visual enlightenment. This also means that in order for Shakespeare to introduce Otherness into poetry, he must subvert and invert the traditional Petrarchan quest for illumination and idealization.

My argument has many ramifications for the current debate on multiculturalism—for Shakespeare clearly insists that the solar poetry of the dead white male threatens to burn itself out or be eclipsed if it does not seek to go beyond its own narcissistic self-enclosure. When Shakespeare states in sonnet 127 that "In the old age black was not counted fair, / Or if it were, it bore not beauty's name, / But now is black beauty's successive heir," he is attacking not only the past metaphorics of color but also his own culture and social value system. Like the African-American activists who declared that "Black is beautiful" in the 1960s, Shakespeare's attempt to consider blackness to be fair can be read as a radical desire to undermine his own racist cultural order.[30]

Of course, this celebration of Otherness and blackness is highly paradoxical in these sonnets and cannot be read as a mere reversal of value. As Fineman points out, the dark lady does not become a pure symbol of truth and beauty; rather, she becomes the embodiment of the "difference" between the fair and the foul (23). She is both the sign of the failure of the old ideal poetry of praise and an indication of a new object of linguistic desire. For her lack of mirroring and idealization results in an undermining of the imaginary mimetic order that holds out the illusion that there is a perfect match between language and its referent. By calling into question this ideal representational order, she highlights what Lacan calls the metonymy of desire; since the wished-for object can no longer be fully represented, one's desire in language is always an impossible one. Fineman reformulates this theory in the following terms:

> Representation carries with it its regretting difference from that which it presents, provoking a desire for that which, as representation, it necessarily absents. Looking at the lady, the poet therefore discovers the loss of a visual ideal, but at the same time this inspires a guilty desire to recover what is lost. (24)

In this structure, the failures of representation create a form of desire that can never be satisfied. Moreover, this lack of satisfaction of desire results in a continuous increase of want and lack.

Lacan posits that the object that we always search for is ultimately a lost part of our own selves: "It is a small part of the subject that detaches itself from him while still remaining his, still retained. This is the place to say, in imitation of Aristotle, that man thinks with his object" (Lacan, *Four Concepts* 62). In this structure, the object of desire is tied to the subject's quest for a sense of completion and totality. Furthermore, if indeed the object that one is in search of is a lost part of one's own self, the quest in romancing the Other is based on a desire to refind an identity in a field of difference.

In her critical monograph entitled *Playing in the Dark: Whiteness and the Literary Imagination,* Toni Morrison follows this logic by arguing that the search for a construction and maintenance of literary whiteness and an American literary self has been centered on an attempt to repress, represent, and utilize a black Africanist presence:

> These speculations have led me to wonder whether the major and championed characteristics of our national literature—individualism, masculinity, social engagement versus historical isolation; acute and ambiguous moral problematics; the thematics of innocence coupled with an obsession with figurations of death and hell—are not in fact responses to a dark, abiding, signing Africanist presence. (5)

In this racist cultural structure, the black Other is reduced to being an object that is the cause both of desire and of anxiety. One needs the Other in order to locate one's identity in difference, yet the Other constantly poses a threat to one's sense of self.

The result of this desire to be like and different from the Other results in what Fineman calls a splitting of the subject between a "visionary and a verbal self" (25). Moreover, in the encounter with the sexual and racial Other, the visual stability of narcissistic self-reflection and idealization is undermined and placed in the space of an "imaginary past." Shakespeare tells us that in the old age, "black was not counted fair," and whiteness was considered ideal. This argument entails that in the old white cultural order there was a constant nostalgic desire to return to the ideal past of likeness and identification. However, with the eruption of Otherness into literature and the dominant social order, the old poetics of vision loses ground to a theory of perception that is determined by verbal difference and loss. When Shakespeare concludes sonnet 127 with the couplet, "Yet so they mourn, becoming of their woe, / That every tongue says beauty should look so," he is marking a transition to a poetry that mourns the loss of old ideals at the same moment that it accepts and names the new source of aesthetic beauty.

One of Shakespeare's critical insights in these sonnets is thus his profound awareness that an encounter with cultural and ethnic difference requires a new form of perception and a different linguistic relation. One can infer from this structure that racial acceptance is in part derived from a refusal to base one's conceptions of the Other on a purely visual quest for sameness. In order for the poet to declare that the dark lady is beautiful, he must move from a vision-based (imaginary) form of perception to a linguistic (symbolic) conception of difference. This transformation of values links the subject's desire to an ethnocentric sense of cultural and visual loss.[31]

The connection between aesthetic mourning and sexual desire is highlighted by the play between "lack" and "black" that we find in sonnet 132: "Then will I swear that beauty herself is black, / And all they foul that thy complexion lack." As Eve Sedgwick points out, this black figure could point to the dark continent of the woman's vagina (32). In this sense, the fear of blackness is also tied to a fear of femininity and the lack of the phallus. What the visual poet hates to see the most is precisely that which blocks his own vision and self-representation.[32]

PERVERSE SEXISM AND RACISM

The encounter with the dark lady shows how the narcissistic white male ego is threatened by the way that blackness and femininity make present the ab-

sence of the phallus and the mirroring self. In order to overcome this encounter with lack and absence, the poet seeks to control his lost object by
eroticizing it in a perverse sado-masochistic structure. In sonnet 132, the
dark lady is equated with the destructive nature of desire and death:

> Thine eye I love, and they, as pitying me—
> Knowing thy heart torment me with disdain—
> Have put on black, and loving mourners be,
> Looking with pretty ruth upon my pain.

(132.1–4)

By associating the blackness of his beloved's eyes to the color of mourning,
the poet is able to transform his masochistic sense of loss and frustration
into a feeling of pity and sympathy, and thus his pain takes on meaning by
being recognized by his Other. However, this recognition is itself a projection of the poet's own desire. The beloved is here reduced to being an empty
object that contains all of the subject's worst fears and desires. In these
poems, the dark lady has no subjectivity herself; rather, she serves as a blank
screen for the poet. By dehumanizing this woman and barring her subjectivity, the poet is able to regain control over his own desire and loss. This poetic
form of sadomasochistic racism is indicative of a larger social process of
using cultural Others in order to express rejected and unconscious forms of
desire and subjection.

We can better understand this perverse form of racist sexism by examining Freud's theory of sadomasochism. According to Freud, the sadist identifies with the barred masochistic subject, while the masochist identifies with
the power of the sadist ("Instincts" 93). In other terms, the masochistic subject gains a sense of empowerment by identifying with the Other who enslaves or controls him or her. For Lacan, all sadomasochistic relations serve
to repeat, eroticize, and master the initial subjection of the subject to the
dominant linguistic law of the father. The subject who calls his lover a
tormenter and celebrates his own sense of pain and humiliation is able to
transform his or her initial state of helplessness in front of the all-powerful
symbolic order of law and language into a new relationship. In order to
show this connection between language and castration, Lacan rereads
Freud's famous fort/da game as the scene where a subject enters into the linguistic order by giving up his or her real object of desire (his mother) in favor
of a symbolic substitute (Lacan, *Four Concepts* 62–63). For Lacan, this
scene of libidinal renunciation and symbolic repetition represents the
essence of culture and the work of the death drive. Furthermore, Symbolic
death not only entails the loss of the real object and the natural realm but
also points to the lack of control that the subject has in relation to the dominant social and symbolic orders.[33]

As a worker of language, Shakespeare's poet realizes that he is barred and transcended by the linguistic order; however, this sense of loss is quickly projected onto the blackness of the dark lady. Sonnet 133 ties together the poet's own sense of loss with the loss of his friend and the absence of the dark lady:

> Beshrew that heart that makes my heart to groan
> For that deep wound it gives my friend and me!
> Is't not enough to torture me alone,
> But slave to slavery my sweet'st friend must be?
> Me from myself thy cruel eye hath taken,
> And my next self thou harder has engrossed.
> Of him, myself, and thee I am forsaken
> A torment thrice threefold thus to be crossed.
>
> (133.1–8)

In this masochistic sonnet, the poet feels that he and his friend are enslaved by the power of desire and that he must suffer a triple form of loss. He has lost his real self by being denied by the frustrating lady. He has also lost his imaginary double through the young man's attraction to the dark lady. Finally, on a symbolic level, he has lost the love of the dark lady of difference. What connects all of these lacks is the way that each loss centers on the lack of subjectivity and self-control.[34]

We can posit that this perverse form of sexism and racism in these sonnets is defined by the way that all forms of cultural, subjective, and linguistic loss are displaced onto a "dark Other" who then is celebrated for her embodiment of castration. In other terms, the obsessional and hysterical racist projects loss and lack onto the Other in an act of fear and debasement. In these structures, the dark Other becomes a source of hatred and anxiety. However, in the perverse form of racism, it is the debased object itself that becomes a source of desire and enjoyment.

Freud describes this perverse celebration of the devalued object in his essay "On the Universal Tendency to Debasemnet in the Sphere of Love." This text begins with a discussion of psychological impotence because Freud discovered that some people are inhibited in carrying out the sexual act with certain people, yet they have no problems with other people (247). He hypothesized that in these cases of impotence, the love-object reminds the lover of the incestuous combination of desire and affection for the mother (248).[35] Therefore, in order to avoid this taboo object, the subject has to split his objects between sensual ones and what Freud calls "tender" or "affectionate" objects. Thus by debasing the object, the subject is able to detach that object from any combined feelings of sensuality and affection:

The sensual current that has remained active seeks only objects which do not recall incestuous figures forbidden to it; if someone makes an impression that might lead to a high estimation of her, this impression does not find an issue in any sensual excitation but an affection which has no erotic effect. The whole sphere of love in such people remains divided in the two directions personified in art as sacred and profane (animal) love. Where they love they do not desire and where they desire they do not love. (251)

This split between love and desire accounts for the fundamental defense of the perverse subject and helps to define the poet's desire for the dark lady.[36]

Freud posits that in order for these subjects to feel sexually free, they have to be with a person who does not represent any form of respect, affection, or judgment: "The man almost always feels his respect for the woman acting as a restriction on his sexual activity, and only develops full potency when he is with a debased sexual object" (255). Freud's explanation for this lack of respect regarding the object of desire is that in order for the subject to avoid the control of his or her repressive ego and conscience, the subject must find a love object that has no relationship to the ideal ego or self. In other words, the perverse subject can only desire an object that is completely different from the narcissistic love-object and that does not remind him of his caring relationship with his mother.

Sonnet 141 begins by highlighting this split between the subject's visual relation to the other and his desire: "In faith, I do not love thee with my eyes, / For they in thee a thousand errors note; / But tis my heart that loves what they despise" (141.1–3). This sonnet shows how the poet's use of the dark lady as a love-object does not represent a pure validation of her dark beauty; rather, the poet desires her precisely because he does not respect or idealize her. While Freud posits that the trauma of incestuous desire causes the splitting of the object into love and desire, I would posit that in these sonnets, the cause of this division is the poet's rejection of his own same-sex desire.[37]

We find a strong indication of the poet's own internalized homophobia in sonnet 35. This poem anticipates much of the imagery of the later dark lady sonnets; however this sonnet is directed toward the poet's love for the young man:

No more be grieved at that which thou hast done:
Roses have thorns, and silver fountains mud.
Clouds and eclipses stain both moon and sun,
And loathsome canker lives in sweetest bud.
All men make faults, and even I in this,
Authorizing thy trespass with compare,

Myself corrupting salving thy amiss,
Excusing thy sins more than thy sins are;
For to thy sensual fault I bring in sense.

(35.1–9)

The sensual fault and sin of the young man can be connected to the poet's own sense of illicit sexual desire. Since he cannot have what he loves, another man, he begins to desire another object that he cannot retain. This structure of the debased love-object implies that an aspect of white racism concerns the way that on an unconscious level, dark people are associated with a loss of idealization and a projection of unwanted same-sex desires. In this logic, blackness serves as the overdetermined transferential object—it is a symbol of sin, failed vision, and repressed desire.

Attached to this process of sexualizing the dark Other, we find the constant literary representation of masochism as a form of artistic control. In the works of Petrarch, Shakespeare, and Philip Sidney, among others, the poet is often represented as someone who suffers at the hands of a frustrating dark lady. In this structure, the excessive sexuality of the dark Other is presented as a traumatic form of desire that the poet attempts to master through symbolic repetition. By transforming the failure of sexual relations into an artistic production of cultural mastery, the poet tries to control on a linguistic level what he cannot control in his own life. However, these poets also realize that they cannot completely master language and that the linguistic order does not decrease their sense of subjection; rather, language becomes another form of servitude. There is thus a vicious circle constituted in the attempt to escape subjection through a system that only serves to further subjection.

UNCONSCIOUS MISCENGENATING DESIRE

Shakespeare's *Sonnets* are not only determined by this cultural cycle of prejudice, they also point to a strategy of subversion that attempts to escape from this rigid order of oppression. The unconscious fantasy that structures most of these sonnets is the idea that the act of poetic inscription can reverse all of the moral, psychological, and linguistic losses and failures that have been accumulated throughout these poems. Due to the materiality and permanence of the written word, all forms of death and decay are overcome:

So all my best is dressing old words new,
Spending again what is already spent;
For the sun is daily new and old,
So is my love, still telling what is told.

(76.12–14)

By spending what is already spent and writing what has already been written, Shakespeare opens up the door for a system of representation and exchange that has no limits. For if one can constantly respend all of the capital
and value that one has already spent, all threats of loss and entropy disappear; the sun of illumination will always reappear just as the name of the
beloved will always be retained in Shakespeare's poetry.[38]

In sonnet 66, Shakespeare bases the celebration of black beauty on the
ability of black ink to immortalize his beloved: "That in black ink my love
may still shine bright." This line serves to resignify the "blackness" so that it
now is attached to the "white characteristics" of light and life.[39] This comin-
gling of colored opposites is foreshadowed in sonnet 27, where the sleeping
poet begins a journey in his head and starts to see the dark shadow of his
beloved:

> Looking on darkness which the blind do see;
> Save that my soul's imaginary sight
> Presents thy shadow to my sightless view,
> which like a jewel hung in ghastly night
> Make black night beauteous and her old face new.
>
> (27.7–11)

In these lines that end by making black beautiful, there is a constant usage of
paradoxical and oxymoronic themes and metaphors: the blind are able to
see, the poet's view is sightless, and the night's old face is made young. Once
again, in this sonnet, standard Petrarchan themes and images are transformed and displaced. On the level of the unconscious, the color-based notions of difference and social hierarchy are collapsed so that the dreaming
poet can transform the old standard of white illumination into a new liminal
figure of black beauty.[40] Moreover, the radical ambivalence of these biracial
figures undermines the perverse attempt to divide the world into the idealized love object and the debased object of desire.

Perhaps the last couplet of sonnet 43 can give us an indication for the
cause of Shakespeare's biracial desire: "All days are nights to see till I see
thee, / And nights bright days when dreams do show thee me." In this cross-
coupled couplet, the very representation of the poet's own self to his Other
rests on the possibility that the illuminated visual object can be transformed
into the repetitive black shadow of an unconscious text.[41] More so, it is on
this level of cross-coupling desire that we can locate the transferential relationship between the text and the reader. What attracts the subject's unconscious to these sonnets is the fact that they offer an escape from the rigid
symbolic order of racial and sexual difference.

This desire for a biracial form of representation is coupled with a call
for a bisexual mode of desire. Shakespeare emphasizes this transgressive desire by playing on his own name "Will." As Stephen Booth insists, the poet

subverts his linguistic self in favor of a pun that points to the thrust of desire, a slang name for the sexual organs of both sexes, as well as the name that he gives to his beloved (466–67). Sonnet 135 opens with a dizzying usage of this term:

> Whoever hath her wish, thou has thy Will,
> And Will to boot, and will in overplus.
> More than enough am I that vex thee still,
> To thy sweet will will making addition thus.
> Wilt thou, whose will is large and spacious,
> Not once vouchsafe to hide my will in thine?
>
> (135.1–6)

On one level, it is clear that the poet wishes to place his will (penis) in a woman's will (vagina), yet at the same time, will is tied to a certain excessive wish or desire, as well as the poet's own name.[42]

In sonnet 20, the poet's repressed bisexual desire comes out into the open: "A woman's face with nature's own hand painted / Hast Thou, the master-mistress of my passion" (20.1–2). Not only does the poet tie his own name to the presence of bisexuality but he also turns the fair young man into a figure that combines both masculine and feminine traits. This combination of sexual opposites is associated to the poet's refusal to accept the phallic signifier of sexual difference:

> And by addition me of thee defeated
> By adding one thing to my purpose nothing,
> But since she pricked thee out for women's pleasure
> Mine be thy love and thy love's use their treasure.
>
> (20.11–14)

Once again in this poem, linguistic ambiguity points to sexual ambiguity; the poet seems to be indicating through the play on the word "prick," that nature has picked his male lover out to be with women due to his sexual organ (prick) as a marker of sexual difference. However, since this marker means nothing to the poet, who seeks out a bisexual object, the difference that it entails should not really bother him.[43]

By subverting his own name and affirming a bisexual form of desire, Shakespeare acknowledges two of the main aspects of the unconscious that often contribute to the generation of prejudices. In order to fight against the anxiety that is caused by confusion over lost identity and sexual disorientation, ethnocentric subjects seek out an imaginary form of racial and ethnic unity. Moreover, in the perverse form of sexist racism, the horror of same-sex desire and of linguistic loss leads subjects to displace castration anxiety onto dark Others. Shakespeare's affirmation of a biracial and bisexual form of identity thus promises to undermine some of the causes of projected racism and sexism.

In these sonnets, what serves to turn disgust into a new desire is the intermixing of opposites that we have located in such terms as Mistress and Master, blind and sight, foul and fair, shiny and black, will, dark and day, light and night, old and young, waking and dream, and black and beauty. These terms not only seek to mediate between oppositions in order to establish a common ground; they also point to a radical difference that is inherent to desire. Following Lacan, we can say that desire is always caused by lack and that desire is always the desire of the Other. Yet we must keep in mind that unconscious desire can neither be destroyed nor satisfied—it can only be metonymically displaced in the signifying chains of language.

Fueling this displacement of desire in the *Sonnets* is an internalized form of cultural homophobia. The destructive nature of this prejudice has been shown to affect all other modes of oppression through the displacement and projection of unwanted desire onto the debased cultural Other. The need to counter homophobia becomes even more pressing when one realizes the role that it plays in other discourses of prejudice.

The *Sonnets* lay the foundations for a cultural study of prejudice by showing the unconscious fears and needs that fuel diverse forms of prejudice. As we have seen, these poems are structured by the circulation of desire within a homosocial, sexist, racist, and homophobic discourse. However, these sonnets also embody an attempt to resist these forms of prejudice through the active positing of biracial and bisexual modes of desire. We can use these poems to fight against oppressive systems of prejudice, if we acknowledge that the perverse splitting of the love object into a debased object is based on the repression of our own repressed bisexual and biracial desires. This acknowledgment of repressed desire can also work to undermine the critical splitting off of intellect from affect that is structured by a cultural form of negation.

In the next chapter, I will examine *The Tempest* in order to explore the ways that this cycle of prejudice is central to the early modern ideology of colonialism and the racist projection of same-sex desires onto the debased cultural Other. The expression and repression of homosexual desires in this play will be connected to the development of a racist form of homophobia and the construction of an ideology of patriarchal control.

The Tempest: Colonial Desire, Homophobic Racism, and the Ideological Structures of Prejudice

In this chapter, I will show how the psychoanalytic structures of prejudice that I have been developing shape the ideological desires that support colonialism and other modes of cultural exploitation. My argument is that in many colonial voyages of discovery, one finds a projection of repressed homoerotic desire onto the debased native population.[1] Moreover, this homophobic racism is fueled by a form of misogyny that sends men off together, not only to find new lands and resources, but also to escape the feared chaotic nature of feminine subjectivity and sexuality. In the cultural-sexual model that I will develop, men move from an initial state of homophobia and misogyny to a form of homosocial male bonding that threatens to release repressed homosexual desires. Furthermore, in order to contain and repress these same-sex temptations, these men constitute an idealized mode of heterosexuality that helps them to reinforce the repression of homoeroticism.

In *The Tempest,* we shall see how Prospero identifies with Caliban at the same moment that he attempts to rid his culture of repressed same-sex desire.[2] This act of identification occurs when Prospero exclaims: "Two of these fellows you / Must know and own, this thing of darkness I / Acknowledge mine" (5.1.274–76). We can read Prospero's acknowledgment of "this thing of darkness" as indicating that he owns his dark slave Caliban and that he has acknowledged his own repressed desires. For throughout this play, Caliban's darkness is equated with an accusation of hypersexuality and a refusal to submit to European control and civilization. As a symbol of foul darkness, Caliban embodies all of the desires that Prospero and his dominant cultural order refuse to accept in themselves.

From a psychoanalytic perspective, we can posit that Prospero's projection of his own desires onto an already devalorized Other represents a fundamental aspect of colonialism.³ In his *Prospero and Caliban: The Psychology of Colonization,* Octavio Mannoni argues that in the colonial situation, the white man projects his own sense of sexual guilt and desire onto the dark man:

> The "inferior being" always serves as a scapegoat; our own evil intentions can be projected onto him. This applies to incestuous intentions; Miranda is the only woman on the island, and Prospero and Caliban the only men. (106)

Mannoni's thesis is that Prospero rejects his own desire for his daughter and projects this same desire onto Caliban who is then accused of trying to rape Miranda. Identification between the two men thus occurs through the identity of their illicit desires.⁴

We can argue with the validity of Mannoni's hypothesis; however, what I believe remains essential is this connection between identification, projection, desire, and racism. For these psychoanalytic processes tend to dominate the entire construction of the play, and yet I do not believe that it is a question of incestuous desire that serves to motivate the movements of repression and projection; rather, I would like to insist that it is the rejection of a certain homosexual desire that is the central cause of the play.⁵

In fact, on the very same page that Mannoni presents his thesis of incestuous desire, he cites the following statement made by Caliban:

> When thou [Prospero] camest first,
> Thou strok'dst me, and mads't much of me; wouldst give me
> Water with berries in't, and teach me how
> to name the bigger light . . . and then I lov'd thee
> and show'd thee all the qualities o' th' isle.
>
> (1.2.334–38)

Mannoni does not interpret Caliban's claim that Prospero once loved and nurtured him, and throughout the play one does not find many indications of a close relationship between these two men; on the contrary, Prospero seems to treat Caliban with only disgust and hatred. We have to ask ourselves whether Caliban is lying or if the relationship between the two men was once one of love and physical closeness.

While the play gives very little evidence of a homoerotic relationship between Prospero and Caliban, it does offer a prolonged discussion of the relation between homoerotism and servitude.⁶ In Act 3, we witness the development of two marriages; the first involves the potential nuptial between Miranda and Ferdinand, while the second concerns Caliban and Stephano. These two marriages are framed in the play by an extended discussion of ideological subjection and masochistic enjoyment. Moreover, marriage will be produced as a sexist form of social control that subjects masochistically enjoy on an unconscious level.

IDEOLOGICAL INVASION

In the Third Act, we find a clear articulation of the ideological process that helps to transform states of social enslavement and loss into a masochistic sense of enjoyment. When Ferdinand discusses his love for Miranda, he ties desire to the inversion of pain into pleasure:

> There be some sports are painful, and
>   their labor
> Delight in them sets off; some kinds of baseness
> are nobly undergone, and most poor matters
> Point to rich ends. This my mean task
> Would be as heavy to me as odious, but
> The mistress which I serve quickens what's dead
> And makes my labors pleasures.

> (3.1.1–7)

Here, Ferdinand articulates the transition of pain into delight, baseness into nobility, poverty into wealth, and labor into pleasure. The key element that allows for all of these inversions is the love that he feels for Miranda. Love thus becomes the "ideological hinge" that represses different social hierarchies and allows for the transformation of social servitude (work) into pleasure.[7] In other words, one of the ways that the dominant social order gets subjects to accept their subjection to certain ideological structures is by motivating these subjects to enjoy their bondage and oppression. This masochistic enjoyment of social inequality lays the foundations for a sexist control of women and other minority groups. In this ideology of love, women are idealized as long as they help men to transform all of their pain and suffering into an experience of enjoyment and control. Furthermore, women and other victims of prejudice may accept their subjected status because they begin to enjoy the consistency and stability of being oppressed.

As Slavoj Žižek has pointed out, this enjoyment of subjection points to the way that many forms of desire serve to reinforce dominant social ideologies. For Žižek, a subject's fantasy life and unconscious desire are often ideologically determined.[8] In fact, one of the most powerful tools that allow for the control and containment of subjectivity and desire is the production of socially determined private lives. Žižek posits that society uses the subject's irrational and incomprehensible desire in order to get him or her to submit to an irrational and incomprehensible social order. Instead of opposing the moralistic superego to the amoral id, Žižek insists that the two often work together:

> This regressive, blind, "automatic" behaviour, which bears all the signs of the Id, far from liberating us from the pressures of the existing social order, adheres perfectly to the demands of the Superego, and is therefore already enlisted in the service of the social order. (*Metastases* 16)

Society therefore controls subjects by producing and containing their irrational desires.[9] When Ferdinand claims that his desire for Miranda allows him to accept the pain of his labors, he is showing how the dominant ideology has gotten him to enjoy his own oppression.[10] Moreover, this ideological production and control of private desires helps to explain Shakespeare's use of transgressive forms of sexuality in his works. By presenting moments of same-sex desire and cross-dressing, Shakespeare is able to call into play and then repress all of the nontraditional modes of sexuality that threaten his social order. The question remains whether he is able to repress completely the diverse forms of desire that he tries to express and contain.

This dialectical relationship between the expression and repression of illicit forms of sexuality feeds the cycle of prejudice that constantly needs to transform threatening modes of desire into ideological systems of control. In this structure, every manifestation of same-sex desire increases the need for a fortification of homosociality and heterosexuality. However, this translation of homoerotic desire into heterosexual relationships (marriage) can only be produced through a masochistic mode of enjoyment. By combining strong elements of control and excitement, erotic slavery and bondage give subjects the belief that they are acting on their own transgressive desires while they are really submitting themselves to a socially produced form of sexuality. This ideological aspect of masochistic modes of desire is displayed by the constant need for these subjects to act out their desires in master and slave relationships. By turning this hierarchy of social power into an erotic relation, masochistic and sadistic subjects gain a sense of control over the dominant social order. Moreover, this strict opposition between the active sadist, who lays down the law, and the passive masochist, who humiliates him- or herself in front of the powerful Other, serves to give the perverse subject a clear sense of identity. In many ways this perverse and sexist division of labor attempts to repress moments of sexual confusion that can be caused by cross-dressing and same-sex desire.

In *The Tempest*, heterosexual love is conceived to be an enjoyable form of servitude and slavery. This becomes evident when Ferdinand declares to Miranda: "My heart fly to your service, there resides / To make me slave to it" (3.1.65–66). As in the tradition of Courtly Love, Ferdinand can only think of his desire in terms of servitude and enslavement, and he induces in Miranda a similar conception of love:

I am your wife if you will marry me;
If not I'll die your maid. To be your fellow
You may deny me, but I'll be your servant
Whether you will or not.

(3.1. 83–86)

Marriage and love are determined here by a relationship of mutual erotic servitude and bondage. In this structure, heterosexual love is based on a perverse form of sadomasochistic sexism. Even though Ferdinand is willing to play the role of the helpless masochistic slave, he still is committed to the rigid opposition between passive masochism and active sadism.[11] He also eroticizes states of bondage by turning pain and work into forms of masochistic enjoyment.

This theory of masochistic ideological enjoyment helps us to understand why victims of prejudice and oppression may unconsciously accept their states of subjection. In the play, Miranda is willing to be a slave to the dominant patriarchal order because she has accepted the ideological equation of desire and enslavement.[12] In other terms, her society bases love on an acceptance of a master and slave relationship that eroticizes diverse states of subjection. One of the causes for this masochistic enjoyment of subjection can be traced back to the religious celebration of the submission to God's will.[13] In the early modern period, subjects are constantly induced to accept and enjoy their submission to the patriarchal forces of God, the father, and the King.

This equation of subjectivity with masochistic subjection entails that as a slave, Caliban embodies the subjected state of early modern subjectivity. In this sense, Prospero's claim that this "thing of darkness" is his own entails that his own subjection is presented by Caliban's presence. Here, the dark slave is the material representation of the master's unconscious awareness of being subjected to the dominant social order. One way that Prospero then seeks to escape and deny his own submission to language and law is by enslaving others and by placing them in a position of being slaves to language. However, this colonialist seeks to justify the subjection of the native population by insisting that these "natural" beings refuse to submit themselves to the laws of culture and language. In the contradictory nature of colonial desire, the slaves represent at the same time the presence of the master's repressed sense of linguistic castration and the absence of linguistic and social control. Prospero thus treats Caliban as a slave at the same moment that he accuses him of not being socially controllable.

Like her father, when Miranda attacks Caliban for not having his own language, she is projecting her own sense of linguistic castration onto her debased Other:

> Abhorred slave,
> Which any print of goodness wilt not take,
> Being capable of all ill! I pitied thee,
> Took pains to make thee speak, taught thee each hour
> One thing or other: when thou didst not, savage,
> Know thine own meaning, but wouldst gabble like
> A thing brutish, I endow'd thy purposes
> With words that made them known.
>
> (1.2.353–58)

By calling Caliban a "thing brutish," Miranda places her dark Other in the position of a natural being that resists all efforts of socialization. Moreover, this description of teaching Caliban how to speak represents the process of linguistic castration. In this colonial structure, the native subject must submit to the dominant will of the Other by submitting to the language of the colonizing culture. Caliban thus becomes the symbol of both the natural being who refuses to be symbolized and the native subject who is subjected to linguistic castration. Moreover, Miranda's patronizing attitude toward this colonized native is based on her inability to recognize that non-Europeans may have a different language and way of doing things. Since, Caliban is denied a native culture and language, he is presented as being a symbol of Miranda's and Prospero's own repressed sense of linguistic and cultural loss.[14]

Caliban not only represents Prospero's repressed awareness that he is himself a slave to the symbolic order, but this dark Other also materializes Prospero's culture's repressed same-sex desires. This connection between homosexuality and social ideology becomes apparent when the marriage between Ferdinand and Miranda is doubled by the mock marriage between Caliban and Stephano:

> Caliban: I thank my noble lord. Wilt thou be pleas'd to harken once again to the suit I made to thee? Stephano: Marry will I. Kneel and repeat it. I will stand and so shall Trinculo. (3.2.40–43)

By having Caliban marry Stephano, the play hints at the way that the homosocial patriarchal order is determined by repressed homosexual desire.[15] Furthermore, this same-sex marriage between a master and a slave points to the way that social institutions are fueled by the rejection and displacement of same-sex desire. In other terms, men bond together in colonial and patriarchal institutions in order to sublimate the desires that they feel for each other. Shakespeare's radical gesture is to reverse this process and to show how the ideological institution of marriage is founded on a cultural lie and deception.

Just as Prospero uses magic to control his daughter's marriage, the dominant social order uses patriarchal ideology to hide homosexuality behind homosociality and heterosexuality. In this sense, the patriarchal order is founded on a lie, because it does not acknowledge the fact that same-sex desire motivates subjects to accept a form of social control (heterosexual marriage) that serves to repress its own foundations (homosexual desire). In other words, social reality is structured by a fundamental fiction that allows subjects to transform one form of desire into its opposite at the same time that the dominant form of desire is being reproduced.[16]

This theory of the fictional nature of ideology and the dominant sexual order helps us to understand how a heterosexist patriarchal system is able to maintain control in our culture. As Žižek argues, the power of many social formations can be derived from the fictitious nature of their foundations; a belief system that is founded on lies cannot be undermined by a revelation of truth. Within the structure of the play, this notion of the fictional foundation of the cultural order is depicted by Prospero's false claim that he is Miranda's father (1.3.55–59). Moreover, Prospero's loss of political power is tied to his brother's false belief that he should be the Duke of Milan:

> Like one
> Who having into truth by telling of it
> Made such a sinner of his memory
> To credit his own lie, he did believe
> He was indeed the duke, out o' th' substitution.
>
> (1.2.99–103)

In this speech, political power is equated with the process of a subject believing in his own lies. Furthermore, Shakespeare stresses the way that the act of telling a lie can create the effect of truth.

This awareness of the fictional nature of truth and the truthful nature of fiction becomes evident in Prospero's famous soliloquy:

> Our revels now are ended: These our actors—
> Are melted into air, into thin air:
> And like the baseless fabric of this vision
> The cloud-cap'd towers, the gorgeous palaces,
> The solemn temples, the great globe itself,
> Yea, all which it inherit, shall dissolve
> And like this insubstantial pageant faded
> Leave not a rack behind: we are such stuff

As dreams are made of, and our little life
Is rounded with a sleep.

(4.1.146–58)

If our vision is a baseless fabrication and our reality is an insubstantial pageant, it is because social reality is shaped out of a series of fundamental fictions. As subjects, we are determined by the dreams and other unconscious productions that we fail to acknowledge. In fact, the globe that Shakespeare refers to is both the name of his theater and the entire world in which we all live. As actors on a stage, our interactions are constantly determined by ideological masks and role-playing.[17] This acknowledgment of the fictional nature of social reality must be thought of in relation to Prospero's role as a colonial patriarch who enslaves his dark Other and who dominates his daughter in a sexist fashion. In other words, the cycle of prejudices that are circulated in the play through Prospero are determined by the social acceptance of a series of fundamental fictions. Within this dramatic work, these fictions are called "magic," and they point to the way that Prospero has gained power by enslaving every subject.

DOMINANT FICTIONS AND THE CYCLE OF PREJUDICE

The first stage of Prospero's conquest over the realm of the Other concerns his defeat of Caliban's mother/witch Sycorax who is known for her dark feminine magic. By taking over her island and son, Prospero is able to tie together the triumphs of colonial expansion with the ascendancy of patriarchal control over the old matriarchal order. In other terms, colonialism becomes a way of reconciling the Oedipus complex; Caliban, the son, must give up his mother and accept the rule of his new father-master.

Schematically we can link all of these power relations together by placing the dominant term over the subordinate term in each equation:

$$\frac{\text{Prospero}}{\text{Sycorax}} = \frac{\text{Patriarchy}}{\text{Matriarchy}} = \frac{\text{Father}}{\text{Mother}} = \frac{\text{Colonialist}}{\text{Native}} = \frac{\text{Heterosexual}}{\text{Homosexual}}$$

These different fractions articulate the ways that Prospero's victory over Sycorax represents the domination of a masculine, heterosexual, colonial regime over the native, matriarchal, and homosexual orders. The project of colonialism thus rests in part on a sexual and psychological foundation: one takes over an island and a native culture not only to find cheap labor and resources but also to extend the power of the heterosexual patriarchal domain and to resolve one's own Oedipus Complex.[18]

This heterosexist resolution of the Oedipus Complex is first presented in the opening of *The Tempest* where we see the different threats that serve to undermine the stability of what I will call the imperialism of the hetero-sexual patriarchal regime. The play begins with a "tempestuous noise" that threatens several men on a sailing vessel and pushes them to exclaim "Where's the master?" (1.1.9–10). This structure sets into opposition the force of nature, in the form of the tempest, and the power of men to instill their mastery. Moreover, this binary relation is doubled by the distinction between articulated and disarticulated sound: "When the sea is Hence! What cares these roares for the name of king" (1.1. 16–17)? Here, the roaring and noise of the sea contends with the name of the king and the mastery of the men in the same way that articulated language of the colonialists will be defined against unarticulated noise of the natives.[19]

The fact that the natural storm threatens the masculine subject's sense of linguistic control shows how the encounter with the real calls into presence a threat of linguistic castration. The violent storm of nature forces these subjects to proclaim their inability to symbolically master the realm of language. Moreover, this equation of nature with linguistic loss serves to reinforce the racist horror of the uncivilized "natural" natives.

A constant theme of *The Tempest* is developed around this difference between the language of the colonialists and the diverse sounds and languages of the natives. At the end of the play, the Boatswain declares: "And mo diversity of sounds, all horrible, / We were awak'd" (5.1.234–35). It is the diversity and difference of the native languages and cultures that horrifies the colonialists and forces them to teach the natives their own language. As Stephen Greenblatt has argued, linguistic colonialism is an essential part of this work:

> In *The Tempest* the startling encounter between a lettered and an unlettered culture is heightened, almost parodied, in the relationship between a European whose entire source of power is his library and a savage who had no speech at all before the European's arrival. (*Learning* 23)

In this colonial opposition, Prospero represent the master of book knowledge, while Caliban is the subject who is excluded from the dominant symbolic order.[20]

What I would like to add to this reading of linguistic colonialism is the idea that in this play, inarticulate sound and the language of the natives are connected to the fear of excessive sexuality. This becomes evident when the men are trying to fight off the sound and the force of the tempest, and Antonio exclaims: "Hang, cur, hang, you whoreson, insolent noisemaker" (1.1.44–45). Here, the excess of sound is tied to the "whore-son" excess of sexuality that the men are struggling to contain.

At the same time that the sea and the storm become representatives of the threat of excessive sexuality, Gonzalo feminizes the boat itself by calling out: "thou the ship were no stronger than a nutshell and as leaky as an unstanched woman" (1.1. 47–49). This metaphorical relationship between the boat and a female is derived from the idea that both can leak and thus threaten men if they are not clogged up. Sound, excessive sexuality, and the flow of female liquids are thus presented here as the major threats to masculine discourse and control.[21]

Upon seeing this storm and its effects on the ship, Miranda sympathizes with it and contributes to the metaphorical equation between the boat and the female body: "I have suffered / With those that I saw suffer: a brave vessel— / Who had no doubt some noble creature in her" (1.2.5–7). The ship has now become a pregnant woman that holds a valuable child inside of her.[22] We can therefore read the opening of the play as centered on the threat of excessive feminine sexuality and the existence of an uncontrollable form of discourse. In this structure, perverse sexism and hysterical racism are linked together through a shared horror of both sexual enjoyment and linguistic loss. The Other is thus hated because he or she presents to the dominant subject his or her own inability to control desire and language.

This association between feminine power and masculine repulsion returns through the figure of Caliban's mother, Sycorax. Prospero points out that she is a foul witch who came from Africa and tried to get Ariel to perform certain "earthy and abhorred commands" (1.2.273). Sycorax is portrayed here as a figure of the primitive maternal superego that the male subject rejects and is horrified by. In order to keep Ariel enslaved, Prospero must remind this spirit of the horrific nature of Caliban's mother: "Refusing her grand hests, she did confine thee / By help of her more potent ministers, / And in her most unmitigable rage, / Into a cloven pine" (1.2.274–77). Prospero conjures up this misogynistic image of the hateful mother in order to further enslave Ariel. In other words, misogyny becomes a source of male bonding and enslavement.

The circuit of power and desire that I have been articulating in *The Tempest* begins with the mythical power of a threatening feminine force (the tempest and Sycorax) that is reacted to by a misogynistic form of male bonding. In turn, this homosocial relation soon turns into a rejected form of homosexuality that is dealt with by instituting a patriarchal heterosexual marriage coupled with a racist displacement of sexuality onto a dark Other. In other terms, men go out to sea to escape the uncontrollable aspects of nature and women, and they end up bonding with each other. In turn, this form of homosocial and repressed homosexual desire causes anxiety that is resolved by setting up certain male-dominated heterosexual institutions.

We can follow a variation of this psychosexual circuit in one of Caliban's speeches to Prospero:

> This island's mine by Sycorax my mother,
> Which thou tak'st from me! When thou camest first
> Thous strok'st me, and made much of me;
> wouldst give me
> Water with berries in't and teach me how
> To name the bigger light and how the less,
> That burned by day and night; and then I lov'd thee
> . . . .
> Curs'd be that I did so! All the charms
> Of Sycorax—toads, beetles, bats—light on you!
> For I am all the subjects that you have,
> Which first was mine own king, and here you sty me
> In this hard rock, whiles you do keep from me
> The rest o' th' island.
>
> (1.2.331–44)

In the structure of this history, the island, the mother (Sycorax), and the native (Caliban) are first united in a foreign feminine space. Prospero comes and institutes a masculine domain by loving Caliban and teaching him the language of binary oppositions (big/less, king/subject). After Caliban tries to rebel, Prospero enslaves him and treats him in a racist fashion. Moreover, one of the ways that Prospero justifies his enslavement of Caliban is by accusing him of sexually assaulting Miranda (1.2.349). Slavery is thus rationalized in this hysterical structure because of the need for civilization to control all forms of sexual excess. This strategy of first projecting unwanted desires onto a debased other and then enslaving the Other on account of their illicit sexuality is a central mechanism that still fuels our own culture's cycle of prejudices. The homophobic and misogynistic projection of repressed desires and fears helps to strengthen the ability of the heterosexist homosocial order to control minority populations by demonizing their sexuality.

STRANGE BEDFELLOWS

In the structure of *The Tempest,* this racist demonization of sexuality occurs through the depiction of Caliban's transgressive same-sex desires. One example of Caliban's homoeroticism can be found in Act II Scene 2, where Trinculo is wandering around looking for shelter from a coming storm. After seeing Caliban, Trinculo decides that he will seek safety beneath this strange "Islander's" cloak: "My best way is to creep under his gaberdine: there is no other shelter hereabout. / Misery acquaints a man with strange bedfellows" (2.2.38–41). Out of necessity, Trinculo decides to hide under Caliban's garments, but what really serves to eroticize this scene is his use of the term "strange bedfellows." We can read this phrase as indicating that out of necessity, men will be forced to sleep together and to share the same physical space. This forced form of male bonding and same-sex eroticism points to the way that many same-sex institutions, like the monastery and the sailing ship, are colored by a constant temptation of homosexual desire. In the case of *The Tempest,* we encounter men that have been sailing together and have developed close homosocial relations but project all of their sexual desire onto the "beastly" natives.

This equation of same-sex desire with the dehumanization of natives is presented when Trinculo first encounters Caliban: "What have we here? A man? or a fish? . . . Were I in England now . . . there would this monster make a man: any strange beast there makes a man" (2.2. 25–32). On one level, Trinculo is claiming that in England he could sell this strange beast in a freak show and that his profit would make him a man. On another level, this reference to Caliban being a beast and a monster points to an act of bestiality and sodomy. After all, Trinculo will follow his description of Caliban by crawling underneath this monster's clothing. As Frankie Rubinstein has pointed out, both the terms beast and monster are often used by Shakespeare in order to stress homosexuality and "unnatural" sexual coupling (22, 164).[23]

This play on homosexuality and the beastly native is continued once Stephano spots Caliban sitting with Trinculo's legs protruding from him. Stephano's first thoughts on seeing this strange monster with four legs is to tame him and to bring him back to England: "If I can recover him and keep him tame, I will not take too much for him; he shall pay for him that hath him, and that soundly" (2.2.78–80). Like Trinculo, Stephano sees in this strange native an opportunity for profit and exploitation. However, in order to turn him into a saleable commodity, he must first trap and tame this dark Other. Colonial exploitation is here once again linked to the control of the native's sexuality.

As Stephano approaches the strange native, he is shocked to hear this Other speak his own language: "Four legs and two voices—a most delicate monster! His forward voice now is to speak well of his friend; his backward voice is to utter foul speeches and to detract" (2.2.91–94). By placing Trinculo and Caliban together in a single body of clothing, the play depicts the combination of the native and the colonizer together. Like a colonized subject whose language has been replaced by the language of the colonizing master, Caliban is placed in the position of being a split subject of double consciousness. Moreover, this divided subject is one that speaks out of both ends of his body. In a way he is a verbal hermaphrodite who employs both an anal and an oral form of discourse.[24]

This combination of opposites in the figure of Caliban's body is soon doubled by Caliban's expression of bisexual desire. After Stephano tells Caliban that he is really the man in the moon, Caliban responds: "I have seen thee in her—and I adore thee" (2.2. 140–41). Once again a master/slave relationship is eroticized, but this time, same-sex desire is revealed to be the key to heterosexual desire. When this man looks at a female object (the moon), what he really sees is another man that he adores. In this structure, repressed homosexuality and homosociality can be seen to be the core of expressed heterosexuality.

Moreover, this hidden kernel of same-sex desire is also essential to the understanding of the relationship between the master and his slave. In a repetition of his claim that he first showed Prospero around the island, Caliban tells Stephano: "I'll show thee every fertile inch o' th' island—and I'll kiss thy foot! I prithee be my god" (2.2.149–50)! As a masochistic slave, Caliban needs to turn his enslavement into an erotic relationship that his master can only follow.[25]

All of this eroticized male bonding is coupled with a plot to kill Prospero, grab Miranda, and take over the island. As in the case of Freud's and Darwin's myths of the primal horde, homosocial bonding becomes the prerequisite for revolution and the overthrowing of the all-powerful primal father.[26] Prospero therefore must resist this plot, not only to save his own power, but also to fight off the threat of same-sex desire. As often occurs in Shakespeare's comedies, marriage is used in an attempt to contain and control the different desires that emerge during the course of the work. In this structure, Prospero reenforces the hegemony of heterosexual desire by planning a marriage between Miranda and Ferdinand and by fighting off the homosocial revolt of Stephano, Caliban, and Trinculo.

Furthermore, Prospero admits that he must create many obstacles to the heterosexual union between Miranda and Ferdinand in order to raise the value of his daughter: "But this / swift business / I must make uneasy make, lest too light winning / Make the prize light" (1.2.451–52). Through his magic, Prospero first creates a discourse of threatened masculinity and menacing homosexuality that will serve to produce the later idealization of his prized possession. Same-sex desires and the fear of feminine sexuality are thus conjured by Shakespeare and Prospero in order to ensure the idealization of the heterosexual couple.

Linked to this idealization of heterosexuality, we find the depiction of Miranda as being inaccessible and narcissistic: "I do not know / One of my sex, no woman's face remember / Save for my glass mine own" (3.1.48–50).

As a subject of pure self-reflection, Miranda appears to be a narcissistic mirror that knows no other representation of femininity. However, we know that this mirror of reflection is closely controlled by Prospero. The lesson of this story seems to be that if men do fall in love with the ideal representation and narcissism of women, this narcissism and idealism is determined by other men. Thus, even when a male subject desires a female object, that desire is dictated by a same-sex relationship.

In Act IV, Prospero clearly tells Ferdinand that he has controlled the young courter's desire from the very start:

> If I have austerely punished you
> Your compensation makes amends, for I
> Have given you here a third of mine own life,
> Or that for which I live, who once again
> I tender to thy hand; all the vexations
> Were but my trials of thy love, and thou
> Hast strangely stood the test. Here, afore heaven,
> I ratify this my rich gift.
>
>   (4.1.1–8)

In this circuit of desire, Miranda is only a gift that is circulated between men, and she serves to ratify a pact that keeps the homosocial order in tact through the mediation of heterosexuality. Here, homosociality uses heterosexuality in order to keep homosexuality repressed.[27]

I have been insisting that the energy that fuels the displacements of the play is sexual desire that circulates between different forms of libidinal relationships. When this patriarchal machine functions "well," homosociality flows into heterosexuality and prevents the emergence of homosexuality. However, when this system breaks down, released homosexuality is transformed into perverse sadomasochism and hysterical racism.

THE DARK ABYSM OF RACISM

A key to Shakespeare's use of racism is the way that he connects the general metaphorical field of "darkness" to unconscious desire. Like Freud, this early modern writer believes that the truth of a subject can be located in dreams, repressed memories, and unintentional speech acts. In this play, Shakespeare clearly shows that dreams are the stuff of which subjects are made.

In the case of Miranda, her only remembrance of her infancy and other females is contained in what Prospero calls the "dark backward and abysm of time" (1.2.50). Darkness is, here, associated to the unconscious and the past, and we can infer from the general thematic of the play that the realm of the dark native is tied to the "backward" period of infancy and unconscious desire. In other terms, like Freud, Shakespeare relates the infancy of the subject to the infancy of civilization.[28] The "primitive" races are thus seen as representatives of the colonizing subject's repressed and unconscious infantile desires. In this structure, the primitive is the unconscious of the colonialist.

Paradoxically, when the colonialist Gonzalo expresses his utopian dream of the perfect civilization, he represents a society that mirrors the "primitive" island on which he has been stranded:

> I' th' commonwealth I would by contraries
> Execute all things; for no kind of traffic
> Would I admit; no name of magistrate;
> Letters should not be known; riches, poverty,
> And use of service none; Contract, succession,
> Bourn, bound of land, tilth vineyard, none.

(2.1.151–156)

This ideal state of nature, where there is no legal authority, property, or scriptural language, is precisely the form of society that repulses these colonial men and helps to create the urge to spread civilization to primitive islands.[29] The paradox of this situation is that this island, and other native islands like it, already have their own forms of government, language, and property; the only problem is that the colonial invaders cannot understand or recognize these different social institutions. What they do recognize in the Other is the projection of their own unconscious desires. Thus, Gonzalo desires a world without authority, and he then sees this nonauthoritarian world on this native island. However, just as he represses his own unconscious desire, he must also repress or hide the manifestations of what he perceives to be an island dominated by a lack of authority.

The contradictory nature of this form of colonial desire is displayed when at the end of the play, Gonzalo celebrates the exact opposite of what he had previously desired:

> O rejoice
> Beyond a common joy, and set it down
> With gold on lasting pillars; in one voyage
> Did Claribel her husband find at Tunis,
> And Ferdinand her brother found a wife,
> Where he himself was lost; Prospero his dukedom
> In a poor isle; and all of us ourselves,
> When no man was his own.

(5.1.206–13)

Instead of celebrating a culture that is devoid of written language, authority, and social institutions, Gonzalo is now rejoicing over cultural inscriptions of marriage, authority, and wealth. Furthermore, he exposes in his speech the main purpose for many voyages of discovery; what one seeks in the Other is to refind one's own lost self.

To be stranded on an island is to experience the loss of one's culture and identity that can be regained by exporting one's dominant culture. To the fantasized island of natural nonauthority, the colonialists bring marriage, regality, and the inscriptions of cultural hegemony ("set it down with gold on lasting pillars"). This process itself is equated by Shakespeare to the very process of going to a theater and seeing a play. In the Epilogue, Prospero addresses the audience in the following manner:

> Now, 'tis true,
> I must be here confin'd by you
> Or sent to Naples. Let me not,
> Since I have my dukedom got
> And pardon'd the deceiver, dwell
> In this bare island of your spell,
> But release me from my bands
> With the help of your good hands!
> Gentle breath of yours my sails,
> Must fill or else my project fails,
> Which was to please.
>
> (Epilogue, 4–14)

If all the world is a stage, the stage is also a world, and this world is not controlled by the playwright but by the audience that has the power to make the play successful or not.

In the context of colonial expansion, this final speech may signal that even though the men of the discovery go to foreign places only to find themselves and their own culture, they are determined by the pleasure of their own home audience. In other words, theater takes people to a foreign place that turns out to be dominated by their own cultural narcissism and the projection of their own repressed desires. This relationship between the playwright and the audience is doubled by the relationship between the reader and the text. Narcissistic reading strategies produce this same type of cultural mirroring and hysterical projection. Perhaps by concentrating on the repressed aspects of our own culture, we are able to undermine this narcissistic quest to avoid encountering all evidences of cultural and subjective loss and excess.

Moreover, the cultural narcissism that is inherent to colonial desire is very different from the narcissism that Miranda and other women are forced into in Shakespeare's world. For Miranda and Desdemona, there is a certain overidentification with the plight of their men that pushes Miranda to see the lost ship as a representation of her own body and allows Desdemona to fall in love with Othello by sympathizing with his tragic life story. On the one hand, these women see the Other as a mirror reflection of their own selves. On the other hand, both Prospero and Othello see reality as structured by a series of cultural fictions that allow them to take a certain distance from their own experiences. We can call this masculine distance ideological because it is founded on the illusion that there is no connection between subjectivity and larger social forces. In other terms, Prospero produces ideology by refusing to acknowledge the ideological effects of his productions. If his and Shakespeare's only goal is to please, the pleasure they produce helps to enslave subjects into vast networks of masochistic subjection.

This masochistic mode of ideological enjoyment has been shown to be essential to all forms of prejudice and social oppression. Shakespeare's play traces the connection between a subject's rejection of linguistic castration, the repression of same-sex desire, and the perverse and obsessional reiteration of various forms of prejudice. In order to avoid linguistic lack and sexual excess, the playwright and colonialist must constantly project loss and sexual debasement onto cultural Others. Moreover, these connections among linguistic castration, racism, and sexism force us to acknowledge that an essential aspect of the work against prejudice must include a subjective acceptance of the way that we are all alienated by language and the dominant symbolic orders.

To overcome perverse and hysterical forms of racism and sexism, subjects must fight against their own masochistic enjoyment of ideological subjection. In other words, cultural critics need to explore the ways that readers are interpellated in texts through the eroticization of various states of enslavement and bondage. Linked to this recognition of cultural masochism is the awareness of the ways that sadists identify with masochists and masochists identify with sadists. In the realm of literary prejudices, this form of sadomasochism often results in an obsessional displacement of loss and lack onto women and debased ethnic Others. One can posit that cultural critics have very little trouble locating examples of racism, sexism, and homophobia in distant cultures and time periods; however, what critics need to do now is to connect these forms of social oppression to our current culture. One way this can be done is by examining our own homophobia and the ways that we project our own feelings of linguistic castration onto Others. This entails that we must guard against the constant racist attempts to argue that the "darker races" cannot speak our language or follow our rules.

Throughout this work, we shall see how early modern theories of subjectivity and sexuality still play a major role in our current cycle of prejudice.

In the next series of texts that I will examine, I will posit that nineteenth-century colonial desire is determined by a similar ideological circulation of homophobia, racism, sexism, and ethnocentrism. The central mechanism in this cultural model of displaced forms of oppression continues to be the projection of same-sex desires and linguistic castration onto the realm of the dark Other.

PART TWO

Colonialism, Slavery, and Racist Homophobia

CHAPTER FIVE

Frankenstein's Homosocial Colonial Desire

In Mary Shelley's *Frankenstein*, we reencounter the same psychocultural model of prejudices that we have detected in the early modern period. However, in Shelley's text this relationship between homosociality, homophobia, racism, and sexism is presented within the nineteenth-century context of colonial exploration and the triangular slave trade between America, England, and Africa. In fact, I will argue that *Frankenstein* offers one of the most subtle and acute analyses of the connection between sexuality and cultural imperialism. For Shelley is able to show how colonial expansion and scientific discovery are fueled by a homosocial attempt to repress same-sex desires and to constitute a patriarchal order that equates women with the natural realm and the foreign lands that men need to dominate and control. Moreover, Victor Frankenstein's monster becomes a symbol of all of the repressed desires that this "discovering male" refuses to accept in himself and that he projects onto his debased Other.[1] We shall see how Shelley also uses the figure of the monster as a victim of prejudice who attempts to escape from his enslaved state.

If this text does indeed represent a veiled analysis of slavery and other colonial enterprises, Mary Shelley has rarely been read as an effective critic of European imperialism. One of the reasons for this failure to acknowledge Shelley's most radical insights can be attributed to the desire to read her as either an early feminist or an early Marxist.[2] While I would not argue against these aspects of her work, they must be attached to her continuous attempt to relate all forms of social prejudice to a psychosexual logic. For throughout this novel, a homophobic repression of same-sex desire results in an idealization of ethnocentric homosociality and a sexist devaluation of women and foreign cultures.

HOMOPHOBIA AND COLONIAL DESIRES

One reason most critics have not discussed Shelley's critical analysis of colonialism and the slave trade is that they have not connected the framing narrative of Walton's voyage of exploration to the story of Victor Frankenstein's creation of the "monster"; However, these two stories of discovery both reflect on a certain "colonial desire" that links the slave trade to the repression of same-sex desire.[3] As a women author surrounded by dominating men, Mary Shelley is able to detect the homosocial and repressed homosexual forces that helped to fuel the spirit of discovery and colonization. Her allegory of creation and domination allows us to see how the hatred of the Other, which is a necessary precondition for the enslavement of the Other, often has at its roots a hatred of the self. The acceptance of one's own rejected desires thus becomes a key to the work against a variety of forms of prejudice and oppression.[4]

In the beginning of the novel, we learn that Walton is sailing to the North Pole, not only to find a quicker route between Europe, Africa, and America, but also to find a friend and a soul mate. In his second letter to his sister, Walton declares: "I desire the company of a man who could sympathize with me; whose eyes would reply to mine. You may deem me romantic, my dear sister, but I bitterly feel the want of a friend" (28). Walton is not just cruising the sea; he is also cruising for another man.[5]

Walton's desire to find someone that he can sympathize with combines strong narcissistic and homoerotic urges. By writing that he wants to find a man whose eyes reply to his own eyes, he is pointing to both a same-sex desire and the need to bond with another person who sees things in the same way that he does. More so, the company that Walton so greatly desires is both a financial and a friendly union. He tells his sister that he wants someone to set him straight and to help "regulate" and cultivate his mind (29). Ironically, the very opposite happens, as the meeting with Victor serves to throw the ship off course.[6]

Throughout the narrative, Walton remains deeply seduced by Victor, and this is in part through the identification that he makes with his fellow European's own desire for knowledge and the domination of natural forces: "One man's life or death were but a small price to pay for the acquirement of the knowledge which I sought; for the dominion I should acquire and transmit over the elemental foes of our race" (35).[7] Just as Victor will attempt to master nature by discovering the secret of life, Walton desires to master the "pathless sea" and to dominate the "elemental" foes of Europe. Meanwhile, thousands of miles to the south, other voyaging men are united together in their quest to enslave the Other and enrich Europe and America.

In fact, Walton hints that his voyage will make a contribution to the navigation of the triangular slave trade. He asks his sister in a letter: "Shall I meet you again, after having traversed immense seas, and returned by the most southern cape of Africa or America?" (31). Either of these two destinations will help to further the slave trade between Europe, Africa, and America. However, before Walton is able to reach his desired destination, he is forced to encounter two beings that we later discover are the monster and Victor Frankenstein. The difference between these two characters is immediately attached to a racial and racist distinction: "He [Victor] was not, as the other traveller seemed to be, a savage inhabitant of some undiscovered island, but an European" (33). On the one hand, the Other is of course the monster that has only been seen from a distance of half a mile (32) but who is already determined to be a savage of some yet to be discovered land. On the other hand, Victor is right away accepted as a "noble creature" that fills Walton with deep feelings of "European" affection and sympathy (35).[8]

I will posit that this instant binary opposition that Walton makes between the savage monster and the noble European is not only based on a sense of a shared culture but also has strong homosocial, if not homoerotic, sources. In the structure of the novel, same-sex desire fuels a form of homosocial colonialism that results in the development of a series of racist and sexist binary oppositions. Using Lacan's schema L, we can map out the central elements of this system:

Same-sex desire S - - - - - - - - - - - a' Homosocial Colonialism

Racial Debasement a - - - - - - - - - - A Sexist Oppositions

This structure depicts the way that same-sex desires (S) motivate a form of homosocial idealization (a') of the same and a sexist devaluation of the Other (A). The fourth element (a) of this structure will be related to the leftover parts of homosexual desire that cannot be displaced into homosociality and thus returns in the racist debasement of the monster. As the novel develops, we shall see how the monster becomes the symbol of the unwanted desires that Victor and his society attempt to repress. In the opening section of this text, it is Walton who expresses this same-sex desire and it is Victor who becomes the symbol of homosocial idealization. When Walton first looks at Victor, he immediately assumes that Victor is the ideal European man (a') who he has been looking for. He also places the monster in the position of being the unknown but debased other (a):

Walton S - - - - - - - - - - - - - a' Victor

Monster a - - - - - - - - - - - A

What will later displace this all-male psychosexual structure is the idealization of women as the symbol of homosocial bonding. In other words, the transformation of the initial system is dependent on the inclusion of a sexist discourse on gender differences that allows for a second displacement of same-sex desire. By introducing heterosexuality into the homosexual and homosocial relation, Shelley is able to show the way that sexual difference is often motivated out of a desire to hide the true psychosexual structure of masculine desire.[9]

THE HOMOSOCIAL IDEALIZATION OF WOMEN

This homosocial "idealization" of women takes place in the second section of the novel, where females are constantly described as perfect beings that need to be saved and protected by men.[10] For example, Victor's mother Caroline was a poor woman who was left alone after the death of her father. Victor relates the way that his father "came like a protecting spirit to the poor girl, who committed herself to his care" (39). The father is seen here as a saving force that protects and mothers his future wife.[11] Not only does the man rescue the woman, he also treats her like a delicate flower:

> Every thing was made to yield to her wishes and her convenience. He strove to shelter her, as a fair exotic, and to surround her with all that could tend to excite pleasurable emotion in her soft and benevolent mind. (39)

This passage begins by arguing that Caroline was in control of all those around her and that the father merely satisfied her desires. However, Victor's mother's power is soon removed from her and she becomes a "fair exotic" who is nurtured by the father.

This notion of the sheltered "fair exotic" is a product of the idealizing aspect of colonial desire. While the masculine monster is immediately associated with the horror of the foreign savage, the women in this novel all tend to be idealized for their differences.[12] In other words, men are able to displace their same-sex desires onto exotic women because they know that they can control and idealize these foreign beings. However, the encounter with native men only serves to enhance the colonialists' homosexual desire and the fear that they cannot control the Other.

This opposition between the fair female and the dark Other is presented in the story of Victor's future wife, Elizabeth. This woman is actually Victor's adopted sister who was chosen by his mother because, we are told, "she appeared of a different stock. The four others were dark-eyed, hardly little vagrants; this child was thin, and very fair. Her hair was the brightest living gold" (40). Victor's future wife and sister is thus picked because of her ideal fair and golden features. Even though she has to be saved from poverty, she still appears to come from the same stock and race as the Frankensteins. In a way, her poverty leaves her open to masculine control and idealization. She also contains in her beauty and her heritage, the gold that these European men are after. Elizabeth and Caroline are therefore both seen as commodities of idealization.[13]

Because, these women are valued only for their fair external appearances, their own will and subjectivity are barred and effaced.[14] In Victor's description of his sister's new family status, he underlines both her captured state and the strangeness of their relationship: "Elizabeth Lanza became the inmate of my parents' house—my more than sister—the beautiful and adored companion of all my occupations and my pleasures" (41). Just as Elizabeth is a prisoner to this house, she is also the object of Victor's pleasures and occupations. The fact that he will love and marry his sister suggests that he can only love something that he feels that he can control and that represents a sense of sameness.[15]

Victor's feeling of entitlement over Elizabeth is strongly presented by Shelley in the following passage:

> On the evening previous to her being brought to my home, my mother had said playfully,—"I have a present for my Victor—tomorrow he shall have it." And when, on the morrow, she presented Elizabeth to me as her promised gift, I, with childish seriousness, interpreted her words literally, and looked upon Elizabeth as mine—mine to protect, love, and cherish. All praises bestowed on her, I received as a possession made to my own. (41)

Elizabeth is for Victor only an extension of himself: when this fair object is idealized, Victor claims the praise as his own possession. She thus becomes his own ideal ego and a representation of his own narcissistic desire.[16]

In the psychosexual logic that I have been developing, women represent the heterosexual Other that fuels homosocial idealization and helps men to repress their same-sex desire:

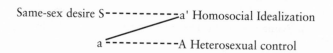

Same-sex desire S---------a' Homosocial Idealization

a ---------A Heterosexual control

Women, as the Other in this structure, have no subjectivity or desire. They are only a means of expressing and displacing masculine desire and idealization.

In "On Narcissism," Freud articulates the relationship between this masculine need to idealize women and the repression of same-sex desires for the service of socialization:

> The ego-deal is of great importance for the understanding of group psychology. Besides its individual side, this ideal has a social side; it is also the common ideal of a family, a class or a nation. It not only binds the narcissistic libido, but also a considerable amount of the person's homosexual libido, which in this way becomes turned back into the ego. The dissatisfaction due to the non-fulfillment of this ideal liberates the homosexual libido, which is transformed into a sense of guilt (dread of the community). (81)

Freud discusses here the reasons why he places homosexual desire in opposition and in relation to social organization. In order for the male subject to idealize the nation and the nation's women, he must repress his same-sex desires; however, this repression is never complete and the left-over residues of homosexual desire create a sense of guilt that further binds the subject to his society. Furthermore, since national and social idealization depend on the sublimation of homosexual desire, there needs to be a constant cycle of the production and repression of same-sex desire.[17] In *Frankenstein,* we witness this continuous oscillation between the eruption and denial of homosexual libido within a structure that idealizes and objectifies women.

Against this background of sexist idealization and heterosexual control, Shelley presents masculine desire as an uncontrollable passion. Victor early on indicates that Walton's passion for geographical exploration is the same desire that fuels his own quest for scientific knowledge: "Unhappy man! Do you share my madness? Have you drank also the intoxicating draught?" (36). Walton and Victor bond over this sense that their passions cannot be controlled and that they are in fact slaves to their own desires. Beneath all of the idealizing rhetoric of heterosexual love and European sameness, these masculine subjects continue to represent their desire as something that is foreign and something that enslaves them.

Returning to our psychosexual diagram, we can now map the different elements of this structure:

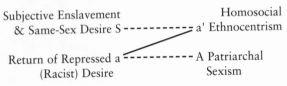

Subjective Enslavement   Homosocial
& Same-Sex Desire S — — — — — — a' Ethnocentrism

Return of Repressed a — — — — — — A Patriarchal
(Racist) Desire   Sexism

Within the context of this novel, Victor attempts to represses his same-sex desires and his feelings of subjective enslavement (S) by bonding with European men on an ethnocentric homosocial level (a'). In order to support this system of male-bonding, women, like Elizabeth and Caroline, are absorbed into a sexist patriarchal order. However, this double assimilation of homosexual desire and feelings of subjective enslavement is never complete, and thus there is always a residue of repressed desire that returns in the form of the racist sexualization of the Other. The initial state of cultural homophobia therefore constitutes the driving force behind other forms of prejudice.

A SLAVE TO PASSION

What still needs to be explained in this structure is the link between the repression of same-sex desire and the displacement of the subjective feeling of enslavement. For Victor, it is clear that he experiences his own desires and passions as enslaving forces that are beyond his control: "Having conquered the violence of his feelings, he appeared to despise himself for being the slave of passion; and quelling the dark tyranny of despair" (36). As a "slave to passion," Victor unconsciously equates his psychological subjection to his inability to repress completely all of his same-sex desires. Homophobia is in this sense tied to linguistic masochism, because it is his submission to the signifying chain that initiates Victor's feelings of subjective enslavement. In other words, Victor attempts to master his subjection to the dominant symbolic order by blaming his sense of linguistic castration on the uncontrollable nature of his illicit desires.[18]

One way that this signifying form of masochism is presented is through Victor's depictions of his strenuous experiments in science and anatomy: "I appeared rather like one doomed by slavery to toil in the mines" (57). Throughout this novel, Victor experiences all of his scientific work as an enslaving passion he cannot control. Moreover, the monster soon becomes the symbol of this type of enslavement to scientific discourse.[19] After the creature asks Victor for a mate, Victor thinks to himself: "My promise fulfilled, the monster would depart for ever. Or (as my fond fancy imagined) some accident might meanwhile occur to destroy him, and put an end to my slavery for ever" (130). As in the classical structure of Hegel's master/slave dialectic, the master has now become a slave because the slave has reversed the balance of power. At one point in the novel, the monster exclaims to Victor: "Slave, I have reasoned with you . . . remember that I have the power; you believe yourself miserable, but I can make you so wretched that the light of day will be hateful to you. You are my creator, but I am your master; obey" (142)! In this passage, the monster has turned Victor into a psychological slave who identifies with the monster's own sense of wretchedness.[20]

This notion of "wretchedness" reflects Victor's homophobic feelings about his own same-sex desires. Throughout the text, he constantly refers to himself in self-loathing terms: "I, a miserable wretch, haunted by a curse that shut up every avenue to enjoyment" (132). In this passage, Victor links his own sense of wretchedness to his inability to pursue sexual pleasure. In other terms, he has no access to enjoyment, or what Lacan calls "jouissance," because he denies his own desire and sexuality. Furthermore, his self-hatred is linked to his feeling that he is a slave to his own uncontrollable passions: "For an instant I dared to shake off my chains and look around me with a free and lofty spirit; but the iron had eaten into my flesh, and I sank again, trembling and hopeless, into my miserable self" (137). As a subject divided against himself, Victor internalizes the master-slave relation that he has with the monster. In this structure, Victor's unconscious desires become the foreign master and monster that enslaves him in a masochistic structure: "By the utmost self-violence, I curbed the imperious voice of wretchedness, which sometimes desired to declare itself to the whole world" (156). Like a good masochist, in order to overcome his overwhelming feelings of guilt, Victor must do mental violence to himself.[21]

This masochistic form of self-hatred is soon replaced in the novel by an even stronger desire for Victor to find and destroy the monster: "I pursued my path towards the destruction of the daemon, more as a task enjoined by heaven, as the mechanical impulse of some power of which I was unconscious, than as the ardent desire of my soul" (170). In this shift from masochistic self-violence to uncontrollable unconscious sadism, we once again encounter the masculine projection of self-hatred onto the hatred of the Other. Since Victor cannot tolerate his own homosexual desire, he displaces his intolerance onto his debased object.

I would insist that this repressed aspect of homosexual desire is only the flip side of the manifest homosocial drive for control and colonization. At the end of the novel when Victor attempts to bully Walton's men into risking their lives in order to pursue the hated monster, he declares:

> Oh! be men or be more than men. Be steady to your purposes, and firm as a rock. This ice is not made of such stuff as your hearts may be; it is mutable, and cannot withstand you, if you say that it shall not. (178)

How may other men have been spurred on to action throughout history by such strong appeals to men's rocklike firmness? This call for phallic power must be related to the mutable surfaces that resist the masculine drive but eventually are overcome.

Linked to this phallic colonial desire, we find Victor's wish to use heterosexuality as a defense against his feelings of homosexual enslavement: "It was the prospect of that day when, enfranchised from my miserable slavery, I might claim Elizabeth, and forget the past in my union with her" (131). In this movement from slavery to marriage, Victor hopes to move from a position of impotency to one of power and control. In a similar fashion, the monster also has a desire to exchange a state of slavery for one of power: "Yet mine shall not be the submission of abject slavery. I will revenge my injuries: if I cannot inspire love, I will cause fear" (124). While Victor desires to efface his feelings of homosexual enslavement by marrying Elizabeth, the monster feels that love is no longer an option for him and that his only choice is thus to seek revenge against his creator.[22]

RACISM AND THE MONSTER

The monster, as a figure of Victor's unconscious, also represents a victim of racial prejudice. Starting with his own creator, everyone who encounters the monster is horrified by his appearance and refuses to look beyond his superficial attributes. Immediately after Victor first creates this new being, he relates that he is disgusted by the creature that he has helped to "author": "his teeth of a pearly whiteness; but these luxuriances only formed a more horrid contrast with his watery eyes, that seemed almost of the same color as the dun white sockets in which they were set, his shriveled complexion and straight black lips" (58). What repulses Victor the most about his creation is the opposition between the whiteness of his teeth and the darkness of his eye sockets. It is color, not the size and proportion of the monster's features, that serve to render him the horrific Other. This horror of color soon spreads to Victor's dream of his beloved Elizabeth: "Delighted and surprised, I embraced her [Elizabeth]; but as I imprinted the first kiss on her lips, they became livid with the hue of death" (58). On the level of his unconscious, Victor displays not only a horror of blackness, and heterosexuality, but also a disgust at his own act of imprinting or writing. What identifies these two horrors as the same is the common contrast between his own whiteness and the blackness of the uncontrollable Other.

In her Introduction to the novel, Shelley herself displays this same fear of creation that we find in Victor's reaction to his own "authorship": "It is true that I am very averse to bringing myself forward in print" (19). This horror of putting her name in black on a white page is in part due to her culture's refusal to take women writers seriously; however, Shelley's horror of writing does have deeper psychological roots that can be tied to the fact that her parents and her husband were all writers who in many ways intimidated her.[23] Furthermore, many critics have related Victor's act of creation to Mary's own troubled relationship with procreation.[24] According to David Collins, Victor "identifies with his mother, recovering her body in his own body as he attempts to become pregnant himself to labor in childbirth, and to watch the child awaken, gesture, and attempt to speak" (248). While there is plenty of evidence to make this association between Mary Shelley and Victor Frankenstein, I will stress the ways that Shelley identifies with the monster and not his creator.

Shelley's identification with the monster is best exemplified by the way that she shifts from Victor's perspective to that of the monster himself (92–124). Through this transition, Shelley is able to narrate the subjectivity of the victim, while she ties the development of a criminal mind to the oppressive forces that produced its criminality. The creature first appears to be an honest and kind man whose only wish is to be accepted by others, but he is shunned on account of his appearance. Due to the fact that everyone judges the creature solely by the way he looks, the monster's only successful interaction is with a blind man, who cannot see the creature's difference. In this allegory of race and prejudice, the sightless man may represent Shelley's desire for a color-blind society. However, even though De Lacey cannot see, the monster knows that the blind man's family will not be able to look beyond his external differences:

> I have good dispositions; my life has been hitherto harmless, and in some degree beneficial; but a fatal prejudice clouds their eyes, and where they ought to see a feeling and a kind friend, but they behold only a detestable monster. (116)

As a victim of prejudice, the monster realizes that no matter what he does to help other people, he will still be considered dangerous and will thus be excluded from interacting with other human beings.

Included in this allegory of prejudice is a commentary on the economic causes of racism and slavery.[25] Since the monster is someone with an open and virgin mind, he is able to see through the divisive class structure that helps to foster various social inequalities:

> I learned that the possessions most esteemed by your fellow creatures were high and unsullied descent united with riches. A man might be respected with only one of these advantages; but, without either, he was considered, except in very rare instances, as a vagabond and a slave, doomed to waste his powers for the profits of the chosen few! (105)

The monster shows himself in this passage to be a natural Marxist, who feels not only the weight of prejudice but also that of a oppressive class structure.[26]

With the continuation of the monster's story, these two forces of racism and classism come together in his retelling of Safie's slave narrative. The reader soon learns that the reason why De Lacey's son is so upset and the family is so poor is that they had been forced to escape from Paris after they helped a Turkish girl named Safie. We also learn that Safie's father was a Turkish man who was imprisoned because of his religion and wealth (107). In this case, the power of money is overcome by the fear of the foreign Other.

De Lacey's son Felix was present at Safie's father's trial and he became enraged by the unjust sentence. After the father was put into prison, Felix visited him but refused to help him escape until he laid eyes on his beautiful daughter. Caught in the throws of sexual attraction, Felix gave up his principles and chose exotic beauty over legality and wealth. He then embarked in a series of communications with Safie, where he discovered that her mother was a slave and that she was bought by Safie's father because of her beauty (108).[27]

In this interwoven story of class, race, and sexuality, the attractive slave woman is able to move out of her servitude solely on the basis of her exotic appearance. In opposition to the monster, whose visual presentation keeps him in his state of enslavement, her external beauty allows her to be free. By combining the forces of sexual desire with the factors of race and class, Shelley is able to endow the monster with a powerful tool for social criticism. Now he is not only a Marxist, he is also sensitive to the questions of gender and ethnicity.

As an early feminist and postcolonial critic, the monster displays a keen analytic desire in his readings of such great literary works as *Paradise Lost, Plutarch's Lives,* and *The Sorrows of Young Werther* (111). As he reads these texts, the monster begins to experience two opposing feelings: on one level, these texts help him to see the similarity between his own sentiments and those of others, yet on another, more profound level, these writings make him feel completely alone and separate (112). These two functions of identification and separation are crucial to the understanding of the way that reading works to both enhance a sense of connectedness and a feeling of disconnectedness.[28]

On one level, we read to see how we are like others; however, at the same time, on another level, reading allows us to detect our own radical difference and separateness. The act of interpretation thus always entails a division of the reading subject between the quest for narcissistic sameness and the unconscious awareness of radical difference. In this structure, reading is a prime example of the way that we deal with Otherness: part of us seeks out sympathetic connections, while the other part denies any similarity. Perhaps Shelley is asking us as readers and social beings to be tolerant of both the similarities and differences between ourselves and others. For the fear of the Other that is at the basis of prejudice is connected to our repressed "uncanny" awareness that this Other is both completely like ourselves and completely heterogeneous.

In order to fight against his feelings of total alienation and solitude, the monster decides that he needs a mate who will be from the same "species" and will have all of the same "defects" (124). We can read the monster's desired solution as an attempt to erase all feelings of difference by finding another that is completely the same. Sexual desire is here based on a resignation to the prejudices and racism of others; since the monster cannot beat the racists, his only choice is to join them in their valuation of superficial appearances.[29]

THE BONDS BETWEEN MEN

Coupled with the monster's and Walton's quests for sympathetic soul-mates, one finds Victor's reconnection with his childhood friend Clevral. This old Swiss friend is singled out by Victor for the way that he resembles Victor's own lost self: "But in Clevral I saw the image of my former self; he was inquisitive, and anxious to gain experience and instruction" (135). Clevral not only acts as a double for Victor's good self, he also serves to unite Walton's discovery narrative to Victor's own pursuit of scientific domination: "His design was to visit India, in the belief that he had in his knowledge of the various languages, and the views that he had taken of its society, the means of materially assisting the progress of European colonization and trade" (135). Like the other scientific and discovering men in this novel, Clevral desires to use his knowledge to colonize and control Other races.

What links Clevral to Victor and Victor to Walton is their shared desire to combine homosocial yearnings with the enslavement of other "inferior" or exotic races. On one level, these characters bond together by actively pursuing similar discoveries; however, on a more repressed and profound level, they are united by their need to determine and control a devalued Other, a need that is itself driven by their desire to deny the homosexual foundations of their bond with each other. Shelley effectively shows how these men's sense of being European and of being men is centered on the exploitation and abjection of other cultures and races.[30]

What then connects this homosocial European drive for conquest to a racist discourse is not only a quest for a shared identity but also a common way of rejecting homosexual strivings that, in turn, results in the projection onto the Other of repressed sexual impulses. The monster, as the missing link between Man and beast, represents the unconscious horror heterosexual men have about their own sexual desire for other men. This subtle theme comes out in the monster's warning to Victor that if he does not make the creature a wife, the monster will be with him on his wedding night (142).

As a figure of the unconscious, we can read the monster as both an insistence of the taboo against incest and a persistence of homosexual longing. Both of these themes come together in the monster's desire to disrupt Victor's planned marriage: Victor will not be able to sleep with Elizabeth because he is afraid that the monster will kill one of them. Moreover, by constantly repeating the monster's phrase "I will be with you on your wedding night," Shelley is able to link together sexual desire, fear, and the triadic nature of the Oedipus complex: the monster is the third term that prevents the dual relation between Victor and his love object.

As many critics have argued, Victor's creation of the monster can be equated with his desire to re-create a relation with his lost maternal object. However, on a more fundamental level, the fact that Victor decides to create a man and not a woman suggests that his desire is more homosexual than heterosexual.[31] In this way, Victor's horror of the monster that he identifies with can be equated with his horror of his own sexuality.

In *Between Men: English Literature and Male Homosocial Desire*, Eve Sedgwick posits that early Gothic stories like *Frankenstein* often contain many of the aspects of paranoia and homosexuality that Freud outlines in his case of Dr. Schreber:

> Each is about one or more males who not only is persecuted by, but considers himself transparent to and often the compulsion of, another male. If we follow Freud in hypothesizing that such a sense of persecution represents the fearful, phantasmatic rejection of an original homosexual (or even merely homosocial) desire, then it would make sense to think of this group of novels as embodying strongly homophobic mechanisms. (91–92)

As Freud argues in his text "Some Neurotic Mechanisms in Jealousy, Paranoia, and Homosexuality," one source of male paranoia is the rejection of strong homosexual desires that results in the reversal and projection of fear and hatred onto a persecuting other (201). This is precisely Victor's story; he rejects his own homosexual desire to create a relation with a man, and in a paranoid way, he experiences the monster as persecuting him.

More important for my argument, Victor's paranoid fear of the persecuting Other is tied directly to the question of race and sexual reproduction: "One of the first sympathies for which the daemon thirsted would be children, and a race of devils would be propagated upon the earth" (140). While a constant theme of the book has been the European man's desire to find sameness and sympathy in those that are like himself, the horror that threatens to reverse this homosocial order is based on the fear that the Other will also seek out likeness and attempt the act of self-reproduction. The fears of other races, of sexual reproduction, and of threats to homosociality all come to-gether in this fear of the monster's desired wife.

The continual reoccurrence of homosociality and repressed homosexu-ality in *Frankenstein* highlights the ways that sexual desire and fear con-tribute to national projects of colonization and racial enslavement. In order to work effectively against these cultural forms of oppression, critics must first realize the ways that the repression of same-sex desires helps to fuel hypermasculine attempts at dominating women and other minority groups. Homophobia thus contributes to a wide range of prejudices and social for-mations that exceed the question of homosexuality.

In the next chapter of this work, I will reexamine this connection be-tween homophobia and colonialism by interpreting Joseph Conrad's *Heart of Darkness* as an example of homophobic panic. This fear of same-sex desire will not only be explored in relation to Conrad's text but also in the critical reception of his work. One of my goals in this project is to show how literary criticism is often dominated by an obsessional university discourse that allows readers to project their own repressed desires and fears onto texts and foreign cultures. This process of intellectualized displacement undermines many of the attempts to use critical theory for the promotion of social change and the fight against diverse structures of prejudice.

CHAPTER SIX

The *Heart of Darkness* and Homophobic Colonial Desire

In this chapter, I will read Joseph Conrad's *Heart of Darkness* as an extended homosexual panic that links together the fear of same-sex desires with the cultivation of a racist and sexist form of ethnocentrism.[1] We shall see how Conrad, his main character Marlow, and his readers constantly repress and express an erotic concern for men's bodies and a horror of bodily holes and anal forms of penetration.[2] Throughout this novella, men's behinds will be equated with a turning away from civilization and an effacement of visual mastery. In this structure, the anus becomes an unconscious source of horror, desire, and masculine vulnerability that forces men to project their own same-sex desires onto debased women and natives.[3] Furthermore, readers of this novella constantly transform the presence of bodily holes into textual gaps in order to avoid an encounter with Conrad's anal erotism. One of the results of this academic form of homophobia is the constitution of an obsessional discourse that associates all forms of sexual and ethnic difference to a threat of anal penetration.

HOMOPHOBIA AND THE OBSESSIONAL READER

As Young-Bruehl argues, obsessional subjects fear being placed in a position where they are the passive objects of the Other's attack from behind:

> Anxiety about being overwhelmed, rendered ineffectual or inactive or passive is the key. Both males and females often express such anxiety in frightening fantasies of anal attack or rape or, in a more disguised form, in fantasies of people sneaking up from behind and stabbing them in the back. (219)

This unconscious horror of anal penetration is in part based on the need for the obsessional subjects to visually control and anticipate the objects of their desire.[4] Preestablished forms of knowledge (i.e., prejudice) and narcissistic modes of pleasure give these subjects a needed sense of bodily mastery and control. Anal penetration, in contrast, can take the form of an attack that cannot be seen or anticipated.[5] To guard against this fear of passive penetration, the readers of Conrad's text are narcissistically interpellated into positions where their own homophobia, ethnocentrism, sexism, and racism are reinforced.

Central to this theory of textual narcissism is the idea that texts are read as reflections of the reader's own body. In other terms, the closure and unity of a text gives the reader a sense of bodily and mental cohesion and completeness. In *Heart of Darkness,* we shall see how bodily and textual closure are continuously provided and then denied. This "self-defeating" strategy constitutes the core of the obsessional discourse that interpellates readers into a masochistic position of self-doubt and incertitude.[6] Each time the symptom of doubt emerges, the subjects are motivated to produce a new knowledge about their textual body. This knowledge then circulates until it runs into the presence of a new hole that produces a new sense of doubt. I will posit that this structure is locked into a vicious obsessional circle.[7]

We can map this logic onto Lacan's discourse of the university:

$$\text{Knowledge } \underline{S2} \text{ ----------} \underline{a} \text{ bodily textuality}$$
$$\text{Doubt } \overline{S1} \text{ ----------} \$ \text{ Bodily holes}$$

In the primary position of agency in this discourse is the circulation of symbolic knowledge (S2).[8] For Lacan, knowledge is defined by the dominance of the signifying chain that links together signifiers in a logical or linguistic system. Obsessional subjects display this dominance of knowledge in their constant attempts to think things out and to submit themselves to a formal system of knowledge.[9] What helps to motivate this structure is the repressed symptom of doubt (S1) that is fueled by the encounter with different textual and bodily holes. Moreover, the knowledge that is dominant in this form of discourse is always directed toward the reduction of the Other into a textual body (a) of narcissistic self-reflection.[10]

Within the context of Conrad's obsessional colonial discourse, the quest for knowledge about the natives and about Kurtz's behavior is determined by Marlow's desire to overcome his own sense of doubt and his fear of the anal hole. In this ethnocentric logic, Marlow is able to envision a world that lacks nothing by subjecting all forms of foreignness and Otherness to a discourse of sameness. This desire to see the Other as the same becomes evident in the narrator's description of the typical imperial sailor:

> Their minds are of the stay-at home order, and their home is always with them—the ship; and so is their country—the sea. One ship is very much like another, and the sea is always the same. In the immutability of their surroundings the foreign shores, the foreign faces, the changing immensity of life, glide past, veiled not by a sense of mystery but by a slightly disdainful ignorance. (19)

By taking their home culture with them, these homosocial colonial sailors are able to imagine a world that is void of all foreignness.[11] However, this narcissistic quest for the same is always coupled with a deep awareness that the Other is absolutely different.

The presence of absolute difference is linked in the text to the heart of internalized darkness: "in some inland post . . . the savagery, had closed round him—all that mysterious life of the wilderness that stirs in the forest, in the jungles, in the hearts of wild men" (21). The obsessional racism that is inherent in this passage is based on the constant threat that the incomprehensible passion of the African might invade the knowledge and the body of the European:

> He has to live in the midst of the incomprehensible, which is also detestable. And it has a fascination, too, that goes to work upon him. Fascination of the abomination—you know. Imagine the growing regrets, the longing to escape, the powerless disgust, the surrender, the hate. (21)

This passage represents an accurate description of Freud's theory of the obsessional subject that he presents in his "Notes Upon a Case of Obsessional Neurosis." For Freud, the obsessional subject is fascinated by what repulses him or her (24). The combination of attraction and repulsion creates the foundations for symptomatic feelings of doubt because the subject fears what he desires and desires what he hates. Within the context of Marlow's colonial exploration, his hatred and fear of the African is based on his rejection of his own unconscious desires and his powerlessness to control his sense of disgust.[12]

In Freud's case of the Rat Man, the patient's unconscious desire centers on his fantasy of being tortured by having a rat shoved into his anus (27). This desire for anal penetration links sexual excitement to fear. Moreover, Freud uses this example in order to establish his notion of unconscious sexual enjoyment: "I could only interpret it as one of horror at pleasure of his own of which he himself was unaware" (27). Freud here clearly articulates Lacan's notion of *jouissance*—a form of sexual enjoyment that is experienced without the subject's knowledge. This concept of unconscious sexual enjoyment is crucial to the structure of the obsessional discourse, which involves an opposition between a knowledge of pleasure and a form enjoyment that has no knowledge.

What, then, threatens obsessional subjects the most is their own (anal) enjoyment that they cannot explain or get to know. In order to overcome this potential loss of knowledge in the face of unconscious desire, the subject attempts to repress this mode of sexuality and to dissociate knowledge from affect:

> The trauma, instead of being forgotten, is deprived of its affective cathexis; so that what remains in consciousness is nothing but the ideational content, which is perfectly colorless and is judged to be unimportant. (54)

This separation of the idea from the affect is one of the key elements in both the obsessional (ethnocentric) and the university forms of discourse.

In fact, the Rat Man is a university student who is dominated by a need to know and to see others. For Freud, the "scoptophilic and epistemophiliac instincts" help the obsessional subject to replace all actions with thoughts (98). Vision and knowledge are thus seen to be regressive defense mechanisms that are employed in order to replace sexual experiences with sexual curiosity. Freud adds that "brooding" is the main symptom of this type of substitution of knowledge for sexual activity (99).

OBSESSIONAL BEHIND SIGHT

This form of obsessional brooding is prominent at the beginning of Conrad's text: "The air was dark above Gravesend, and farther back still seemed condensed into a mournful gloom, brooding motionless over the biggest, and the greatest town on earth" (17). In this passage, the narrator projects his own obsessional sense of doom onto nature, thus affirming his affect at the same time that he denies it. Furthermore, this sense of brooding and gloom is placed behind the narrator, which returns us to the general threat of anal penetration. For we shall see in the following paragraphs that this form of seeing from behind serves to translate the unknown fear of anal attack into a known sense of subjective brooding.

What I would like to stress in these opening scenes is the way that Conrad's narrator employs what Lee Edelman has called "(be)hind-sight." Edelman uses this term in order to emphasize the homoerotic aspects of Freud's theory of the primal scene and the way that Freud always discusses psychological trauma as an event that only becomes traumatic after the fact through a process of hindsight (95). Homosexual encounters thus imply for Freud not only a reversal of sexual positions but also a reversal of temporal relations. Furthermore, Edelman points out that Freud himself insists that children first believe that sexual intercourse takes place from behind (101). In the development of sexual knowledge, this early theory of anal procreation is replaced by the child through a transformation of sexual positions where the behind becomes the vagina and the parents take on specific gendered roles. "Thus in the first instance the primal scene is always perceived as sodomitical, and it specifically takes shape as a sodomitical scene between sexually undifferentiated parents" (101). Edelman effectively shows in his reading of Freud that the primal scene of sexuality for the subject always entails an element of bisexuality and the penetration from behind.[13]

In her *Male Subjectivity at the Margins,* Kaja Silverman posits that the traumatic nature of the primal scene can reduce the viewing male subject to the passive role of the one who knows but cannot act (157).[14] In this form of masculine masochism, the passive male subject is always looking at others from behind and with hindsight in order to transform the primal scene of anal penetration into an imaginary fantasy of visual control. Silverman uses this theory to discuss Henry James's constant references to "going behind" his characters and the placement of his narrative voice and eye in the position of a passive onlooker who sees and hears but cannot act (157–58). One reason for this form of masculine passivity is James's horror of his own sexuality—he knows that his desire is illicit but he cannot help returning to scenes of repressed homosexual desire. Like the child in the primal scene who is forced to watch sexual acts that are outside of his or her control, James places his characters and his narrative voice in a position of visual and representational nonmastery (165).

In Conrad's text, we find this same emphasis on masculine passivity and visual hindsight: "We four watched his back as he stood in the bows looking seaward" (17). The sailors here watch their captain from behind as he himself watches the sea from the front of the boat: "It was difficult to realize that his work was not out there in the luminous estuary, but behind him, within the brooding gloom" (17). Once again, the darkness behind the captain is connected to the subjective symptom of brooding in a personification of nature. Throughout this text, the view of the back of men causes Marlow to translate his sexual desire into the intellectual act of obsessional doubt and worry.

This latent connection between anal eroticism and symptomatic doubt is soon repressed by the reaffirmation of the homosocial bond between the sailing men:

> Between us there was, as I have already said somewhere, the bond of the sea. Besides holding our hearts together through long periods of separation, it had the effect of making us tolerant of each other's yarns—and even convictions. (18)

Through their mutual connection to the sea, these men are able to accept each other and even love each other. In a way, the sea, represents the "see"— a common way for these men to view the world. By affirming this shared homosocial vision, they are able to repress the potential same-sex desire that is always threatening to rise to the surface. Moreover, as readers of this text, we are also called into the position of identifying with Conrad's/Marlow's yarns and convictions. To read this text, we have to attempt to visualize what Conrad is trying to represent, and in this act of visualization, we begin to see things from his perspective. This bonding through vision also serves to place us in the same masochistic position of watching the unfolding of events without the ability to act or change them.[15] Moreover, by being interpellated into this text on an imaginary level, we are motivated to share Conrad's/Marlow's ideas and his body of knowledge.[16]

FROM THE MASTER TO THE UNIVERSITY

One of Marlow's bonding beliefs is the idea that the nineteenth-century form of colonialism is much less brutal and more efficient than older modes of colonial exploration:

> They were colonialists; their administration was merely a squeeze, and nothing more, I suspect. They were conquerors, and for that you only want brute force—nothing to boast of, when you have it, since your strength is just an accident arising from the weakness of others. (21)

This passage indicates that colonial rule has moved from the pure brutality of the discourse of the master to the rational bureaucracy of the discourse of the university. In Lacan's theory of the discourse of the master, the master signifier of power and language is placed in the dominant position of agency, while knowledge is located in the position of the Other:

Master Signifier S1 – – – – – – – S2 Knowledge of other
Barred subject $\overline{\$}$ – – – – – – – a Produced Lost Object

In this older form of mastery, language and power serve to render the subjects of these forces blind and barred. In other words, the subject of language cannot control the effects of the discourse that he or she uses. This lack of control forces the masters to find more brutal ways of controlling the Other subjects and reducing them to fixed knowable, objects.[17]

Marlow points to this relation between the master and the Other in the old form of colonialism:

The conquest of the earth, which mostly means the taking it away from those who have a different complexion or slightly flatter noses than ourselves, is not a pretty thing when you look into it too much. What redeems us is the idea only. An idea at the back of it. (21)

Marlow here makes a distinction between the brutal force of racist colonialism and another mode of colonial rule. While the first type of imperialism concerns the symbolic and physical mastery of the Other, the second type of control involves the acceptance and maintenance of a certain idea: "an unselfish belief in the idea—something you can set up, and bow down before, and offer a sacrifice to" (21). This glorification of the idea represents the absorption of the discourse of the Master into the obsessional discourse of the university (and the universal).[18]

As Lacan has argued, the transition from the discourse of the master to the discourse of the university entails a shifting or rotation of discourse, with knowledge (S2) instead of the master signifier (S1) now occupying the dominant position:

$$\text{Master Signifier } \underline{S1} \text{ ------- } \underline{S2} \text{ Knowledge of other}$$
$$\text{Barred subject } \$ \text{ ------- a Produced Lost Object}$$

$$\underline{\text{Discourse of the University}}$$
$$\text{Knowledge } \underline{S2} \text{ ------- a Narcissistic object}$$
$$\text{Doubt S1} \qquad \$ \text{ Textual Holes}$$

This shifting of the master signifier (S1) from a position of dominance to one of subservience below the realm of symbolic knowledge (S2) entails the sign of mastery being replaced by a symptom of doubt (S1). This also means that knowledge is now directed toward the translation of the Other into a narcissistic object (a) of self-coherence that represses the failures (\$) and lacks of discourse and the body. This structural shift entails a movement from the symbolic racism of the discourse of the master to the obsessional ethnocentrism of the discourse of the university. The master stresses the radical difference of the Other, while the university attempts to represent the Other in a form of universal sameness. Furthermore, Lacan posits that this shift in discourses is based on the new, bureaucratic form of knowledge, which can function all alone without the need for a master.[19]

This distinction between the discourses of the master and the university is crucial for the understanding and undermining of different forms of prejudice. In the case of the racist master, criticism must be able to show the way that all forms of mastery are motivated out of a sense of subjective loss (\$)

and a subjection to the realm of language that no one can control. In the case of the obsessional homophobe and xenophobe, symbolic knowledge of the causes of prejudice will only serve to strengthen their university discourse. What has to be stressed is the unconscious desires and fears that fuel the demand for more knowledge and the repression of unconscious forms of enjoyment. By motivating obsessional subjects to acknowledge their own repressed anal and passive desires, the ethnocentric horror of the Other may be reduced.

THE HORROR OF THE ANAL HOLE

Another way of working against this obsessional discourse that attempts to split off unconscious affect from conscious forms of knowledge is to reconnect affect to intellect by concentrating on the traumatic elements that lead to their splitting. In the case of Conrad's text, these moments of trauma surround the horror of anal penetration. One example of the displacement of the encounter with this hole occurs in the description of a deserted native village: "the huts gaped black, rotting, all askew within fallen enclosures" (24). The blackness of these structural holes will be a reoccurring theme throughout the novella.[20] All forms of destruction return Marlow to his own horror of the hole of darkness, and his prejudice and racism are connected to this association between the anus and blackness.

The anal hole and the blackness of the natives are equated in Marlow's mind partly because of their mutual mysteriousness: "I avoided a vast artificial hole somebody had been digging on the slope, the purpose of which I found it impossible to divine. It wasn't a quarry or a sand pit, anyhow. It was just a hole" (31). In a way this impossible hole is Marlow's master signifier—he cannot help but focus on the presence of this absence even though it blocks his desire for understanding and bodily closure. Moreover, since this hole has been ripped away from its true signification, it represents a pure obsessional idea that is separated from its affective content. It is just a hole because this signifier has lost its signification.[21]

This dissociation between the signifier and the signified infects all of Marlow's representations and allows him to develop an ironic and surface-oriented discourse. Conrad hints at this superficiality by claiming that for Marlow "the meaning of an episode was not inside like a kernel but outside, enveloping the tale" (20). Marlow thus keeps things on an external and surface level in order to avoid the attachment of his signifiers to their affective signifieds. This stress on the external also helps to account for the way that he views the natives: "They shouted, sang; their bodies streamed with perspiration; they had faces like grotesque masks . . . They were a great comfort to look at" (28). What gives Marlow pleasure in his viewing of these Africans is the fact that he denies them any level of subjectivity and thus can see them as pure signifiers and masks that have no internal content.[22]

Marlow thus splits his world into the manifest realm of the pure signifier and his latent feelings of horror regarding his own sexual desire, which he projects onto nature and the natives. Throughout the text, nature becomes the main depository for the projection of Marlow's own rejected feelings:

> All along the formless coast bordered by dangerous surf, as if Nature herself had tried to ward off intruders; in and out of rivers, streams of death in life, whose banks were rotted into mud, whose waters, thickened into slime, invaded the contorted mangroves, that seemed to writhe at us in the extremity of an impotent despair. (29)

This personification of nature allows Marlow to express his own horror of muddy bodily fluids and untamed natural forces. Like an obsessional xenophobe, Marlow sees the Other as a penetrating and invasive force that threatens the subject's sense of bodily unity and self-control. Freud attaches this fear of penetration and flowing fluids to the need to master one's bodily secretions through the act of toilet training.[23] The muddy, slimy rivers can be read as the projection of Marlow's horror of his own impotency and inability to control his bodily fluids. The fear of anal erotism may therefore be connected to a horror of uncontrollable bodily functions.

For the obsessional subject, anal retention represents a desire to master the body through the transformation of the anal flow into monetary objects of value.[24] In the popular conception of anal retention, people who horde their money display a great need to hold onto things and to control their rate of expenditure. This type of an "anal economy" is explored in Freud's Rat Man case and is connected to the subject's desire to control the circulation of money and the equation of his feces with gifts (70). In Conrad's text, this same transformation of anal fluids into monetary objects is produced in his description of the ivory trade:

> Everything else in the station was in a muddle,—heads, things, buildings. Strings of dusty niggers with splayed feet arrived and departed; a stream of manufactured goods, rubbishy cottons, beads and brass-wire set into the depths of darkness, and in return came a precious trickle of ivory. (33)

This trickle of ivory helps to regulate the muddle of things that enter into the colonial system. This muddle can be connected to the muddy river and the murky depths of Marlow's anal erotism that is repressed by his depiction of the ivory trade. In order to overcome the threat of natural and native darkness, the obsessional colonialists must produce a white product of capital accumulation.

As Mark Bracher points out, Conrad's constant descriptions of bodily fragmentations and natural flows reproduces in the reader a threat of moral and corporal disintegration (148). The reader is thus interpellated into the text through a shared sense of repressed imaginary bodily fragmentation and dismemberment. Once again, these threats to the reader's body and mind help to reinforce the desire to repress these unconscious elements by returning to a state of imaginary completeness and unity. However, the reader may also identify with these depictions of bodily fragmentation on a masochistic level. By seeing scenes of corporeal fragmentation presented in the discourse of the Other, the subject can confront his or her own feelings of bodily disintegration in a safe and abstract way.[25]

Marlow hints at this form of vicarious masochism when he addresses his audience directly:

> Kurtz whom at the time I did not see—you understand. He was just a word for me. I did not see the man in the name any more than you do. Do you see him? Do you see the story? Do you see anything? It seems to me I am trying to tell you a dream—making a vain attempt, because no relation of a dream can convey the dream-sensation. (42)

In his obsessional discourse, Marlow indicates to the reader that Kurtz was just a pure signifier for him and that he could not imagine what this symbol could mean.[26] Furthermore, Conrad reveals here his failed desire to present his unconscious world (his dream) in his text. He thus posits that his story both approaches the unconscious and fails to attain it, and it is this play between the revelation and concealment of the unconscious that serves to intellectually titillate the reader.

The failure of the text to present what it is supposed to represent celebrates a failure of textual closure. However, this linguistic lapse succeeds in covering over the bodily gaps that the writer is trying to avoid: "Not it is impossible to convey the life-sensation of any given epoch of one's existence— that which makes its truth, its meaning—its subtle and penetrating essence" (43). In a way, Conrad is arguing here that the Real of one's existence is impossible to symbolize. However, his use of the term "penetrating essence" may indicate a return of a repressed form of real anal erotism within the texture of his symbolic discourse. I am calling this form of anal penetration "real" because it functions in the text as the form of sexuality that is impossible to represent directly.

Due to the impossibility of describing his own anal desires, Marlow continuously returns to a displaced description of behinds and backs:

> Yes—I let him run on . . . and think what he pleased about the powers that were behind me. I did! And there was nothing behind me! There was nothing but that wretched, old, mangled, steamboat I was leaning against. (43)

By claiming that there is nothing behind him, Marlow is able both to present the signifier of his desire and to repress its content. Moreover, what makes the boat behind him so wretched is the fact that it is filled with holes: "What I really wanted was rivets, by Heaven! Rivets. To get on with my work—to stop the hole" (43). This clogging up of the boat's anal hole through an act of work represents the very task of the obsessional critic who must interpret every gap in the text in order to refind a preestablished sense of textual unity.

Marlow himself indicates that this desire to work in order to fill all holes comes out of the narcissistic need to find one's own self in the tasks that one performs: "I don't like work—no man does—but I like what is in work—the chance to find yourself. Your own reality—for yourself, not for others" (44). Within the obsessional university discourse, this need to work for Others always hides a desire for narcissistic gratification. This narcissistic structure of knowledge is most evident in the critical reading strategies that stress the greatness of the Author and the Great Ideals of Great Books. When one finds greatness in the Other, one also is able to find greatness in one's self through the process of narcissistic identification. However, the cost of this form of reading narcissism is that it must refuse to take into account the nonideal aspects of every subject's desire and unconscious enjoyment.[27]

Conrad appears to be aware of this problematic nature of idealizing literature, and thus he allows himself to describe some of the "darker" passions that he is trying to contain. His radical ambivalence comes out in the following passage, which seems to say more than he wants to say: "To tear treasure out of the bowels of the land was their desire, with no more of a moral purpose at the back of it than there is burglars breaking into a safe" (46). These lines allow Conrad's association of colonialism and anal desire to come to the surface but in a hidden and displaced way. His horror of Kurtz and the old discourse of the master can be traced to this unconscious connection between colonial conquest and anal rape.[28]

I would like to suggest that readers and critics have struggled with Conrad's seemingly ambivalent stance toward racism and colonialism because they have not taken into account this distinction between Marlow's and Kurtz's discourses and prejudices.[29] In his depiction of Kurtz, Marlow displays a hatred of his anal savagery:

> As for me, I seemed to see Kurtz for the first time. It was a distinct glimpse: the dugout, four paddling savages, and the lone white man turning his back suddenly on the headquarters, on relief, on thoughts of home—perhaps; setting his face towards the depths of wilderness towards his empty and desolate station. I did not know the motive. (47)

In this passage, the back is represented as indicative of a turning away from morality and the home culture; Kurtz becomes the embodiment of the man who has "gone native" and has decided to turn his back on his European society and to claim the darkness of African passions as his own.

HOMOPHOBIC RACIAL PROJECTIONS

Shortly after Marlow gives this description of Kurtz, he begins to suffer what we may call a displaced homosexual panic:

> I sweated and shivered over that business considerably, I can tell you. After all, for a seaman, to scrape the bottom of that thing that's supposed to float all the time under his care is the unpardonable sin. No one may know of it, but you may never forget the thump. (50)

Without making the play between "seaman" and "semen," we can still detect a strong undercurrent of anal erotism and fear in this passage. The unpardonable sin is for Marlow to scrape his (boat's) bottom and receive a thump from the Other.[30]

The central mechanism that Conrad/Marlow uses in order to escape from the throes of this unpardonable sin is the projection of unwanted desires onto the "prehistoric" natives and the dark realm of untamed nature:

> The earth seemed unearthly. We are accustomed to look upon the shackled form of a conquered monster—there you could look at the thing monstrous and free. It was unearthly and the men were— no they were not inhuman. (51)

As many readers and critics have realized, this description of nature and of the Africans represents a racist displacement of the narrator's own rejected desires onto the realm of the debased Other. In fact, Marlow continues by directly equating these inhuman humans with his own wild passions: "They howled and leaped, and spun, and made horrid faces; but what thrilled you was just the thought of their humanity—like yours—the thought of your remote kinship with this wild and passionate uproar" (51). By calling attention to the audience's own wild passions, Marlow exposes one of the main ways that prejudice can be reproduced in the text. On one level, he does reveal the fact that people project their repressed desires onto Others; yet, this revelation does not stop the process.[31] In other words, he exposes his obsessional displacement of desire at the same time that he reenacts this displacement.

In this structure, there is very little room for the reader to reject this racist process, because Marlow continues by further implicating everyone into his discourse: "Yes, it was ugly enough; but if you are man enough you would admit to yourself that there was in you just the faintest trace of a response to the terrible frankness of that noise" (51–52). Here, Conrad is bullying his readers into being manly and facing up to their own dark desires.[32] In his obsessional homosocial discourse, Marlow needs other people to feel the same hatred and revulsion toward his own wild passions. Racism is produced here within a homosocial structure and an attempt to reestablish a sense of European masculinity.

In making this connection between the natives and his readers' own rejected desires, Conrad/Marlow functions as an obsessional agitator who warns people of the threat of foreign invasion: "The danger, if any, I expounded, was from our proximity to a great human passion let loose" (59). The text works on this level by constantly telling the reader that the Other represents a threat and that one must be vigilant about allowing this loose passion to enter into one's own body.[33]

As the novella progresses, Kurtz becomes the embodiment of the internalization of this natural, native threat:

> They only showed that Kurtz lacked restraint in his gratification of his various lusts, that there was something wanting in him—some small matter which, when pressing need arose, could not be found under his magnificent eloquence. (74)

Kurtz represents, in this passage, the perverse colonialist who cannot control his drives and who satisfies his lusts without any Western moral restraints. This lack of a moral core or code turns him into a hollow being and the personification of the anal hole: "the whisper had proved irresistibly fascinating. It echoed loudly within him because he was hollow at the core" (74). In this structure, Kurtz becomes the bodily hole that Marlow refuses to acknowledge in himself; Marlow cannot accept the erotism of his own anal hole because this orifice has been equated with amorality and a turning of one's back on one's home culture.

Kurtz's embodiment of Marlow's hole is also connected to the displaced horror of Kurtz's mouth: "I saw him open his mouth wide—it gave him a weirdly voracious aspect, as though he had wanted to swallow all the air, all the earth, all the men before him" (76). Once again in these lines, the open orifice or bodily hole represents a complete threat to Marlow's narcissistic order. We find in this passage, not only a primitive threat of oral devouring but also a displacement of the eroticized orifice from the anus to the mouth.

In order to block the presence of Kurtz's hole, Marlow concentrates on his voice and his final words: "Kurtz discoursed. A voice! a voice! It rang deep to the very last. It survived his strength to hide in the magnificent folds of eloquence the barren darkness of his heart" (85). Here, the master signifier of Kurtz's voice, his pure word, serves to hide the true dark hole of his heart and body.

INTERPELLATING ETHNOCENTRIC READERS

It is this celebration of Kurtz's and Conrad's voice and eloquence that has also allowed readers and critics the ability to repress the more threatening aspects of this text. By concentrating on Kurtz's final words, the audience and Kurtz's Intended, attempt to locate in this text a "supreme moment of complete knowledge" (86). In fact, I would like to argue that Conrad's final depiction of the faithful intended/reader tries to place the audience in the position of the one who truly believes in Kurtz's mission and racist ideology.

In the last section of the novella, Kurtz's Intended is described in the following way:

> I know that the sunlight can be made to lie too, yet one felt that no manipulation of light and pose could have conveyed the delicate shade of truthfulness of those features. She seemed ready to listen without mental reservations, without suspicion, without a thought for herself. (90)

This passage defines the reader of Conrad's text as one that must assume a passive and accepting "feminine" position. In order for us to follow his signifiers, we have to remove all of our mental reservations and suspicions about his project. The white light of truthfulness shines on those readers who agree to remove themselves from the reading process.

This reading relationship is structured by a sexist division between the man's world of literary communication (Kurtz speaks and Marlow writes) and the female's role as the passive receiver.[34] Throughout the novella, women have been openly placed in a position of exclusion in order to emphasize the homosocial bonding between Marlow and his male audience:

It's queer how out of touch with truth women are. they live in a world of their own, and there had never been anything like it, and never can be. It is too beautiful altogether. (27)

The only place left for these women in this text is to blindly follow what their men say.

I am therefore using the Intended as the named interpellation of the reader into Conrad's story. She is the one that needs to know Kurtz's story and his final words. The Intended is also the one who idealizes Kurtz in every possible way: "Ah, but I believed in him more than any one on earth—more than his mother, more—than himself. He needed me! Me! I would have treasured every sigh, every word, every sign, every glance" (94). The Ideal and idealizing reader is truly one who treasures every word and sign of the author. However, the price that the writer has to pay for this type of narcissistic reading relationship is the transformation of the truth of history into a lie of self-recognition.

When the Intended insists on hearing Kurtz's last words, Marlow cannot tell her the truth about Kurtz's horror and blackness and he decided to tell her a lie: "The last word he pronounced was—your name" (94). In order to gratify his reader, Marlow returns to the master signifier of self-reflection—the reader's own name. He thus chooses repression over revelation and narrative deceit over historical truth. In typical obsessional fashion, the ending of the novel places us in a position to question the validity of the subject's entire preceding discourse. Did Conrad write this entire story so that we would be trained how to replace the horror of the hole with the pronouncement of our own names? If this is true, then we must insist that this text presents a literary form of obsessional homophobic prejudice.

In order to work against this type of ethnocentric discourse of the university that is presented in Conrad's text and in our literary institutions, we need to resist the homosocial reading relationship. This form of resistance requires an awareness of the multiple ways that texts attempt to interpellate us and the constant call that these texts make for us to renounce and repress our own unconscious enjoyments.

In the next series of texts that I will be considering, we will encounter the ways that African-American subjects have internalized and resisted the diverse forms of prejudice that I have been analyzing. This shift from British to African-American literature will also entail a movement from modernist to postmodernist forms of textuality and subjectivity. I will posit that in our current postmodern condition, the older cycle of prejudices is transformed by the increased dominance of a global symbolic order and a growing sense of subjective fragmentation. One of the results of this transformation is that the fundamental source for projective racism is no longer solely homophobia but is now centered on an increased sense of linguistic castration. In other terms, the postmodern subject does not just project repressed same-sex desires onto a debased cultural Other; this Other also becomes the depository for the subject's projection of his or her sense of subjection to the symbolic order of law, language, the mass media, and global capitalism. The horror of the Other in postmodernism becomes the horror of failed communication, multiple languages, and diverse ethnic modes of enjoyment.

PART THREE

Postmodern Prejudices

CHAPTER SEVEN

Internalized Racism and the Structures of Prejudice in *The Bluest Eye*

In the previous chapters, I have concentrated on the production of prejudice within dominant literary discourses. In this section of readings, I will
change my focus and concentrate on the way that the victims of different
forms of prejudice both suffer and resist diverse modes of oppression. This
dialectic between the internalization and the subversion of racist discourses
is a central element of Toni Morrison's *The Bluest Eye*. In interpreting this
novel, I will reexamine the interplay among ethnocentrism, classism, racism,
and sexism from both a psychoanalytic and Marxist position.

ETHNOCENTRISM AND THE BEAUTY INDUSTRY

The Bluest Eye is centered on the connection between America's political
economy and its racial, aesthetic, and sexual systems. This work displays
how the ethnocentric idealization of whiteness not only is an aesthetic or a
racial formation but it also has clear sexual and economic roots.[1] Through
her descriptions of advertising, children's toys, and literature, Morrison ties
capitalism to the circulation of desire in a color-coded structure. We learn in
Morrison's text that postmodern capitalism not only works by producing
new desires and new objects for consumption but it also serves to produce
these desires within a racist and ethnocentric order.[2]

The "beauty industry" is the prime example of the way that global capitalism has linked itself to a cycle of prejudices. In this postmodern structure,
the homosocial and ethnocentric celebration of whiteness and heterosexuality is tied to a mass-mediated form of racial desire. Morrison shows that all
modes of representation (books, toys, movies, billboards, stores, magazines,
newspapers, etc.) in our current culture tend to idealize whiteness and devalue blackness. Her text thus relates the internalization of racism to the

105

power of postmodern capitalism in the shaping of unconscious subjective desires and fears.[3]

One of the central ways that this connection between beauty, capitalism, and racism is constituted in the novel is through the portrayal of children's toys. Thus, when Claudia, a young African-American child, receives from her parents a Raggedy Ann doll, she decides to tear it apart in order to see what inside of it makes it so desirable for others:

> I had only one desire: to dismember it. To see of what it was made, to discover the dearness, to find the beauty, the desirability that had escaped only me. Adults, older girls, shops, magazines, newspapers, window signs—all the world had agreed that a blue-eyed, yellow-haired, pink-skinned doll was what every girl treasured. (20)

The beauty of the white doll is derived from the advertisements (shops, magazines, newspapers, window signs) that produce desire.[4] Claudia rejects this celebration of white beauty, but she does not realize that this form of idealization is socially constructed and not the product of some inner quality. In her attempt to locate the source of beauty in the material object, she shows the ways that children (and adults, as well) confuse symbolic constructions with real or natural qualities.[5]

Claudia's confusion between the representation of beauty and the materiality of the object points to the ways that racism attempts to naturalize socially constructed value judgments. Like the unconscious, which Freud argues treats words as if they were real things, Claudia participates in the postmodern attempt to transform symbolic representations into real presences (Freud, "The Unconscious" 147). For this young girl, the white beauty of her dolls must be derived from some internal property (real things) and not from an external representation.

According to Jean-Louis Baudry, postmodern consumer culture functions by "offering the subject perceptions which are really representations mistaken for perceptions" (315). The prime example of this form of postmodern simulation for Baudry is the cinema that is based on a "psychotic" transformation of symbolic codes into real perceptions.[6] In Morrison's text, television and film play an essential role in the production of internalized racism. When Pauline, Pecola's mother, goes to the movies, she becomes seduced by the popular culture's conception of beauty and ideal love:

> There in the dark her memory was refreshed, and she succumbed to her earlier dreams. Along with the idea of romantic love, she was introduced to another—physical beauty. Probably the most destructive ideas in the history of human thought. Both originated

in envy, thrived in insecurity, and ended in disillusion. In equating physical beauty with virtue, she stripped her mind, bound it, and collected self-contempt by the heap. (122)

By calling beauty the most destructive idea in history, Morrison offers an insightful criticism of the beauty industry. Not only do films and the popular media render females insecure about their bodies, they also create racial self-hatred.[7]

The consumer culture's ethnocentric idealization of white beauty transforms the vision of all of the subjects in Morrison's novel. In Pauline's case, "she was never able, after her education in the movies, to look at a face and not assign it some category in the scale of absolute beauty" (122). For Pecola's mother, this stress on the visual presence and judgment of beauty is produced in a female homosocial structure: "Pauline did not really care for clothes and make-up. She merely wanted other women to cast favorable glances her way" (118). In this homosocial structure, we do not have the traditional displacement of male homosexual desire into heterosexual competition; rather, we find heterosexual desire mediated by a female-to-female relationship.[8] Within the sphere of the beauty industry, women are not only commodified as objects of desire but they also become consumers and producers of beauty.

Just as beauty becomes an ethnocentric capital commodity, "ugliness" and blackness are produced as forms of economic failure and devaluation. Morrison constantly reiterates that the Breedlove family are considered poor, black, and ugly:

The Breedloves did not live in a storefront because they were having temporary difficulty adjusting to the cutbacks at the plant. They lived there because they were poor and black, and they stayed there because they believed they were ugly. (38)

By placing this family in an abandoned storefront, Morrison shows how they represent the opposite of the consumer culture's celebration of white beauty. Since they live in a window of capital exchange, the Breedloves become objects that are displayed for the public; however, they are not objects of consumption or idealization but objects of hatred and racist debasement.[9]

For the surrounding community, Pecola becomes the central emblem of black ugliness:

And all of our beauty, which was hers first and which she gave to us. All of us—all who knew her—felt so wholesome after we cleaned ourselves on her. We were so beautiful when we stood astride her ugliness. Her simplicity decorated us, her guilt sanctified us, her pain made us glow with health, her awkwardness made us think that we had a sense of humor. (205)

Since these black subjects cannot gain a sense of beauty from the dominant culture that celebrates only whiteness, their beauty is derived from debasing other people in their own community. In this structure, Pecola and her family function as the scapegoats for the whole community's self-hatred. Moreover, by showing that Pecola's ugliness and weakness made everyone else feel beautiful and strong, Morrison displays how the idealization of the self is dependent on a devalorization of a debased Other.

We can read Pecola as an example of the way that the most disempowered people in our society become the easy targets for the projection of our worst cultural fears and failures.[10] As Slavoj Žižek argues, the social out-group represents the materialization of all of the central conflicts that structure a given society: "The basic trick of anti-semitism is to displace social antagonism into antagonism between the sound social texture, social body, and the Jew as the force corroding it, the force of corruption" (*Sublime Object* 125). In this obsessional scapegoating structure, the "black" subject becomes the source for all of America's social problems. An example of this logic can be found in the desire to blame African Americans on welfare for the country's deficit and for the break-up of the American family.

ECONOMIC FORECLOSURE

Within *The Bluest Eye*, Pecola functions as this abjected fantasy object for both the whites and the African Americans. In her attempt to buy candy from a white man, we see how she embodies the failures of both America's racial and economic orders:

> Slowly, like Indian summer moving imperceptibly toward fall, he looks towards her. Somewhere between retina and object, vision and view, his eyes draw back, hesitate, and hover. At some fixed point in time and space he senses the need not to waste the effort of a glance. He does not see her, because for him there is nothing to see. (48)

Pecola's attempt to interact economically with this white man results in the total negation of her presence; her ego can find no validation in the look of the Other. Instead, she is reduced to an instant sense of self-erasure: "She looks up at him and sees the vacuum where curiosity ought to lodge. And something more. The total absence of human recognition—the glazed separateness" (48). This refusal of the Other to look at her contributes to the destruction of her imaginary sense of subjective unity.[11] This means that she is not only excluded from the symbolic world of consumer capitalism but she is also denied an entrance into the imaginary realm of self-reflection and ego-unity.[12]

Pecola quickly associates this loss of her ego and sense of self-unity to the blackness of her skin:

> All things in her are in flux and anticipation. But her blackness is static and dread. And it is the blackness that accounts for, that creates, the vacuum edged with distaste in white eyes. (49)

In this phenomenological description of the experience of racism, Morrison allows us to see how blackness offers the subject an abject sense of identity. The only thing that Pecola knows for sure is that she is black and that white people hate her blackness.[13] Moreover, her blackness becomes a fixed object for the white man's vision.

In order to analyze the psychoanalytic ramifications of racism for a child, we can examine the relationship between Pecola's blackness and the white store owner by using Lacan's schema L:

Female Disempowerment S - - - - - - - - ⇒ a' White Beauty

Black Ugliness a ⊏ - - - - - - - - A White Male Power

In the imaginary relation, we find the opposition between the ethnocentric idealization (a') of white beauty and the racist de-idealization (a) of black ugliness. This aesthetic binary is matched by the social opposition between the power of the white male Other (A) and the disempowerment of the black female subject (S). When Pecola (S) attempts to interact with the white male storekeeper (A), we see how the symbolic relation of social power links up with the imaginary relation of aesthetic beauty. Furthermore, the white male's refusal to acknowledge Pecola's presence pushes her into the position of representing the abjected object (a) of cultural desire.

By concentrating on the look of the white man, Morrison highlights the ways that the symbolic consumer culture manipulates subjects on an imaginary and visual level. In this text, the subject's "eye" and "I" are the center of vulnerability and social control. Pecola desires to have blue eyes, because she wants to reverse the relationship that has reduced her to nothing in front of the eyes of her white Other. If she receives blue eyes, she will become white and beautiful and thus she will become the celebrated object (a') of white ethnocentrism.[14]

Coupled with Pecola's desire to become white, we find her psychotic attempt to foreclose her own black body:

"Please God," she whispered into the palm of her hand. "Please make me disappear." She squeezed her eye shut. Little parts of her body faded away. (45)

This fading away of her own subjectivity and body represent the first stages of her psychotic withdrawal from social reality. For it is Freud's argument that the first phase of any psychosis is something a kin to the destruction of the subject's psychological world that then has to be re-created through an imaginary fantasy or delusion ("On Narcissism" 57). What Pecola destroys in the primary stage of her psychosis is her identification as a black subject.[15] This destruction of the self is then followed by the delusional attempt to see herself in the mirror with blue eyes. Pecola thus hallucinates on a perceptual level the reconciliation of the social division between white and black Americans.

This connection between Pecola's blackness and her psychotic desire for blue eyes is tied to her family's economic abjection. In the case of the Breedlove family, Morrison connects homelessness to a state of socially in-duced nonhumanness: "Cholly Breedlove, then, a renting black, having put his family outdoors, had catapulted himself beyond the reaches of human consideration. He had joined the animals" (18). In this culture, the people in the lowest socioeconomic class are perceived to be animals because they have no connection to the dominant economic and linguistic order. In other terms, the Breedloves have become foreclosed by the dominant economic symbolic order, and thus they are no longer considered to be human subjects.

This notion of foreclosure or radical rejection introduces a psychotic form of internalized racism.[16] Like the psychotic subject who rejects the symbolic order of castration and the name-of-the-father, the Breedloves have been foreclosed from the symbolic consumer culture and thus they are pro-jected into the "outsideness" of the real: "Outdoors we knew was the real terror of life . . . Outdoors was the end of something, an irrevocable physical fact" (17). This description of the outside is strikingly similar to Lacan's de-finition of the primitive real and the state of psychosis: "The Other no longer exists. There is a sort of immediate external world, of manifestations per-ceived in what I call the primitive real, a non-symbolized real" (*Seminar I* 66–67). For Lacan, the real is defined by its opposition to the symbolic order of language and law.[17] In the case of psychosis, what occurs is that the sub-ject is not able to accept the Name-of-the-father that functions as the anchoring point between the real and the symbolic orders. Without this sta-bilizing factor, the subject becomes "unglued" and is spoken and controlled by the discourse of the Other. In Pecola's case, her family's economic status and her own blackness place her in a position to be rejected from the dominant symbolic order of white capitalism.

It is the fear of being placed in this position of radical psychotic outsideness that motivates the other subjects in the novel to guard against any intrusion of the real. "The threat of being outdoors surfaced frequently in those days. Every excess was curtailed with it. If somebody ate too much, he ended up outdoors" (17). This horror of being placed outside of the symbolic order is therefore tied to the threat of the indulgence in certain forms of enjoyment or what Lacan calls *jouissance* and what Morrison later relates to the "eruptions of funk" that the middle-class subject Geraldine tries to eliminate.[18] By linking economic foreclosure to sexual enjoyment, Morrison effectively displays the connection between unconscious sexuality and racism.

OBSESSIONAL RACISM

In fact, in her description of Geraldine, Morrison accurately outlines the major components of an obsessional neurosis:

> The careful development of thrift, patience, high morals and good manners. In short, how to get rid of the funkiness. The dreadful funkiness of passion, the funkiness of the wide range of human emotions. (83)

Central to the development of an obsessional neurosis is the desire to repress eruptions of uncontrollable sexuality and emotion through rituals of purification and classification.[19] The thriftiness, morality, and manners of the obsessional all represent attempts of the subject to comply with the social Other in order to build up a wall of defense against the emergence of uncontrollable unconscious impulses. Within the structure of internalized racism, these African-American middle-class subjects accept the dominant order's connection between blackness and excessive sexuality.[20]

Morrison gives this obsessional structure of internalized racism a psychoanalytic foundation in her description of Geraldine's social group:

> Whenever it erupts, this Funk, they wipe it away . . . they hold their behind in the fear of a sway too free; when they wear lipstick they never cover the entire mouth for fear of lips too thick, and they worry, worry, worry about the edges of their hair. (83)

In discussing the control of the excessive movements of their behinds, their lips, and their hair, Morrison connects this need for propriety and properness to the neurotic desire to control one's body through an acceptance of the rules of the social Other. Within this structure, the obsessional fear of losing control of one's bowels is directly linked to the presence of blackness and excessive sexuality.[21]

Geraldine's middle-class internalized racism is connected to her desire to separate her son from any sense of debased blackness:

> His mother did not like him to play with niggers. She had explained to him the difference between colored people and niggers. They were easily identifiable. Color people were neat and quiet; niggers were dirty and loud. He belonged to the former group; he wore white shirts and blue trousers. (87)

The obsessional fear of dirt and excess is directly associated to the internalization of the social connection between blackness and the lack of bodily control.[22] Furthermore, Morrison argues here that African-Americans who try to act and look white are only playing into the obsessional stereotypes that oppress them. Ultimately, this desire to take on the whiteness of the other fails because the black ego is alienated by the visual idealization of the white body.

In the novel, this failure to attain white narcissism is connected to Geraldine's attempt to whiten the skin of her son:

> In the winter his mother put Jergens Lotion on his face to keep the skin from becoming ashen. Even though he was light-skinned, it was possible to ash. The line between color and nigger was not always clear; subtle and telltale signs threatened to erode it, and the watch had to be constant. (87)

In order to affirm her son's white beauty, Geraldine has to obsessionally watch for any signs of blackness. The result of this obsessional prejudice is that Geraldine becomes separated from both her own sexuality and her own "black" culture.

Implied in Morrison's text is that the middle-class blacks have to surrender their own emotions, looks, and sexuality, in order to fit in with the proper and property-owning classes. Any excessive desire and expression of passion is seen as a threat to the middle-class and represents a return to the psychotic real of "outsideness": "Knowing that there was such a thing as outdoors bred in us a hunger for property, for ownership" (18). These middle-class values of personal property and home-owning sets up a psychological class hierarchy that internalized racism feeds off of. In this structure that divides and conquers, the middle-class has a horror of the lower class because they do not want to be faced with the possibility of being thrown outside into the unknowable terrifying real.

Linked to this structure of internalized racism, we find Morrison's analysis of the ways that prejudices can trickle down from the upper classes to the lower classes. In her description of Soaphead Church, we encounter an upper class form of internalized hysterical racism.[23] Soaphead comes from "mixed-blood"; his grandfather, Sir Whitcomb, was a white "decaying British Nobleman" who helped to produce a "mulatto bastard" (167). This mulatto child was Soaphead's father, who was dedicated to "hoarding" his white blood and who married a Victorian woman who learned from her husband "how to separate herself in body, mind, and spirit from all that suggested Africa" (167). This family history is thus determined by a certain act of hysterical splitting, where the subjects, who are produced out of a mixing of races, desire to split off one of the racial components from their subjectivity. The result of this process is an idealization of the master race: "They transferred this Anglophilia to their six children . . . they married "up," lightening the family complexion and thinning out the family features" (168). In this description of Anglophilia, the white race and the upper class are linked together through the mutual idealization of a master signifier and the visual debasement of their own "dark" sexuality.

Using Lacan's discourse of the hysteric, we can begin to define this structure of internalized hysterical racism:

$$\text{Split Subject } \$\text{ ------- S1 Ideal Signifier}$$
$$\overline{\text{Traumatic Object a}} \qquad \overline{\text{S2 Knowledge}}$$

In the structure of hysterical neurosis, the subject's encounter with a traumatic form of sexuality (a) leads to a state of self-division ($\$$) that results in the formation of a symptom around a master signifier (S1) cut off from the subject's own knowledge (S2).[24] In the case of Soaphead's grandfather, the initial sexual trauma concerns miscegenation. This mixing of blood produces in the next generation a series of subjective divisions that are repressed by the formation of a symptomatic idealization of whiteness. Whiteness, in this structure, represents a master signifier that functions as a symptom for the racially divided subject.[25]

This symptomatic glorification of whiteness results in Soaphead's family's belief that "all civilizations derive from the white race, that none can exist without its help" (168). In this hysterical internalization of white ethnocentrism, whiteness is a symptom of something that only exists for the subject on the level of a repeated but failed form of identification. Since, Soaphead's father never feels completely white, he must constantly attempt to present and prove his whiteness. I will posit that this theory of reiterated white identification is central to Morrison's critique of African Americans who try to act and look white.[26]

PERVERSE SEXISM AND RACISM

Linked to this depiction of the hysterical desire to affirm a false sense of white identity, we find Morrison's articulation of a perverse form of internalized racism. In her descriptions of both Soaphead Church and Cholly Breedlove, Morrison shows how perverse racists and sexists project their own sense of humiliation and loss onto vulnerable people in their own community. Soaphead's sexual molestation of Pecola will be directly attached to his own hatred of blackness and his desire to escape from his memories of being abused by his own father: "He responded to his father's controlled violence by developing hard habits and a soft imagination. A hatred of, and a fascination with, any hint of disorder and decay" (169). This double fascination and hatred of disorder and moral decay is central to perverse forms of subjectivity. In sadomasochistic relations, the sadist often plays the role of the moral authority who forces the masochistic subject to submit to his or her will.[27] From this perspective, perversion serves to reinforce the power of law to regulate the actions and sexuality of the subject. However, these perverse scenarios often include a moment where sexual enjoyment transgresses the law that is supposed to contain it. The perverse subject literally "over-comes" the law by transforming legal subjection into physical enjoyment.[28]

Freud posits that many perverse scenarios can be read as an attempt to symbolically master the scene of castration by reenacting the original relationship between the active (masculine) castrating father and the passive (feminized) masochistic child: "This happens particularly if he has developed a strong identification with his father and plays the part of the latter; for it is to him that as a child he ascribed the woman's castration" ("Fetishism" 356–57). Freud thus affirms that castration and fetishism center around the primary identification with the father who castrates a feminized Other.

In Lacan's rewriting of Freud's theories of sexuality, he places at the center of the castration complex the realm of language that serves to enslave both the subject and the object of representation. In this theory, sadomasochistic perversion is an attempt to act out in an intersubjective relationship the intrasubjective dialectic between the subject and the linguistic order. For Lacan, we are all slaves to language, and one way that we attempt to retroactively master our own bondage is by enslaving ourselves and others in highly structured sexual situations. In other terms, the fetishist who identifies with the sadistic father represents the imposition of the symbolic order of language and law, while the suffering masochist can be identified with the subject who submits to the law of the Other. What fuels and supports the rigid binary logic of sadomasochism is a fundamental rejection of linguistic loss and a projection of lack into the realm of the Other. To hide the presence of their own linguistic castration, perverse sexists need to impose a strict division of structured symbolic differences.[29]

We can use this theory of perverse sexism in order to explain the ways that the internalization of racism can result in the abuse of members of one's own community. In the case of Soaphead Church, he projects his own sense of debased blackness and linguistic castration onto young girls whom he controls and disciplines by raping them. In his sexist perverse structure, he constantly sexualizes religion and religiously practices sexuality: "He equated lovemaking with communion and the Holy Grail" (170). One of the reasons Soaphead needs to connect religion to sexuality is in order to escape his strong belief that all physical forms of contact are by their very nature evil. Religion allows him to displace this belief by giving him a symbolic discourse that purifies his own self-image while it demonizes the blackness of Others.[30]

Morrison's development of this perverse form of sexism and racism sets the stage for Soaphead's encounter with Pecola, who comes to him in search of beauty and blue eyes. For this deranged counselor and wish-fulfiller, Pecola represents "a little black girl who wanted to rise up out of the pit of her blackness and see the world with blue eyes" (174). Here, blackness is directly tied to the moral and social lowness of internalized racism. What the perverse racist hates in the other is precisely the manifestation of their own sense of depravity. Within Morrison's description of internalized racism, the cultural debasement of blackness results in the perverse subjects attempt to escape from his own sense of corruption by corrupting others. This displacement of guilt and shame is manifested when Soaphead writes a letter to God and declares that his love for young girls is based on "a Thing To Do Instead. Instead of papa, instead of the Cloth, instead of Velma" (179). Thus Soaphead's abuse of this little girl reenacts his own past losses of his father, his profession, and his wife (Velma) with the loss of another. First he has Pecola sacrifice a dog and then he sacrifices her. He justifies this in the typical perverse way by declaring that he is only the "instrument" of God's will (174) and by affirming, "I needed a comfortable evil to prevent my knowing what I could not bear to know" (180).[31] Sexual abuse is posited as a way of escaping from one's own self-knowledge concerning past abuses and humiliations. By affirming himself to be the instrument of a higher power, Soaphead can connect his desire to reject his own past with a displacement of responsibility.

One way that Soaphead is able to escape from his shame and his past is by loving little girls who are not in a position to judge or condemn him: "There wasn't any look—any funny look—any long funny Velma look afterward. No look that makes you feel dirty afterwards" (181). This effacement of the abused girls' vision is an essential aspect of Soaphead's and

Pecola's father's form of sexual abuse. Both men feed on the supposed innocence of young girls in order to deny their own sense of degradation.

In the case of Cholly, Pecola's father, his incestuous rape of his daughter
is motivated out of an early traumatic experience. When he was a young boy,
he was caught by two white men performing a sexual act:

> When he was still very young, Cholly had been surprised in some
> bushes by two white men while he was newly engaged in eliciting
> sexual pleasure from a little country girl. The men had shown a
> flashlight right at his behind. He had stopped, terrified. (42)

Part of the traumatic nature of this scene is the fact that Cholly is being
watched and humiliated by others. The light at his behind represents a combination of homoeroticism, white superiority, and black humiliation.[32]

After these men force Cholly to continue to have sex in front of their
watching eyes and flashlight, Cholly does not become angry at them; rather,
he takes out his fury on the girl that he is with: "For some reason Cholly had
not hated the white men; he hated, despised, the girl" (42). In this displacement of anger and humiliation, we find the same perverse logic that dominates Soaphead's sexuality. Both men use sex as a way of mastering past
traumas by repeating them in a displaced and reversed scenario. In Cholly's
rape of his daughter, this reversal becomes apparent when Cholly becomes
the one who approaches a helpless victim from behind:

> The sequence of his emotions was revulsion, guilt, pity, then love.
> His revulsion was a reaction to her young, helpless, hopeless pres-
> ence. Her back hunched that way; her head to one side as though
> crouching from a permanent and unrelieved blow. Why did she
> have to look so whipped? . . . The clear statement of her misery
> was an accusation. He wanted to break her neck—but tenderly.
> Guilt and impotence rose in a bilious duet. (161)

On one level, Cholly feels that his daughter's miserable condition reflects directly on his own inability to provide for her. However, on a deeper level, he
identifies with her helpless and hopeless state. His desire to break her neck is
a displacement of his desire to efface his own existence. After all, it is his
own guilt and impotence that he reads in her beaten-down condition. For
Cholly, Pecola embodies his own failures to be a father and to defend himself
against the people who oppress him. Cholly thus internalizes, in a self-hating
way, the ideological fantasy that the dominant order produces.

In order to escape from his feelings that he has failed his daughter and
that he is a member of a debased race, Cholly attempts to efface his daughter's existence by refusing to look into her eyes: "If he looked into her face,
he would see those haunted, loving eyes. The hauntedness would irritate

him—the love would move him to fury" (161). Like Soaphead, Cholly equates vision with moral judgment and responsibility. And like the sexual sadist, he needs to blindfold his victim so that she cannot see or predict what he is about to do. This effacement of the vision is a form of castration that forces the subject to submit to an all-powerful Other and to take on the castration that the sadist refuses to acknowledge. Pecola in this context exemplifies the African-American subject who is castrated and humiliated by the dominant symbolic order. She is a subject not only to language but also to Cholly's internalized racist ideology.

What also pushes Cholly to rape his daughter is his feeling that his daughter looks like his wife Pauline when they first met. This detail indicates that perverse sexuality is based on repetition and memory: "The confused mixture of his memories of Pauline and the doing of a wild and forbidden thing excited him" (162). Cholly is able to overcome his traumatic past at the moment that he overcomes his daughter's will and the law against incest; his desire is one of transgression but the things that he is transgressing are not determined by him.[33] In other terms, his rape of his daughter represents his attempt to master the white men's humiliation of his sexuality. Like Soaphead, he is an instrument of the white Other's desire and his rape of his daughter can be traced back to the white men's destruction of his own self-esteem and masculinity.[34]

In her description of the Breedlove family, Morrison continues her elaboration of the perverse nature of their internalized racism. At first we are told that everyone in this household is profoundly ugly: "It was as though some mysterious all-knowing master had given each one a cloak of ugliness to wear, and they had each accepted it without question" (39). Ugliness here functions as the abject object (a)—a form of identity that is produced by society and affirmed by the subject's unconscious. Morrison points out that it is the master signifier of white power that places these subjects in their abjected status. However, I would argue that it is on an unconscious level that this abjected identity takes on its full power. For there is a certain masochistic form of enjoyment that is produced by the subject's acceptance of their abjected status; since their social order does not allow them to gain a sense of identity and identification in the symbolic and the imaginary, they are forced to find a stable sense of self in the real.[35]

This logic helps to explain why some people internalize the racist prejudices that help to victimize them. In Pauline Breedlove's case, ugliness represents an essential tool that she uses in her dealings with other people: "Mrs. Breedlove handled hers as an actor handles a prop: for the articulation of character, for support of a role she frequently imagined was hers" (39). In this masochistic structure, blackness becomes a symbol of her central defining characteristic, which is a sense of martyrdom and sacrifice. Therefore, the narrator points out that Mrs. Breedlove needed her husband's sins and atrocious behavior in order to define herself as good:

> If Cholly had stopped drinking, she would never have forgiven Jesus. She needed Cholly's sins desperately. The lower he sank, the wilder and more irresponsible he became, the more splendid she and her task became. (42)

Pauline's own sense of self-glorification (all goodness) is thus derived from her acknowledged difference between herself and her hateful husband. Yet, in true perverse form, she is completely dependent on her husband's sadistic and vile nature.

In many ways, the Breedlove marriage excludes all possibility of neurosis and narcissism by constituting itself through certain sadomasochistic rituals:

> An escapade of drunkenness, no matter how routine, had its own ceremonial close. The tiny undistinguished days that Mrs. Breedlove lived were identified, grouped, and classed by these quarrels. They gave substance to these minutes and hours otherwise dim and unrecalled. They relieved the tiresomeness of poverty, gave grandeur to the dead rooms. In these violent breaks in routine that were themselves routine, she could display the style and imagination of what she believed to be her true self. (41)

In this depiction of the perverse sadomasochistic couple, Morrison highlights the structural aspects of symbolic routine, ceremony, identification, classification, and style, demonstrating that perversion is an attempt by subjects to control their unconscious sexuality by ritualizing it and thus giving it a symbolic logic.[36]

If Mrs. Breedlove does indeed play the role of a masochistic martyr, it is Cholly who is the perverse sadistic father who beats his wife and rapes his daughter. Morrison strongly develops this character by highlighting the way that his hatred for his wife is a displaced hatred of the white men that forced him to have sex:

> She [Mrs. Breedlove] was one of the few things abhorrent to him that he could touch and therefore hurt. He poured out on her the sum of all of his inarticulate fury and aborted desires. Hating her, he could leave himself intact. (42)

Instead of Cholly being the victim to the Other's desire, he subjects his daughter and his wife to his own flights of violence and depravity. In this perverse form of racism and sexism, Cholly attempts to master his wife and daughter by destroying the grounds of their subjectivity. His own sense of humiliation, emasculation, and defeat thus push him to humiliate and destroy others.

Perverse racism and sexism also represent a reaction to the postmodern forms of psychotic, obsessional, and hysterical modes of prejudice.[37] In this perverse discourse of the master, the subject projects loss and lack onto a debased Other:

$$\text{Master Signifier S1} \text{-------} \text{S2 Signifying Chain}$$

$$\text{Barred Subject } \$ \text{-------} \text{abject object}$$

Lacan posits that the master is someone who attempts to appropriate the master signifiers (S1) that control language and social relations (S2) by forcing the Other to submit to the signifying chain of law and language (S2) and by displacing his or her sense of subjective loss ($\$$) onto a produced abject-object (a). In Cholly's case, he attempts to force all of his sexual enjoyment into a symbolic ritual (S2) that allows him to transfer his repressed sense of humiliation and impotence ($\$$) onto his wife and daughter who function as a debased object (a) for him. Furthermore, by accepting whiteness as a master signifier for goodness, Cholly forces his own sense of "blackness" onto Others.

On the one hand, we have found that in this structure of perverse internalized racism, the subject attempts to erase any sense of subjective fragmentation by placing the blame for loss and lack onto the realm of the abjected object (a). On the other hand, in the case of hysterical internalized racism, we have seen how subjects desire to identify with an impossible signifier of idealized whiteness. In the extreme case of psychotic racism, this desire for whiteness results in an act of total self-negation. Moreover, all of these modes of internalized racism feed off of each other and create a vicious cycle of prejudice.

In many ways, *The Bluest Eye* provides the necessary first step for the active work against these diverse forms of internalized racism by providing the psychodynamic grounds for different systems of prejudice. Within the structure of this text, blackness is often equated with the unsymbolizable realm of sexual excess in the same way that homosexuality has been shown to function in the early modern and modern cycles of prejudice. In the next chapter, I will examine the ways that in *Beloved,* Morrison constructs a psychoanalytic form of communal therapy that goes beyond the description of forms of prejudice and attempts to posit ways to overcome diverse modes of oppression.

CHAPTER EIGHT

Beloved: Psychoanalytic Cultural Criticism and the National Unconscious

Toni Morrison's *Beloved* allows us to articulate some of the central strategies that victims of prejudice can use in order to escape from their states of oppression.[1] Through her discussions of memory and history, Morrison outlines a theory of African-American subjectivity that is centered on a postmodern and psychoanalytic recognition of the impossibility to symbolize the real of certain historical and personal traumas.[2] Moreover, her theories of memory are dedicated to her desire to locate slavery and racism as the repressed heart of American culture and history.

By claiming that slavery represents the repressed trauma of American culture, I am positing that there is such a thing as a national unconscious. In fact, Slavoj Žižek has argued that every nation is organized around a series of unconscious fantasies and desires that serve to hold a given community together: "This relationship towards the Thing, structured by means of fantasies, is what is at stake when we speak about the menace to 'our way of life' presented by the Other" (*Tarrying* 201). For Žižek, what unites a nation is not a shared set of values and beliefs; rather, the unifying factor in all social groups is "the unique way a community organizes its enjoyment" (201). Furthermore, this form of enjoyment that unifies nations represents an unconscious mode of sexual pleasure (jouissance). While Žižek often concentrates on the "positive" unconscious modes of enjoyment (pubs, food, music) that binds a community together, I would like to focus on the more "negative" unconscious fears and desires that support the national unconscious.[3]

In this study of literary prejudices, we have witnessed how most forms of oppression are generated out of the avoidance of linguistic castration and the repression of sexual enjoyment. Within the context of the American national unconscious, both of these founding causes of racism have been projected onto the body of the black slave. In other terms, blacks and slaves

121

have served to represent both the loss of linguistic mastery and the presence of an excessive form of sexuality.[4] Due in part to the Puritan foundations of American culture, there has been a constant refusal to acknowledge that we are all castrated by language and that we all have a diverse range of sexual desires. In the dual American quest for mastery and innocence, castration and sexual enjoyment have constantly been repressed and thus they continue to be projected onto debased out-groups.[5]

We have found that in the case of narcissistic and perverse forms of sexism, women are seen as the feared embodiment of both castration and hypersexuality. This figure of the female who is placed outside of linguistic control and is portrayed as being sexually excessive reappears throughout Western culture, society, and literature. The function of this debasement of femininity is to counteract the masculine horror of loss and excess. Combined with this sexist devalorization of women, we have also located the strong narcissistic and perverse desire of men to bond together in ethnocentric homosocial groups. In other words, in order for men to avoid encountering castration and excessive sexuality, they form social groups that exclude women and all aspects of sexual and ethnic difference. One of the results of this process is the production of a cultural form of homophobia that serves to repress same-sex desires and to celebrate heterosexual unions.

This foundational homophobia plays a central role in the American national unconscious. The fear of same-sex relations and anal penetration helps to police the possible relationships that men can have with each other. We have also seen how homophobia provides the psychical material for other forms of prejudice. In the case of obsessional anti-Semitism and homosocial ethnocentrism, the homophobic fear of anal penetration results in a displaced fear concerning the invasion of foreign people into one's own nation. In this obsessional structure, the nation as a national body is perceived to be threatened by the internalization of outside forces that serve to threaten bodily integrity and cultural homogeneity. Likewise, in the case of hysterical racism, the horror of one's own homosexual desire often leads to the displacement of that rejected enjoyment onto one's debased cultural Other.

In Morrison's *Beloved,* we see how the return of the oppressed slave manifests a cultural symptom that ties together these diverse modes of prejudice. I will argue that the dead daughter/slave/ghost, Beloved, represents the embodiment of America's repressed national sense of linguistic loss and excessive sexuality. Moreover, Morrison's call for us to claim this Beloved as our own is founded on her attempt to establish a national form of communal psychoanalysis that is designed to overcome the destructive effects of racism, sexism, and ethnocentrism.

In order for Morrison to develop this national therapy, she first must produce a psychoanalytic and postmodern "slave narration" that radically calls into question traditional conceptions of history, language, and subjectivity, while it makes a call to America to remember repressed moments of its past. Like the philosophical reaction to the Holocaust, the traumatic nature of slavery has undercut many of the transcendent signifieds that once grounded our sense of history.[6] For one can argue that postmodern and poststructuralist theories are the result of the loss of belief in the unifying principles of truth, historical progress, God, justice, and social morality.[7] In the case of the Holocaust, one of the most technologically advanced countries in the world embarked on a path that showed a complete lack of concern for truth, justice, and morality, and therefore technological advancement became dislocated for many people from any belief in the linear progression of history. Likewise, one can posit that slavery, as the extension of capitalism in its extreme form, has helped to reveal the separation between political economy and any moral and ethical ground.[8]

If we now think about both the traumatic nature of the Holocaust and the Middle Passage, I believe we will be able to see how a "historical" text like *Beloved* could only have been written in a postmodern style that reveals the absent ground of our current culture. Thus, if in the twentieth century there has been a turn toward the study of language and discourse that is cut off from the ability to represent the real, this separation has a historical foundation. Likewise, the New Historicist stress on the interlinking of power, knowledge, improvisation, and discourse has been generated from the awareness that in the postmodern era, political might has continuously overcome the restraints of moral rights.[9]

The challenge of *Beloved* is then how to represent the reality and truth of slavery, while taking into account our new conceptions of history and representation.[10] I will argue that Morrison is able to successfully negotiate between these two extremes of a groundless history and a language of the real by developing a double strategy of narration. Through her writing she reveals the failures of representational language at the same time that she develops a form of cultural (re)memory that does not allow us to forget any of the past. Furthermore, in her recounting of the unrepresentable aspects of slavery, she both highlights the limits of all forms of representation, while she stresses the materiality and sensuality of language.[11]

SLAVE NARRATION

If we consider *Beloved* to be a slave narrative, then we must insist that this novel is bound to all of the problematics inherent to the tradition of slave writing.[12] A central problem in this genre is that the writing-subject must often use the very words and metaphors that have helped caused his or her servitude in order to escape from his or her oppression. Moreover, these words and concepts prove themselves to be ultimately unable completely to represent the traumatic events that lie at the heart of the narrative quest.[13] This inability of language to do what it is suppose to do is thus a historical fact that has a linguistic structure.

However, the inverse aspect of the failure of language fully to represent its referent is the production of a historical form of consciousness that materializes the past in the form of the present. This collapsed theory of postmodern temporality is at the center of Morrison's novel and is given the name "rememory." In the following passage, we can see how this new theory of history results in an unconscious discourse where words are treated as real things:

> Where I was before I came here, that place is real. It's never going away. Even if the whole farm—every tree and grass blade of its dies. The picture is still there and what's more, if you go there— you who never was there—if you go there and stand in the place where it was, it will happen again; it will be there for you, waiting for you. (36)

Ostensibly this passage is addressed to Sethe's daughter Denver; however, I would like to interpret this statement as directed mainly toward the reader. It tells us that the past is always present, and that even if we repress it, it will return. There is thus no escape from history, which is equated with an unsymbolizable "real place."[14]

In Morrison's case, this implies that even though we do not have the narratives of the sixty million who perished in the Middle Passage, their presence is still felt among us. In fact, when it becomes a question of leaving the haunted house, Sethe's mother-in-law declares that: "Not a house in the country ain't packed to its rafters with some dead Negro's grief" (5). The haunting of 124 Bluestone must be read as a specific instance of the general phenomenon of American mourning. We are all threatened with the return of the dead who have not received a proper burial or commemoration. At the heart of our postmodern souls, lies this unassimilated kernel of the real.[15]

We must keep in mind that America is a country that has been founded on the attempted genocide of one race (Native Americans) and the enslavement of other races (mostly African). This history entails that "Americaness" has been constructed through processes of exploitation, murder, and racism. Furthermore, racism itself is dependent on the projection of socially constructed symbolic values onto a particular group that is then realized through different signs encoded on a individual subject. In its extreme form, the symbols of racism appear on a body through the presence of scars and lacerations that we can now read as the material residues of enslavement.[16] In the case of *Beloved,* Sethe's back is a writing surface that presents the textual body of slavery and the repressed history of America.

Mae Henderson has pointed out that because this writing is literally behind her, Sethe needs others to read it for her (67). On one level, this inability to read her own history forces her to connect with other characters in the novel who can attempt to interpret her story. However, I would like to argue that on a more profound level, it is the reader of Morrison's text who is called into the position of filling in the gaps that this subject can only circle. We must therefore go behind Sethe in order to read the message that has been inscribed on her back.

WE ARE ALL SLAVES TO LANGUAGE

One way that we can attempt to perform this type of communal reading is to explore how we all are enslaved.[17] In her second epigram that precedes the actual text of *Beloved,* Morrison points to our own implication in the story by quoting Romans 9:25: "I will call them my people which were not my people; and her beloved, which was not beloved.[18] "In this cross-coupling biblical passage that follows Morrison's reminder of the "Sixty Million and more" who died during the Middle Passage, we are called to consider all of the people who have died to be our own ancestors, even if in reality they are not. Furthermore, this passage asks us to love those who we have not loved before.

The radical transvaluation of our conception of the "beloved" that this novel calls for represents a postmodern ethics of diversity. Since so much of our own self-conception is based on the way that we view, idealize, and devalue Others, any revaluation of a cultural ideal (the beloved) entails a transformation of our own selves. The beloved is, in this sense, a mirror image of our own ego, just as the "people" whom are not our people represent the Other that is opposed to our own subjective positions.[19] Using Lacan's schema L, we can map the structure of reversed relationships that this biblical passage asks us to make:

$$\text{Subject S} \text{-----------} \text{a' Ideal Image of ego/other}$$
$$\text{ego/other a} \text{----------} \text{A Social other}$$

In the traditional theory of psychic development, this structure depicts the way that the ego (a) gains a sense of self by mirroring an ideal image of the other (a'). Likewise, in order to become a social subject, one must break with this imaginary structure and affirm the symbolic laws and language of the social Other (A). One of the results of this process is that the initially free and undefined subject (S) becomes barred ($) and subjected to the realm of culture.

What the biblical passage from Romans and Morrison's text asks us to do is to reverse and displace the movements of both of these phases of psychical development. It tells us that we should take for our ideal image (the beloved) precisely what is not ideal, the object (a) that has no specular or idealized image. More so, it asks us to replace the cultural Other that causes our subjection with another Other with which we do not normally identify.[20]

I would like to argue that this double movement of cultural revaluation serves to structure Morrison's entire novel and helps to provide the foundations for the cultural work against prejudice. In order to overcome our constant ethnocentric attempt to idealize white sameness (a') and debase all forms of difference (a), we need to affirm the value of objects (a) and people that have served as the screens for the projection of our rejected desires and fears. This implies that in order to culturally change, we must be able to reevaluate both our ideal images and our symbolic conceptions of the Other. However, since Morrison cannot represent in the traditional symbolic order the "sixty million or more" who died in the Middle Passage, she must turn to a magical and postmodern form of representation that seeks to destroy the separation between the material world and the fictional-spiritual world.

The embodiment of Beloved's ghost is the central magical figure that runs throughout the novel. In psychoanalytic terms, we can say that this animistic spirit represents the projection of the subject's rejected memory of a beloved.[21] Thus, Freud argues in *Totem and Taboo,* that societies believing in animism, fear that the people they have harmed and who have since died, will come back to terrorize them. In Lacanian terms, we can say that the return of the living dead represents a rejection of a certain symbolic element that returns in the real in the form of a hallucination.[22] A classic example of this structure is the Wolf Man case, where this subject's inability to accept the symbolic law of castration results in his hallucination that he has actually cut off his finger (Freud, "Infantile Neurosis" 275).

If we now apply these psychoanalytic theories of animism and symbolic foreclosure to the novel, we must ask what is the symbolic element that has been rejected and returns in *Beloved*? On one level, we can say that Sethe hallucinates Beloved's presence because she has attempted to foreclose her act of infanticide; thus, her refusal to remember and represent this act results in her psychotic projection of her unconscious "rememory." The only problem with this theory is that in the case of the novel, Sethe is not the only one who sees and feels this haunting presence.

The fact that Denver, Baby Suggs, and Paul D. also share in this same psychotic formation points to the idea that we need a communal explanation for this foreclosing structure.[23] As I have begun to argue, Beloved's unassimilated murder represents a particular example of the general loss of all of the people who died during the Middle Passage and American slavery. Since, as a culture we have not symbolized and represented these deaths, they are now returning to us in the form of ghosts and spectral presences. This means that Morrison's own text represents a psychotic hallucination of an unconscious memory that our culture has foreclosed. This cultural return to animism and a postmodern mode of magical realism is thus founded on our inability to mourn our own dead.[24]

Morrison's use of magical realism and other nontraditional forms of narration points to the connection between postmodernism and psychoanalytic theory. Throughout this chapter, I will argue that what we often call postmodernism often entails the cultural employment of unconscious forms of textuality and representation. One of the defining characteristics of both postmodernism and psychoanalysis is the radical critique of the classical modernist subject who has been defined as an independent white male ego (181).[25] In opposition to this conception of the unitary self-enclosed subject, we have the postmodern idea that the distinction between the self and the Other has been collapsed, so that no easy boundary can be drawn. [26] This destruction of the traditional separated self, surfaces in *Beloved* when Paul D. states: "This here new Sethe didn't know where the world stopped and she began" (164). Thus, in the postmodern world, we are the Other, because our self-conceptions are entirely dependent on the social roles and constructions that we affirm or deny.

This theory of the postmodern destruction of the self and Other opposition points to Lacan's psychoanalytic claim that "the unconscious is the discourse of the Other" and Žižek's notion that social reality is structured by subjective fantasies. Taken to its logical extreme, both psychoanalysis and postmodernism offer a form of subjectivity that denies the intentionality of the ego and present the subject as linguistically and socially divided or barred. In other words, postmodern subjectivity requires an affirmation of the type of linguistic castration that is most often denied by prejudiced subjects.

In the context of Morrison's novel, Sethe represents the general figure of this barred and castrated subject.[27] Sethe's divided subjectivity points to the notion that as a culture, we no longer know where we start and where the Other begins. The enslaved subject is thus the extreme example of our general condition of being determined by the metaphors and representations of an Other. Moreover, Lacan insists that we are all enslaved by the signifying chains of the Symbolic order. What happens in the case of slavery is that this structural relationship of subjection is translated into a lived experience.

In fact, when Lacan attempts to illustrate his theory of the death drive and the signifying chain, he turns to the body of the slave:

> Like the "message-slave" of ancient usage, the subject who carries under his hair the codicil that condemns him to death knows neither the meaning nor the text, nor in what language it is written nor even that it had been tattooed on his shaven scalp as he slept. (*Ecrits* 302)

Lacan employs this image of the slave that has his own death sentence written on his head, as the general condition of the subject of the unconscious, whose subjective death is determined by his or her relationship to language. Lacan's idea is that because our bodies and experiences are represented through an inanimate language, we are always already dead in our relation to the symbolic order (301). Yet, in this allegory of the slave-message, the subject does not know that this death sentence is tattooed on his head. For Lacan, this lack of knowledge represents the unconscious' relationship to the deadly aspect of language. We do not know what is in our unconscious because it is written in a place that we cannot see. Thus, in order for us to be able to read this repressed message, we must turn toward Others who can help us to decode our own blind spots.[28]

Lacan's theory of the dialectical nature of language and analysis returns us to the writing on Sethe's back. Inscribed on her body, is the message that calls for her own symbolic death: "He rubbed his cheek on her back and learned that way her sorrow, the roots of it . . . none of which Sethe could feel because her back skin had been dead for years" (17–18). As Jean Wyatt points out in her interpretation of this passage, Paul D. attempts to read Sethe's slave narrative by feeling the dead skin on her back (478). This subject's death drive and submission to the symbolic order is thus materialized in this extreme form of a "body language." In other terms, Sethe's back presents in the real, her submission to the symbolic death drive.

This synthesis of the symbolic and the real is at the heart of Wyatt's reading of Morrison's text and is a central component of many postmodern discourses. In Wyatt's terms, Morrison rejects the strict Lacanian opposition between the real and the symbolic, because this theory she argues does not take into account the "Maternal Symbolic" (474). Wyatt seeks to account for a different form of language that allows one to combine the abstract symbols of culture with the materiality of the natural body. In this conception of writing, figurative representations are treated as real things.

I prefer to call this form of writing, unconscious textuality instead of feminine writing, in order to remove it from the binary opposition of sexual difference. In Morrison's case this stress on the collapse of sexual difference is even more necessary because she desires to use Beloved in order to represent all of the people whose lives were lost in the Middle Passage. In fact, in the central cultural primal scene that determines the novel, Morrison describes the way that the slave ships and slavery in general worked to destroy sexual identifies and any concept of individuality: "I am not separate from her there is no place where I stop . . . her face is my own . . . storms rock us and mix the men into the woman and the women into the men" (210–211). In the horrid conditions of the slave ship, all differences between self and Other, male and female are broken down and eliminated. The sexless, egoless subject that some postmodernists celebrate is in the case, a result of a cruel system that dehumanizes its victims. Once, again Morrison shows in her broken and disjunctive writing the extreme reality of postmodern theory.

THE PAST IS ALWAYS PRESENT

In fact, this section of *Beloved* can be seen as a primer to different postmodern themes and writing strategies. As Brenda Marshall argues, one of the central characteristics of this new form of discourse is that temporal differences and historical time periods are often collapsed into an eternal now. "Perhaps the most obvious critique here of traditional history in the form of counter-memory is the blurring of pastpresentfuture. There is nothing in *Beloved* that denies the past, nor negates a future" (183). As an example of unconscious textuality, *Beloved* displays how culture forgets nothing and that desire and memory can never be destroyed.

In the *Interpretation of Dreams,* Freud clearly points out that the only temporal dimension that the unconscious knows is the present (589). This is why he can say that the subject never forgets anything and always returns to its first objects of desire. In its postmodern context, this theory results in the juxtaposition of radically different texts and contexts together. Morrison uses this nontemporality in Beloved's recounting of the Middle Passage: "All of it is now it is always now there will never be a time when I am not crouching and watching others who are crouching too" (210). This eternalization of the past, that is linked with the destruction of the difference between self and Other, serves to implicate all of us into this traumatic period of American history. We cannot escape the past because all of us retain it in our cultural unconscious. "Rememory" must be considered to be a general figure for the intertextuality of postmodern and psychoanalytic history.[29]

Morrison's text is thus centered on a psychoanalytic theory of historical repression and repetition. From a cultural perspective, we can posit that slavery is the repressed trauma of American history, and that this form of repression has helped to generate a whole series of social prejudices. For example, the structure of hysterical racism has been shown to be connected to the splitting of the subject in front of a traumatic cause. The result of this division is that the hysterical subject divides his or her own self into a good white half and a repressed evil black half. In the context of American culture, we can posit that the traumatic nature of slavery has helped to solidify this subjective division on a national level. In other terms, America itself is split between an idealized good white self and a debased black unconscious.

Within the structure of obsessional ethnocentrism, the horror of slavery can be related to the fear of passivity and the threat of bodily penetration. The remembrance of slavery must be repressed in this structure because it threatens the quest for bodily and national unity. The slave also represents for the obsessional subject the materialized presence of his or her own sense of linguistic and sexual castration. In this sense, the slave presents in the real every subject's subjection to the death drive and the dominant symbolic orders. Furthermore, this connection between the slave's body and the linguistic castration feeds into perverse and narcissistic forms of sexism that serve to deny all forms of difference by fixating on bonds that reinforce sexual and cultural sameness. The repression of slavery thus helps to generate and reinforce a wide range of social prejudices.

In order to counter some of the destructive effects of cultural repression and repetition, critics, readers, and teachers can use a text like *Beloved* in order to articulate the unconscious, preconscious, and conscious aspects of diverse forms of prejudice. As I have argued throughout this work, traditional educational means of overcoming racism, sexism, homophobia, and ethnocentrism have often failed because they have not taken into account unconscious levels of subjectivity. Due to this nonrecognition of the role played by unconscious desires and fears, many forms of criticism have only served to reinforce what they are trying to undermine. However, a text like *Beloved,* shows a profound awareness of the connection between conscious and unconscious forms of subjectivity and sexuality.

Thus, in her text, Morrison constantly connects the plight of slaves to the undermining of her reader's own sense of linguistic and representational control.[30] This removal of the stable ground of representation can be related to Morrison's claim that she opens up the novel in such a way that it upsets the reader and puts her or him in the position of the slaves who were taken from Africa and placed on the slave ships:

> The reader is snatched, yanked, thrown down into an environment completely foreign, and I want it as the first stroke of shared experience that might be possible between the reader and the novel's population. Snatched just as the slaves were from one place to another, from any place to another, without preparation and without defense. No lobby, no door, no entrance. (Morrison, "Unspeakable" 32)

Although we have learnt to be wary about discussing the intentionality of the author, this interpretation by Morrison of her own work makes a clear call for the reader's participation in the emotions and experience of the slave population.

Morrison's desire to place her reader in the position of the displaced slave points to one of the ways that her work attempts to provide for a communal psychoanalysis of prejudice. By forcing subjects to encounter their own sense of linguistic loss and confusion, her text provides a space for the working through of subjective feelings of fragmentation, disorientation, and de-idealization. Since many forms of prejudice are derived from the desperate attempt to escape from linguistic and subjective loss coupled with a projection of loss and lack onto a debased cultural Other, Morrison's text pushes her readers to confront the foundations of their own prejudices. In fact, her novel works by returning onto the reader the sense of unconscious disruption that the reader projects onto the slave and the devalorized black body.[31]

Linked to this desire to have her reader experience the lost emotions and unconscious feelings of slaves is Morrison's commitment to a community-based form of interpretation and textual analysis. In fact, this desire for a communal mode of writing and reading has been one of the constant themes in African-American literature and criticism. Danielle Taylor-Gutherie lists this role of the community in her discussion of the different aspects of black writing that repeat throughout Morrison's work:

> A participatory quality between a book and a reader; an aural quality in the writing; an open-endedness in the finale that is agitating; an acceptance and keen ability to detect differences versus a thrust towards homogenization; acknowledgement of a broader cosmology and system of logic in touch with magic, mystery, and the body; a functional as well as aesthetic quality; an obligation to bear witness; service for a conduit for the 'ancestor'; uses of humor that are frequently ironic; an achieved clarity or epiphany and thus a tendency to be prophetic; and an ability to take the 'tribe' via art through the pain of historical experience that has been haunted by race to a healing zone. (x)

Several of these characteristics that are listed in reference to African-American writing are classical paradigms of a postmodern psychoanalytic aesthetics. For I have been arguing that in African-American literature, the poststructuralist deconstruction of the subject is coupled with a need to reclaim history on the level of a collective experience. Aesthetics are thus historicized and politicized the moment that different textual strategies get applied to the mission of representing the real of a collective past.

NOT A STORY FOR AMERICA TO PASS ON

Within in postmodern structure, I would like to read the ending of the novel as an extended address that is made to all of America. *Beloved* can therefore be read as reminder of a part of American history that has never been fully dealt with and so it rests "disremebered and unaccounted for" (275). When the narrator reminds us that, "Everybody knew what she was called, but nobody knew her name. Disrembered and unaccounted for, she cannot be lost because no one is looking for her" (274), we as readers are called to remember her name and to pass on her story. Yet, Morrison repeats the phrase "It was not a story to pass on" three times in order to stress the fact that this horrific story cannot be forgotten at the same time that it cannot be remembered.[32] We are afraid to pass this story on to other people because we do not want to deal with this dark chapter of our past. However, we cannot pass over this history, because it threatens to return.

Morrison centers this cultural repression and return of the Middle Passage to our individual unconsciouses by claiming that people have forgotten Beloved in the same way that they try to forget a bad dream (274). "Remembering seemed unwise. They never knew where or why she crouched, or whose was the underwater face she needed like that" (275). Perhaps the face that Beloved continuously searches for in the Other is our face as a nation of readers and receivers of history. In order for the broken fragments of Beloved's history to be re-membered and reorganized, we as a nation need to face up to the facts and begin a form of communal healing.

The third part of Morrison's novel concerns the possibility of a communal response to personal and historical pain. In the opening of this section, Sethe attempts to make up for her own evil actions by repeating her story to Beloved over and over again. "Sethe pleaded for forgiveness, counting, listing, again and again her reasons" (242). Beloved's response to Sethe's apologies and subservience is to demand more and more and to break up and destroy the house (242).

Due to the fact, that Beloved's desires become insatiable, she begins to literally eat Sethe and Denver out of house and home. The only way that this situation can be maintained or rectified is if Denver ventures outside of 124 Bluestone and looks for a job or some food from the community. Morrison expresses this need for the family to go outside of the home in order to survive with the following phrase: "Whatever was happening, it only worked with three—not two—and since neither Beloved nor Sethe seemed to care what the next day might bring (Sethe happy when Beloved was; Beloved lapping devotion like cream), Denver knew it was on her" (243). This call for the need of three, can be read as a restating of the classical Freudian and

Lacanian argument that the symbiotic dual relation between the mother and her child needs to be broken by the paternal third term. Yet, it is clear that the "three" that must come into place in the novel is a purely symbolic function that will soon be filled by the entire female community that surrounds this family.[33]

This cultural process of communal healing only begins once Denver decides to tell her story to Janey, who will in turn, circulate this history orally among the other people of the community. By having Denver act as a mediator between Sethe's constant retelling of her story and Beloved's constant need to have more, Morrison is able to connect the social process of history telling to a personal quest for absolution. Of course the result of Denver's narration of the story is a proliferation of different histories and different readings:

> It took them days to get the story properly blown up and themselves agitated and then to calm down and assess the situation. They fell into three groups: those that believed the worse; those that believed none of it; and those like Ella, who thought it through. (255)

This distinction between three different forms of reading and interpretation relates to three different psychological structures. The subjects who do not believe in Denver's story foreclose history in a psychotic way. The result of this foreclosure is a return of the repressed history in the form of hallucinated presences. However, the subjects who only believe in the worst parts of history become locked into a hysterical or masochistic structure. In *The Bluest Eye,* we found that this mode of enjoying historical pain is often determined by a neurotic or a perverse form of internalized racism. These first two mode of historical memory are undermined by Ella's attempt to think through and accept Denver's story.

It is precisely this latter form of reception that Morrison's own writing calls for us to perform. As a nation we must begin to think through the difficult parts of our history. One place where this process has already begun is in the teaching, writing, and reading of literature that openly recalls the past and questions the present. Cultural history can thus be a form of communal therapy that helps us to redefine the very meaning of our national and individual identities.

By refusing to repress the traumatic aspects of our national past, we can start to work against the structures of prejudice that I have been analyzing. Form a postmodern and a psychoanalytic perspective, this project requires an acceptance of our diverse unconscious desires and an acknowledgment of the ways that we are all alienated in the discourse of the Other. Once we have affirmed this notion of linguistic castration, the next step is to refuse to project our sense of loss and lack onto other subjects. In the case of literary studies, this refusal of projection requires a rethinking of the way that we use literary texts in order to work out our own unconscious fears and desires in an intellectual and alienated way. Literary criticism must move beyond the mere diagnosis of social problems and forms of prejudice and begin to posit alternative modes of social interaction.

CHAPTER NINE

Conclusion

Throughout this work, I have argued for a form of literary criticism that is no longer content with finding examples of prejudice in cultural texts but rather seeks to explore ways to undermine diverse modes of oppression. In order to work effectively against these different forms of prejudice, I have posited that it is necessary to first distinguish between psychotic, neurotic, and perverse modes of discrimination and then show how these different structures feed off each other.

We have found that in perverse forms of prejudice, the subject's refusal to accept the fact that all human beings must submit their own bodies and enjoyments to the alienating effects of language results in an attempt to enslave others in sexist sadomasochistic relationships. In this structure, women and minorities are attacked for refusing to conform to the dominant forms of language and law. We have also seen that this accusation of linguistic failure is most often tied to the claim that these same subjects are hypersexual. This equation of linguistic castration and sexual excess is derived from the patriarchal and sexist need to control women and nontraditional forms of desire by mastering all aspects of language and law.

To overcome both linguistic and sexual modes of perverse racism and sexism, we need to acknowledge the fact that we are all enslaved by language and that we all have transgressive desires and enjoyments. This double awareness of linguistic castration and illicit sexuality also implies an insight into the homophobic equation between same-sex desires and a lost sense of gender identification. The fact that men can desire men and women can desire women threatens the heterosexual logic of the dominant symbolic order. I have posited that this generation of symbolic confusion in the face of same-sex desire often results in a perverse attempt to reinforce rigid gender and sexual oppositions.

In many ways, homophobia is still an accepted form of prejudice that helps to govern and police our culture's sexuality and gender constructions.

Throughout this work, we have witnessed the ways that this fear of same-sex desire feeds into neurotic modes of oppression and prejudice. In the case of obsessional ethnocentrism, I have argued that the unconscious connection between anal penetration and lost social status is based on the imaginary equation of the body and the nation. For the obsessional ethnocentrist, any threat to the unity and purity of the nation and its borders is experienced as a threat of bodily invasion and fragmentation. In this structure, the Other is experienced as an alien force that is trying to penetrate the subject from behind. To work against this type of prejudice, we need first to undermine this imaginary conception of the nation and then explore the fears of penetration and passivity that haunt obsessional subjects.

In the case of hysterical forms of prejudice, the projection of repressed desires and fears onto the debased Other is often structured by class differences. For the hysterical subject, the poor or the foreign Other embodies the excessive sexual enjoyment that the hysteric does not want to accept in him- or herself. In order to work against this need to project repressed desires onto Others, these subjects must first acknowledge the unconscious desires and fears that they refuse to admit. Part of this work entails an awareness of how all modes of enjoyment and fear are shaped by the dominant symbolic order's need to regulate and produce sexual desire.

I have argued that one of the most effective ways that societies interpellate and control subjects is through the manipulation of their most private desires. In the case of psychotic forms of prejudice, we see how the cultural rejection of same-sex desire results in a paranoid discourse that forces subjects to reject and project their own homosexual desires. Moreover, the cultural equation of heterosexual relations with symbolic coherency implies that same-sex desires will be connected to a sense of linguistic confusion and subjective fragmentation. In order to counter this psychotic form of homophobia, cultural critics can show how homosexuality has represented an essential aspect of our shared culture.

Another way that critics can help to fight these various forms of prejudice is to refuse to project their own culturally stigmatized modes of enjoyment onto foreign lands and distant historical periods. In order to fight against this intellectual displacement and projection of unconscious fears and desires, critics must constantly relate literary depictions of prejudice to current social and subjective issues. We have argued that criticism becomes most effective when it uses the past in order to talk about the present and not the other way around.

To stop the compulsive repetition of destructive modes of prejudice, I have been arguing that we must not only uncover the repressed desires and fears that constantly return in our culture but also explore the ways that subjects enjoy the diverse modes of prejudice that oppress them. By using Slavoj Žižek's theory of masochistic ideological enjoyment, I have articulated how subjects cling to internalized forms of racism and sexism in order to gain an illusory sense of symbolic mastery over real trauma. Psychoanalysis teaches us that subjects will repeat, on a symbolic representational level, the unresolved unconscious conflicts that they cannot resolve in their own lives. Furthermore, I have examined how the central trauma that subjects try to symbolically repeat and master is the trauma of linguistic castration. In order to avoid the fact that no one can control the alienating effects of language, subject's constantly project their own sense of linguistic inadequacy onto debased cultural Others.

The type of cultural criticism that I am arguing for cannot be developed without a constant awareness of the dialectical relationship between subjective structures and social forces. By examining the ways that minority subjects become the scapegoats for a diverse range of social and political problems, we can more effectively help to alleviate these forms of social injustice. In many ways, Toni Morrison's work can serve as a guide on how to undermine this process of scapegoating at the same time that one develops an alternative psychoanalytic model for social and political change. Through the creation of a communal form of psychoanalysis, we can work though the social and subjective fears and desire that still haunt our current culture.

Notes

CHAPTER ONE

1. It is impossible to provide here a list of the different critical essays that have analyzed racism, homophobia, and sexism in literary texts because of the incredible number of these works. I am not arguing that this form of literary criticism is without value; rather, I am positing that this form of criticism is a necessary first step but not a sufficient one.

2. In *The Acoustic Mirror*, Kaja Silverman argues that Lacan posits a form of linguistic castration and Symbolic murder that predates the discovery of sexual difference:

> With Lacan . . . there is a castration which precedes the recognition of anatomical difference—a castration to which all cultural subjects must submit, since it coincides with separation from the world of objects, and the entry into language. (1)

The first form of castration thus represents the original separation between the real world of things and the symbolic world of language and not primarily the separation between the mother and the child or the separation between the sexes.

This initial mode of castration is then only recast in terms of sexual differences after-the-fact through its symbolic repetition. As in the case of the repetition-compulsion, the desire to repeat the scene of castration is dependent on a desire to master the initial anxiety of a trauma through its symbolic reproduction.

3. For a description of the way that this process of projection works in the structure of prejudice, see Silverman *Male Subjectivity*, 45–47.

4. Silverman adds that this structure of repetition takes the form of a fetish: "It projects male lack onto female characters in the guise of anatomical deficiency and discourse inadequacy" (1). In other words, because men do not want to face the possibility that they are not in control of language and that they are in fact castrated by the Symbolic order, they project their own sense of loss and lack onto a debased Other. We can also hypothesize along these lines that if women are often equated with the unsymbolizable

real, they are placed in this position in order for men to ward off their own feelings of linguistic alienation.

5. Central to Silverman's argument is the idea that Freud himself, in his theory of castration and fetishism, acts out his own process of denial and projection:

The malice Freud himself exhibits toward the female subject in the course of his essay on anatomical difference—the "triumphant contempt" he encourages the male subject to entertain for the "mutilated creature" who is the sexual other. This set of emotions attests to nothing so much as a successfully engineered projection, to the externalizing displacement onto the female subject of what the male cannot tolerate in himself: castration or lack. (16)

In other words, the entire theory of anatomical castration is based on a displacement of linguistic castration by the male subject, who this time happens to be Freud.

6. Lacan argues that this initial subject of the unconscious can be equated with "ineffable, stupid existence" (*Ecrits* 194). Lacan's argument here is that the primary subjective state is defined by the real and the impossibility of symbolizing this originary form of existence.

7. The Oedipus complex itself represents the imposition of a third term to break up the imaginary relationship between the child and the mother. For Lacan, this intervening third element links paternity to the dominance of language and law in the shaping of subjectivity.

8. By transforming Lacan's model of subjectivity into a sociocultural structure, I hope to show how prejudices are taken in a dialectic of social and subjective forces. Since every form of prejudice has both a social and a psychological cause, we can not easily separate one end of this dialectic from the other.

9. Young-Bruehl shows how most theories of prejudice have utilized the post–World War II theory of anti-Semitism in order to examine other forms of prejudice that have a different structure and etiology.

10. Young-Bruehl explains that racist subjects refuse to acknowledge their own repressed impulses and thus constantly blame others for the feelings that they do not want to admit in themselves. These "Others" that become the target of hysterical prejudices are most often people who have a lower class status than the prejudiced subject and who are from a different cultural or ethnic background (222). In this structure, hysterical subjects split off a part of their own desire and sexuality and then see it acted out in the realm of an Other who has been placed in a position of social inferiority or weakness.

11. Young-Bruehl posits that central to this structure of hysterical racism is the notion that this Other is in some way associated with the sub-

ject through a mutually shared space or geographical location: "The objects of hysterical character's prejudices are—in one way or another, literally or symbolically—domestics. They live in a distinct part of the household, whether in fact or fantasy or social theory or myth, whether in familial, community, or national image" (22). This close physical association between the hysterical racist and the victim of racism is necessary in order for the Other to be placed in the position of being an outside threat that has been internalized. Domestics or slaves are outsiders who are inside the house and have no power to combat their subjected status. These internal outsiders become the physical and psychological repository of the hysterical subject's unconscious.

12. One of the differences between the hysterical and the psychotic forms of projection is that the psychotic experiences his or her projected desires as a real perception and not as an imaginary fantasy.

13. Lacan's theory of psychosis is outlined in *The Seminar of Jacques Lacan. Book III: The Psychoses.*

14. Young-Bruehl argues that homophobia does not represent a unified psychological structure; rather, it can take on several different forms: "Homosexuals are all-purpose targets" (240). While I also think that homophobia does play a role in a diverse range of prejudices and psychological structures, I will argue throughout this work that the basic structure of this form of prejudice is tied to a cultural mode of psychosis. In this structure, the dominant social order forecloses same-sex desire and this act of foreclosure is coupled with a projection of illicit sexuality onto debased Others.

15. In "Subversion of the Subject and Dialectic of Desire," Lacan insists that what the obsessional subject "does not want, and what he strenuously refuses to do, until the end of analysis, is to sacrifice his castration to the jouissance of the Other" (*Ecrits,* 323). The obsessional subject thus attempts to disconnect his or her *jouissance* from castration by refusing to submit both to the will of the symbolic Other.

16. Miller's comments have been published in Žižek's *Tarrying* 203. I would like to argue that Žižek appropriates Miller's theory without differentiating between the diverse forms of prejudice that I have been articulating.

17. Sedgwick defines homosociality as "social bonds between persons of the same sex" (1). She adds that this form of relations can include both homophobia and latent forms of homosexuality (1). I will be using homosociality as defining the link between repressed same-sex desire, homophobia, and the idealization of the bonds between subjects of the same gender.

18. One of the main differences between neurotic and perverse subjects is their different modes of defense. In neurosis, the primary way that a subject deals with trauma is by repressing any threatening stimuli into the

unconscious. However, in perversion this mode of repression is replaced by a splitting of the subject into the intellectual and affective parts of the personality. Furthermore, in neurotic forms of prejudice, one must first get the subject to see what he or she is repressing (castration and *jouissance*). However, in the analysis of perverse subjects, there is very little repression; rather, one has to help the subject see how he or she is repeating and displacing the scene of castration.

19. In *Between Philosophy and Psychoanalysis,* I examine Freud's and Lacan's theories of perversion as they relate to the symbolic order of sexual difference and linguistic castration (107–131).

CHAPTER TWO

1. By stressing the way that social forces shape subjective structures, I am not downplaying the importance of individual psychological components in the formation of prejudices; rather, I am trying to establish a dialectical relationship between subjective and social forces.

2. I do not want to give the impression here that all societies must repress homosexuality; rather, I am arguing that in our current Western culture, this structure of idealized heterosexuality and debased homosexuality is a dominant form of ideological control.

3. Young-Bruehl argues that there are hysterical, narcissistic, and obsessional homophobes, but she does not consider the psychotic and perverse structures that this prejudice can take. In order to correct this limitation, I will be articulating the relations among psychotic (paranoid), neurotic (obsessional ethnocentrism and hysterical racism), and perverse (sexism) forms of homophobia.

4. The United States government decided that the military would not ask military personnel what their sexual preference was but they could discharge anyone who was caught performing a homosexual act. In other terms, the act, and not the person, was deemed illicit.

5. One result of Young-Bruehl's theory of homophobia as a pathology of categorization is that the mere act of defining what homosexuality is can be considered an act of homophobia. For example, Foucault's claim that the homosexual was invented in the nineteenth century implies that the psychiatric production of this term was itself a homophobic act. Furthermore, by letting the homophobic establishment define homosexuality, Foucault falls into the trap of reproducing a form of prejudice. As Tim Dean has argued, queer sexuality is queer precisely because it calls into question many of the ways that we define subjectivity and identity.

6. Following Foucault, many recent theorists have argued that it is wrong to speak of homosexuality and homophobia in the early modern period because this form of identity was not yet solidified. Jonathan Dollimore repeats this theory, when he states, "Recent studies emphasize the different ways homo/sexuality was conceptualized in early modern England—a difference so considerable in fact that 'homosexuality' becomes anachronistic, since at times there was neither the concept nor, exactly, the identity it signifies" (237). I believe that this argument is both wrong and counterproductive. It is based on the misguided notion that homosexuality can only be analyzed if it takes on its modern form and nomination. I will counter that early modern subjects and authorities were acutely aware of homosexual desires and practices but that they simply had a different way of characterizing all forms of sexuality and subjectivity. More important, modern readers cannot help but project their current understandings of same-sex desires onto early modern texts, and since I am concerned with the current interpretations of texts and prejudices, I will focus on the ways that homosexuality and homophobia are conceived of today.

7. I do not want to equate homosexuality with anal penetration; rather, I am arguing that homophobic subjects often see no difference between the two.

8. This displacement of prejudices from one subject to another manifests the dialogical nature of all forms of social oppression and subjective pathology. In his *Problems of Dostoyevsky's Poetics*, Mikhail Bakhtin insists that literary ideas and ideologies always represent intersubjective dialogues between different minds and characters. In fact, for Bahktin there is no such thing as a unified subject of consciousness; rather, all subjects are dialogically constructed. If we take this theory to heart, then we must begin to reexamine some of the fundamental ways that we read and critique all forms of literature. Bakhtin eloquently argues that we need to develop a form of criticism that is as dialogical as the texts that we are reading.

9. According to Young-Bruehl, people with obsessional prejudices "imagine the conspirators as having the capacity to penetrate them, get into their bowels and their privacies" (34).

10. In Iago's case, his hatred for Othello stems from his interest in his own status in the Venetian military hierarchy:

> Three great ones of the city,
> In personal suit to make me his lieutenant,
> Off-capped to him; and by the faith of man,
> I know my price; I am worth no worse a place.
>
> (1.1.8–12)

Iago's obsessional concern with his social position is determined by his belief that he deserves to be in a higher rank than Cassio. Furthermore, by stressing the fact that he knows his price and value, his concern over his social status is linked to an economic calculation.

11. In "Character and Anal Erotism," Freud posits that the obsessional concern over order, money, and the body is derived from an attempt to transform the subject's early anal erotic stimulation into an acceptable form of control: "Cleanliness, orderliness and trustworthiness give exactly the impression of a reaction-formation against an interest in what is unclean and disturbing and should not be part of the body" (212–13). In this structure, the obsessional subject sublimates his or her anal erotism by substituting money for feces as the dirty object of desire.

12. While Young-Bruehl writes about psychological traits and character structures, I will be focusing on psychoanalytic structures of subjectivity and psychopathology. The difference in our approaches stems from her use of "normal" forms of subjectivity. From a Lacanian perspective, this notion of the "normal" does not exist; every subject is either perverse, psychotic, or neurotic.

13. Iago's concern with his place within the larger social structure is presented throughout the opening scenes of the play. His obsessional discourse locks him into a conservative desire to retain the old feudal order of fixed rank and status. In this light, Iago complains about the new system where "preferment goes by letter and affection / And not by old gradiation" (1.1.36–37). In many ways, this statement is an accurate account of the early modern transition between a static feudal order of rank and the new order that undermines old forms of social control. We shall see that the power of Iago's discourse is that he often combines real social concerns with subjective states of fear.

14. The constant reference to animals and beasts in this play points to both a racist and a homophobic discourse. For these early modern subjects, any form of excessive sexuality is connected to a loss of social prestige. Cassio makes this point when he exclaims, "O, I have / Lost my reputation! I have lost the immortal part of / Myself, and what remains is bestial" (2.3.52–54). This statement is structured by the opposition between an ideal state of reputation and the debased form of animal existence.

15. According to Young-Bruehl, in order for hysterical subjects to control and contain their projected unconscious, they need to enforce strict rules concerning marriage, social hierarchy, and political power. The domestic Other or outsider must be contained within the house or the nation in a fixed location or position. Young-Bruehl adds that the ultimate threat to this form of social control is an intermarriage where an outsider becomes associated with an insider: "The quintessential act of transgression is intermarriage between the higher and the lower. Marriage represents equality for the partner and thus destroys the main theme of the hysterical character's prejudice—

'They have a place and they must stay in it'" (224). This fear of intermarriage is therefore in part determined by the desire for social inequality and the need to keep the Other in the role of being the target of projected desires.

16. Throughout this work I will be arguing that every society unconsciously desires what it renders illicit or amoral. In the case of this play, interracial marriage and same-sex relations represent two of the repressed aspects of Shakespeare's own culture.

17. Shakespeare's use of hysterical racism shows how the symptoms of hysteria are in part culturally determined.

18. Mario Digangi argues that in seventeenth-century satiric comedy there is a constant play between the "ass" as representing the fool and a part of the male anatomy: "satiric wit that makes asses of men is vectored towards a man's ass—an overdetermined part of the body in which sexual, sadistic, and scatological activities converge" (179). This use of the ass is still at work today as a symbol of humiliation, punishment, control, illicit sexuality, and foolishness.

19. The power of this phrase rests in part on the combination of Othello's internalized racism with a form of discourse that combines symbolic names and visual faces. Blackness as the symbol of both sin and racial difference is an object that circulates throughout this drama and receives its power through its ability to be both visual and symbolic at the same time. I would like to posit that the black object in this work functions as an excluded center of discourse that ultimately helps to ground the constant displacement of signification and subjective identity. Just as Othello needs "ocular proof" for Desdemona's infidelity, all of the characters seek out a form of language that can be both seen and signified.

20. *Othello* shows that every subject must seek out his or her self-representations in the discourse of the Other (A). At the end of the play, Othello himself becomes aware of this contradictory structure of subjective representation by stating: "That's he that was Othello, here I am" (5.2.284). In this anticipation of Descartes's cogito, Othello displays the subjective division of his identity while he affirms the way that he has been identified by the Other characters in the play. Moreover, from the very start of this work, Othello is aware of both the potentiality of his own nothingness and the way that he can construct himself through the discourse of the Other: "Not I; I must be found. / My parts, my title, and my perfect soul / Shall manifest me rightly" (1.2.30–32). These lines indicate that Othello's identity is not given, rather it has to be dialogically discovered through the manifestation of his public reputation.

21. This form of dialogical self-fashioning has been strongly articulated by Stephen Greenblatt; in his essay "The Improvisation of Power," Greenblatt sees Iago and not Othello as the great improviser:

Iago is fully aware of himself as an improvisor and revels in his ability to manipulate his victims, to lead them by their noses like asses, to possess their labor without their ever being capable of grasping the relation in which they are enmeshed. (*Renaissance* 233)

It would be difficult to argue with this assessment of Iago's ability to control and dictate all of the actions of the other characters in this play. It is Iago's strange combination of empathy and cynicism that allows him to determine what others will believe and what they unconsciously fear. Yet, there is a problem with Greenblatt's need to posit a strong sense of intentionality and self-awareness in Iago's character. For to say that Iago is fully aware of himself and his acts of improvisation is to deny the very ground of self-fashioning that Greenblatt will later posit.

It is significant that when Greenblatt turns toward Lacan in order to explain his own theory of self-fashioning, he also switches his discussion from Iago to Othello:

I would propose that there is a deep resemblancebetween the construction of the self in analysis—at least as Lacan conceives it—and Othello's self-fashioning. The resemblance is grounded in the dependence of even the innermost self upon language that is always necessarily given from without and upon representation before an audience. (244–45)

The fact that the subject always defines him- or herself in a discourse that comes from the Other would mean that all forms of intentionality are rendered suspect. We must then question why Greenblatt denies Othello the intentionality that he attaches to Iago.

22. One way that the encounter with feminine desire and subjectivity is controlled in early modern society is through the formation of all-male institutions like the military and the monastery. For Othello, it is clear that his manly military actions must be separated from his sexual desire. This becomes evident when he requests that Desdemona not be allowed to come with him to battle:

I will your serious and great business scant
when she is with me. No, when light-wing toys
Of feathered Cupid seel with wanton dullness
My speculative and officed instruments.

(1.3.266–70)

Within the sexist structure of the male-dominated military homosocial order, Desdemona represents a threat to Othello's ability to work and to think.

23. Jyotsna Singh posits that Othello's subjectivity is determined by a series of psychic and social divisions that place him simultaneously inside and outside of Venetian culture. Playing on Homi Bhabha's notion of post-colonial liminality, Singh declares that we cannot speak of Othello as a singular identity, "for his 'otherness' as a black man cannot be contained within the dominant, Western fantasy of a singular, unified identity" (288). As a culturally divided subject, the other characters in the play simultaneously define him as being a loyal military hero and a debased black animal.

Moreover, critics have also followed this strategy of dividing and conquering Othello by placing him within a strict Euro-centric binary logic that pits the Christian Western civilized world of Venetian law and reason against the barbarian non-Christian realms of Turkey and Africa. Singh points out that in the Introduction to the Signet Classic edition of *Othello*, one finds the following ideological description of this binary opposition:

Here then are the two major reference points on the map of the world of *Othello:* out at the far edge are the Turks, barbarism, disorder, and amoral destructive powers; closer and more familiar is Venice, the City, order, law, reason (qtd. in Singh 289).

The excluded third term in this description is, of course, Cyprus, which represents in the play the meeting of these two opposing worlds. This Signet Introduction adds that in Cyprus:

passions are more explosive and closer to the surface than in Venice, and here, instead of the ancient order . . . of the City, there is only one man to control violence and defend civilization—the Moor Othello, himself of savage origins and a converted Christian. (Qtd. in Singh 287)

One has to wonder if Iago himself wrote this highly ideological introduction that is determined by the opposition of Christianity and Savagery.

In order to work against this form of binary racist logic, we must return to our original desire to see how this play concentrates on the relationship between characters and ideologies and not on the fixed and stable grounds of individual figures and stereotypes. Dialogically, one can examine how Iago's deconstruction of Venetian ideology relates to Othello's self-fashioning and Desdemona's victimization without losing sight of the different social and historical factors that both separate and connect these different subjective positions. In other words, I am arguing for a form of critical theory that mimics the theatrical interplay between different characters and ideas.

24. Valerie Traub posits that Othello both idolizes and mistrusts his beloved and that he thus leaves himself open to Iago's manipulations (33–43). Traub reads the following lines as indicating that Othello believes that feminine deception and inconstancy represent the very foundations of

marriage: "O curse of marriage, / That we can call these delicate creatures ours, / And not their appetites!" (3.3.274–76). In this passage, Othello highlights the difference between the social control of the married subject and the uncontrollable nature of sexual desire. Furthermore, from a certain perspective, every female has to deceive and leave their first love-object (their father) in order to be with their husband. Desdemona shows her awareness of this conflict when she declares to her father: "I do perceive here a divided duty. / To you I am bound for life and education . . . But here is my husband" (1.3.181–85). Desdemona's own subjective division is thus determined in part by her dual subjection to both her father and her husband. Othello, in turn, does not trust her because he realizes through Iago that she has a double nature.

25. According to Mary Ann Doane, Frantz Fanon insists that "Racism is the result of the surplus sexual guilt of the white man which is generated in the process of building culture" (281). Since culture itself requires a certain renunciation of sexual desire, this lost "uncivilized" part of sexuality becomes projected onto the black man who becomes what Fanon calls "the genital nigger." In Othello's case, we have the situation of a highly civilized black man who represents himself as someone who has renounced most of his sexual energy: "Not to comply with heat—the young affects / In me defunct" (1.3. 263–64). Since, Othello actively works against the stereotype of being the "genital Moor," he is forced to project this excess of sexuality onto Desdemona.

26. Traub argues that Othello's idealization of Desdemona and his attempt to compare her to a jewel is based on his need to contain her mobile sexuality: "By imaginatively transforming Desdemona into a jewel—hard, cold, static, silent, yet adored and desired —Othello is able to maintain both his distance and his idealization of her" (39–40).

27. The effect of this transformation of Desdemona into a subjectless object, however, results in a displacement of violent desire back onto Othello himself:

> O cursed, cursed slave! Whip me, ye devils,
> From this possession of this heavenly sight!
> Blow me about in winds! roast me in sulphur!
> Wash me in steep-down gulfs of liquid fire!
>
> (5.2.278–81)

I would like to read this passage as indicating that once Othello reaches his ultimate goal of turning Desdemona into an immobile pure white surface, all of his own violent passions and racial fears become mobilized. He now affirms himself to be the slave and black devil that everyone in the play has been accusing him of being. This final act of internalized racism is therefore linked to the ideological idealization of white fairness.

28. By labeling Othello a postmodern subject, I am calling into question the usage of such historical terms as early modern and postmodern in order to highlight the continuity of certain psychosocial models in Western culture. In particular, I have been arguing that our culture is still dominated by the same cycle of prejudices that are circulated in Shakespeare's text.

29. In his essay "Othello, Bakhtin, and the Death(s) of Dialogue," Thomas Cohen insists that we can locate in the first letter of Othello's name the symbol that marks both the circularity of all forms of discourse and the negation or zero-ground of dialogue itself: "The circle or letter 'O' may suggest less the completed rehabilitation of Othello's old image . . . than a voiding of the fiction of the self, like a zero" (12). This "O" that repeats throughout the play can be read as the ultimate symbol of the subject who cannot be defined in the circulatory discourse of the Other. For Cohen, "*Othello* dismantles the ideology of dialogue as an inter-subjective communicative model" (13). I would not argue with this deconstructive reading; however, I would like to stress that the "character" who enacts this form of criticism in the play is none other than Iago, who declares: "For I am nothing if not critical" (2.1.119). Following Iago's own self-avowal, I would like to read his character as a proto-deconstructionist critic who uses his rhetorical skills in order to entrap Othello into a discourse of self-hatred and doubt.

CHAPTER THREE

1. This splitting of the subject and the lifting of repression that occurs in the process of negation often indicates a perverse form of subjectivity. Moreover, according to Slavoj Žižek, it is this perverse form of discourse that determines the postmodern theory of subjectivity and sexuality:

> In post-liberal societies . . . the agency of social repression no longer acts in the guise of an internalized Law or Prohibition that requires renunciation and self-control; instead, it assumes the form of a hypnotic agency that imposes the attitude of 'yielding to temptation'—that is to say, its injunction amounts to a command: 'Enjoy Yourself.' (*Metastases* 16)

This connection between the superego and the command of enjoyment can be best seen in the realms of advertising and the mass media where subjects are told what to consume and what to enjoy.

2. I am using the term "Other" to indicate here, the symbolic order, other people, and the encounter with people that have a different racial, ethnic, or sexual identification.

3. Since Shakespeare's sonnets were originally distributed among a white male coterie of readers, it is easy to see why his poems are directed toward a homosocial reading relationship.

4. Throughout this chapter, I will be equating the celebration of the young man's fairness with the idealization of racial and ethnic whiteness. For more on this question of race in the *Sonnets*, see Hall 62–122.

5. Bracher posits that the critical turn toward new historicism produces a form of textual analysis that is often void of any real political consequences: "According to some critics, the currently prominent form of cultural criticism, new historicism, is successful only in giving its practitioners the illusion that their work is socially transformative, while in fact taking them in the opposite direction" (4).

6. This notion of a psychoanalytic theory of reading and criticism has been outlined by Bracher (1–16).

7. For an extended analysis of the way that this cultural system functions, see Sedgwick.

8. Both Sedgwick's and Rubin's excellent studies of homosociality tend to divorce this question of male boning from the analysis of racism. Throughout my work, I will posit that we must link the homosocial celebration of sexual and cultural sameness to the racist debasement of sexual and ethnic otherness.

9. This example may seem crudely obvious; however, it is the obviousness of this type of everyday occurrences that is often left unexamined by cultural and literary critics. In order to break down the borders between academic criticism and social reality, we must constantly force ourselves to use theory to discuss our own lives and cultures.

10. All citations from the *Sonnets* come from Booth's edition.

11. Joseph Pequigney has discussed this movement of sexual desire in the *Sonnets*; however, he does not stress the role played by homosociality and racial difference in these poems.

12. Lacan may argue that the unconscious is the discourse of the Other but he also affirms that the subject always desires things that resist the dominant symbolic orders. By defining the subject as a hole or a lack in the structure of the symbolic Other, Lacan affirms Freud's theory of unconscious desire.

13. By stressing the relationship between the unconscious of the reader and the unconscious of the text, I am arguing for a purely psychoanalytic theory of transference. Many current psychoanalysts and literary theorists have moved away from Freud's initial insights into the role played by the unconscious in all truly psychoanalytic phenomena. These same critics have also failed to realize the ways that the unconscious represents that part of the subject that rejects the dominant symbolic order.

14. The paradox of the unconscious rejection of the symbolic order is that nothing can be rejected from the symbolic order without a return in the

real of the foreclosed element. In other terms, the subject who refuses to submit to castration, experiences the act of castration in his or her dreams and fantasies.

15. My reading of the *Sonnets* is highly influenced by Fineman's *Shakespeare's Perjured Eye: The Invention of Poetic Subjectivity in the Sonnets*. In his analysis of these poems, Fineman follows the traditional method of dividing them into two major subsequences: sonnets 1–126 are written to and about a fair young man, while the last 28 sonnets are addressed to a dark lady. Fineman does not try to determine the biographical source of either of these two characters; rather, he attempts to see them as two interrelated figures of sexual and rhetorical difference. What I would like to do is to take Fineman's "literary" argument and transform it into a historical and cultural commentary. In this sense, we can begin to read the figure of the fair young man as the representative of white homosocial male-bonding and narcissistic self-reflection, while we interpret the figure of the dark lady as a symbol of ethnic and cultural difference.

16. For a detailed discussion of the Lacan's use of logical squares, see my *Between* 79–83.

17. I have been arguing that the Western culture is dominated by a destructive racist metaphorical system that opposes an idealized form of whiteness to a debased form of blackness. In the early modern period, this color-coded distinction between white fairness and black foulness has aesthetic as well as social ramifications. Even when an artist employs a color-based metaphor for purely aesthetic reasons, this metaphor often serves to reinforce racist systems of oppression. In fact, the metaphorical distinction between white goodness and black evilness contributed to the ability of European explorers to colonize and enslave a number of foreign people. As many travel narratives show, once the Europeans equated whiteness with humanity and darkness to animals and the devil, they were able to rationalize their treatment of people in a nonhumane way.

Many of the initial encounters between white explorers and dark natives were predetermined by a cultural and literary system of color difference. This means that before "race" was solidified into a coherent category, dark and light colors were attached to a series of moral and political value judgments. Kim Hall has shown that in the exploration narratives of Richard Hakluyt and John Pory, Africa is constantly equated with the darkness of ignorance, while whiteness is attached to the enlightening effect of Christianity. In his *Geographical Historie,* Pory declares, "Now that we have declared the miseries and darkness of Affrik, it remaineth that we set downe that little light of true religion which there is" (qtd. in Hall, 49). This statement shows how the early explorers and colonizers of Africa where influenced by the religious and literary division between white enlightenment and dark ignorance. These color-coded signifiers and significations were both produced and circulated by the growing literary canon. Literature thus played a significant role in the exploitation and dehumanization of a large number of people.

Not only did this system of metaphorical difference help to shape the conscious interpretations of race by writers, explorers, and readers, but it also had destructive unconscious effects. The production of a binary system of moral and racial difference laid the groundwork for the projection of unwanted desires onto debased ethnic groups. Time and time again in early modern texts we find the darker races accused of having darker passions—excessive sexuality in these works is tied to a lack of moral light and white purity. In this system, the dark Other becomes an overdetermined symbol for moral depravity, sexual perversion, and erotic desire.

18. The brilliance of Shakespeare's *Sonnets* may be based on his uncanny ability to represent the structures that serve to channel and repress our culture's deepest fears and desires.

19. In current literary debates, we find this same desperate attempt to hold off the effects of time through the idealization of a past form of white male literature.

20. The constant threat of losing the idealization of whiteness in the *Sonnets* is reflective of the general economy of loss that dominates these poems. Thomas Greene points out that:

> the procreation sonnets display with particular brilliance Shakespeare's ability to manipulate words which in his language belong both to the economic and the sexual/biological semantic fields: among others, 'increase,' 'use,' 'spend,' 'free,' 'live,' 'dear,' 'house,' 'usury,' 'endowed,' along with their cognates. (76–77)

Greene partially accounts for this abundance of economic metaphors by arguing that Shakespeare displays a "bourgeois desire" to accumulate and "store" up all resources and excesses. Part of this desire may be derived from the poet's own feelings of poverty and a certain level of class anxiety.

Many of the recurrent themes of the earlier and later sonnets revolve around a sexual, economic, and rhetorical system that threatens to result in an internal state of bankruptcy. From the very first sonnet we are told that the young man "Mak'st waste in niggarding." What this youth is wasting is his semen and his own beauty that he only spends on himself. Masturbation and narcissism are here linked to an economic model that is determined by scarce resources and a constant need for redistribution. Shakespeare shows himself to be a keen proto-Marxist because he realizes that the accumulation of capital can only result, in the long-term, in a loss of surplus value and profits. In order to overcome this movement toward economic and sexual entropy, the poet thus tells his young lover that he must quit his acts of autoeroticism and go out and spread his seed and capital around.

The first sonnet also sets into motion a system of distribution that constantly results in loss and self-consumption. In his narcissistic economy, the young man is accused of "Making a famine where abundance lies" (1.7). While it is not clear if Shakespeare is attacking the old feudal order for hoarding all resources or whether he is warning against the new individualistic capitalist class, it seems certain that he is critical of any mode of economic distribution that does not circulate and share its resources.

The second sonnet adds to this economic and sexual theory of use and loss an aesthetic dimension. The poet begins by warning his beloved that his beauty will be destroyed by age and "Thy youth's proud livery, so gazed on now, / Will be a tattered weed, of small worth held." Like the value of stored capital and semen, beauty itself needs to be expended or it will soon be lost. This drive toward consumption and production is soon countered and restricted by a warning against "thriftless praise." In other words, praise as a form of idealization and poetic conceit must be rationed out in a just and careful manner. In fact, the poet goes onto to tell his beloved that only an act of procreation will help him to balance his books: "How much more praise deserved thy beauty's use / If thou couldst answer 'This fair child of mine / Shall sum my account, and make my old excuse" (2.9–11). In this strange system of exchange, the production of a child clears one's social debts that have been incurred through self-consumption and the unwise expenditure of praise.

21. This need to contain the increase of ethnic difference and maintain the dominance of white culture is apparent in Queen Elizabeth I's proclamation of 1596: "Understanding that there are lately divers blackamoors brought into this realme, of which kinde of people there are allready here too manie, considering howe God hathe blessed this land with great increase of people of our own nation as anie countrie in the world, whereof manie for wante of service and meanes to sett them on worck fall to idleness and to great extremytie . . . that those kinde of people should be sente forth of the lande" (qtd. in Shyllon 2). The Queen's racism is tied to a classic fear of economic competition coupled with the desire to maintain and increase her own population.

22. This displacement from same-sex desire to a form of love that is mediated by men but directed toward women is a central theme of Eve Sedgwick's *Between Men: English Literature and Male Homosocial Desire.* I would like to add to Sedgwick's theory by showing how Shakespeare's *Sonnets* help to expose contradictions inherent in Western culture's homosociality and racial hegemony. In other terms, I will add a race-based component to Sedgwick's sex-based theory.

23. Throughout the *Sonnets,* procreation is equated with the act of writing and the copying of poetic verse. Sonnet 13 clearly ties creative reproduction to the act of sexual procreation: "She carved thee for her seal, and meant thereby / Thou shoudst print more, not let the copy die" (11.13–14). This poem implies that cultural reproduction depends on a social form of narcissism that will allow the white male ego to look into the realm of the other in order to copy its own perfect reflection. Racial narcissism in this system aligns itself with homosociality and the reproduction of a contained cultural order.

24. This movement from narcissism to allo-eroticism may indicate a transformation and not a replacement of the narcissistic pleasure principle.

25. Lacan has shown that the narcissistic subject defines him- or herself solely through the reflection and responses of others. When this type of subject can no longer receive the desired feedback of the other, there is a radical sense of loss and nothingness. For more on this dialectic between narcissism and nothingness, see my *Between* 59–74.

26. This constant stress on youth and beauty is relevant to our own current culture's beauty industry. Shakespeare's work allows us to see that this idealization of youth and beauty may be derived from internal feelings of loss and self-disgust.

27. Bracher has argued that one of the central ways that a reader is interpellated into a text is through this form of mirroring identification (31–40).

28. Temporality is often employed in literature and literary studies as an attempt to displace onto history problematics that are inherent to the very structure of language itself. Therefore, the argument that poetry was once able to realize its ideal by matching the idealization of the object with the idealization of the subject is itself an attempt to escape from an awareness that all forms of representation depend on an imaginary and illusionary quest for total recognition and illumination. Likewise, the claim that insists that in the literature of "dead white men" there was a form of language that was unproblematic and in many ways ideal, represents a failure to see that literature has always been telling a story about its own failures and its own imaginary attempts to cover those failures.

I am hypothesizing that what literary history most often entails is an attempt to displace and project the negating and desubjectivizing aspects of language onto some cultural Other. In this sense, Shakespeare's sonnets can be read as a text that serves to both reveal and conceal the most threatening and destabilizing aspects of language. These poems are able to point to the failure of traditional metaphors as well as the very process of metaphorization itself. Yet at the same time, they hide these discoveries by acting them out in certain sexual and racial encounters and relations. Moreover, this lit-

erary strategy of projecting linguistic loss onto the cultural Other is a fundamental aspect of all forms of racism and social prejudice.

29. This opposition between white and black can be read in the distinction between the young man sonnets and the dark lady sonnets; however,
people have been resistant to read any form of racial signification in these
poems. One of the reasons literary critics may refuse to read these sonnets in
terms of race relations is that they do not want to challenge the cultural
idealization of Shakespeare by implicating him in the "real world" of social
relations.

30. Like the political activists of the 1960s, Shakespeare's claim of black
beauty points to the relation between racism and the ethnocentric beauty
industry.

31. For an extended analysis of the relation between the imaginary
order and questions of racial difference, see Silverman, *The Threshold* 9–37.

32. Lacan attaches the failure of vision to castration in his theory of the
gaze. For Lacan the gaze itself is an example of the "lack that constitutes castration anxiety" (*Four Concepts* 73). This indicates that the inverse relation
between vision and the gaze is doubled by the binary opposition between the
phallus and castration. In Lacan's theory, the gaze proves castration by undermining the visual presence of the phallus and the mastery of the visual
field. "In our relation to things, in so far as this relation is constituted by the
way of vision, and ordered in the figures of representation, something slips,
passes, is transmitted, from stage to stage, and is always to some degree
eluded in it—that is what we call the gaze" (73). The gaze is therefore the object that is eluded by all forms of representation and vision—it is the lack or
the limit that is inscribed into the phenomenology of consciousness.

Moreover, Lacan posits that voyeurism is predicated on the presentation of the unseen object that undermines the intentionality of the ego:

> What he is trying to see, make no mistake, is the object as absence.
> What the voyeur is looking for and finds is merely a shadow behind
> the curtain. . . . What he is looking for is not, as one says, the phal-
> lus—but precisely its absence. (182)

In other words, what the voyeur is looking to see is the absence of the ideal
image or phallus and not its presence. The male voyeur thus looks into the
place of the Other, not to see the ideal image of the woman, but rather to see
her absence.

33. Lacan insists that the symbolic control of objects and the self in
Freud's fort/da game does not give the subject power over language: "The
function of this exercise with this object refers to an alienation, and not to
some supposed mastery, which is difficult to imagine being increased in an
endless repetition" (*Four Concepts* 239).

34. These poems of loss and servitude create a context for a culture of prejudice and slavery that valorizes states of submission and domination. The poet does not mind if he has to suffer and be enslaved if he can turn his subjection into a written document of pain. Sonnet 141 returns to this theme of masochistic slavery by celebrating the power of desire to undermine all of the subject's reason and will:

But my five wits nor my five senses can
Disuade one foolish heart from serving thee,
Who leaves unswayed the likeness of man,
Thy proud heart's slave and vassel-wretch to be.
Only my plague thus far I count my gain:
That she that makes me sin awards me pain.

(141.9–14).

In this poetic tradition, to write about pain is to transform a real experience of loss into a symbolic form of profit. The introduction of pain into this structure allows for a displacement of erotic energy into another mode of intense excitation. For Freud, the unconscious does not recognize the difference between pain and pleasure, it only acknowledges the intensity of a stimulation. Masochism can therefore be considered to be an unconscious form of sexual enjoyment that serves to valorize a variety of forms of subjection and slavery.

35. I will use masculine pronouns here because Freud only relates this theory to the desire of men and he does not fully articulate how this relation works with women.

36. Freud also concludes in this text that this process of splitting cannot be avoided by any subject: "I shall put forward the view that psychical impotence is much more widespread than is supposed, and that a certain amount of this behavior does in fact characterize the love of civilized man" (253). In other words, splitting and debasement are a "normal" part of every sexual relation.

37. It is a common belief that in a great number of cases of homosexual men and woman that during childhood their own sexuality was a great source of shame and inhibition and that they denied their own sexuality to themselves and to their parents. However what is often not looked at is that individuals have to split their personalities and their object choices in order to overcome their initial inhibitions to their own sexuality. The result of this may be a tendency toward debased objects and anonymous sex, where sensuality and respect or love have to remain separate.

38. The irony of Shakespeare's insistence on memorializing his beloved's name is that no one knows for sure who this lover is.

39. In sonnet 108, this celebration of writing is directly attached to the representation of the ink that is used in order to produce written characters on a blank surface: "What's in the brain that ink may character, / Which hath not figured to thee my true spirit?" As Jonathan Goldberg argues, this line can be read as indicating that for Shakespeare, "figures" and "characters" are primarily forms of inscription and not actual people or metaphorical tropes of rhetoric (*Voice Terminal* 91–94). The power of language is then tied to the power of the written word that inks its character in the form of black lines.

40. This insistence of the black letter in the unconscious of the subject is presented in the *Sonnets* through a series of dreams where black beauty becomes a symbol of unconscious desire. Sonnet 43 pushes us to read the later figure of the dark lady as the material representation of the poet's own textual unconscious:

But when I sleep, in dreams they look on thee,
and darkly bright, are bright in dark directed.
Then thou, whose shadow shadows doth make bright—
how would thy shadow's form form happy show
To clear the day with thy much clearer light,
when to unseeing eyes thy shade shines so.

(43.3–8)

As in the case of the oxymoronic phraseology of sonnet 27, this sonnet breaks down colored differences through the process of the repetition of the same word in order to signify something different. The shadow that shadows and the form that forms point to a collapsing of the difference between nouns and verbs. We may say that language that shadows its object sees only shadows (Booth 204) and that what we see in language is always based on the absence of the object; but we are still left with Shakespeare's strange desire to reverse and collapse racial, sexual, and linguistic differences (Fineman 236–237).

41. Fineman labels the rhetorical trope the "cross-coupler" a "miscegenating mixture of figurative "kinds""; however, he does not examine the racial or social implications of this biracial figure (37–38).

42. Fineman calls this play of the overdetermined "will," the "languageness of language" and he affirms that it is this form of "verbal density and texture" that determines the "peculiar literary quality" of Shakespeare's sonnets (27). Furthermore, by concentrating on the actual materiality of writing, Shakespeare is able to merge together his concern for vision with his love of verbal language. In his deconstruction of this binary opposition, the written word becomes both a visual and a verbal presence.

43. Some critics have read this line as an indication that the poet/lover only loves the young man in a purely Platonic way, that is, he had no need

for this man's prick. Yet at the same time, other readers have insisted that the poet may not have favored his lover's penis but was more interested in other parts of his anatomy (Pequigney). This body language, or shall we say bawdy language, points to a form of erotic poetry that forgoes a traditional kind of idealizing homosexuality, for what Fireman calls a poetry of pure difference (273–75). This does not mean that these figures do not have a certain cultural and historical importance; rather, it points to the absence of their grounding that allows for their movement. For I would like to argue that the cultural conventions and roles that these figures invent, subvert, and recirculate have crucial social values. For example, the groundless fixation and reiteration that connects the figure of blackness to the notions of evil, ignorance, horror, and savagery performs a social function that categorizes an Other in a negative and destructive manner. On a certain social and existential level, it does not matter that this series of cultural associations is made possible by the pure will to power of a master discourse. The ground of the stereotype may be unfounded but its power is not diminished. In fact, the very groundlessness of the figure's definition makes it in many ways even more oppressive. As Nietzsche has argued, it is through sheer acts of power that particular terms and objects take on particular values and meanings. The power to control language is dependent on one's ability to idealize the signifiers that represent one's self, while one debases the signifiers that represent one's Other.

The flip side to this argument is that political power rests on unstable grounds and that social definitions and conventions are always open to being transformed and replaced if one is in the right position to do this. In many ways, when we read Shakespeare's work, we are witnessing this active attempt to displace and transform different cultural ideals and definitions. However, the power of the writer's acts of resignification still rests in part on the ideology and receptiveness of the reader. Shakespeare can continuously transform women into men and blackness into whiteness but if the reader resists these movements, the transformation of value does not take place.

CHAPTER FOUR

1. In *Sodometries: Renaissance Texts, Modern Sexualities,* Jonathan Goldberg examines this connection between repressed same-sex desires and colonialism in relation to the discovery of America and the persecution of the Native American population (179–222).

2. In Jonathan Dollimore's insightful reading of this play, he argues that Caliban becomes the target for all of the dominant order's projections concerning their own social conflicts:

> The perverse, unredeemable nature created for Caliban within language is more than a strategy for justifying his enslavement . . . We also discern in it a displacement of disorder from within the dominant onto the subordinate. (111)

The stress on Caliban's savage nature serves to call for his enslavement, at the same time that it allows the dominant order to displace its own conflicts onto the dark Other.

3. This colonial projection of same-sex desire onto the dark native can take on both a hysterical and psychotic structure. In Prospero's case, there seems to be evidence of a hysterical splitting of the subject into an all-good white self and a repressed "dark" self.

4. This notion of the identification between two illicit desires supports Slavoj Žižek's claim that society is held together through perverse forms of illegal enjoyment (*Metastases* 54).

5. Freud's and Mannoni's stress on the repression of incestuous desire does not undermine my concentration on the repression of homosexual desire because early desires for the mother and the father often include strong same-sex desires.

6. For an extended discussion of the relationship between servitude and same-sex desire in the early modern period, see Digangi.

7. Following Zizek and Althusser, I will be defining ideology as an unconscious system of beliefs that help to shape subjectivity and desire. The subject's acceptance of diverse ideological systems helps us to account for the ways that desire is always the desire of the Other.

8. For an extended analysis of this relation between ideology and unconscious desire, see Žižek, *Sublime Object* 11–53.

9. By locating this production of ideological desire in the early modern period, we begin to see how the postmodern superego has its roots in a much earlier time period. This postmodern form of subjection is connected to the consumer culture's need for subjects to desire and to enjoy more and more unneeded products.

10. As Dollimore argues, the play functions by first constructing conflicts within the dominant culture and then displacing these problems onto subordinate groups. In Ferdinand's speech, we find the social conflicts between sport and work, poverty and wealth, and pleasure and labor. Throughout the play, these social binary oppositions will be displaced onto the opposition between the Europeans and the natives.

11. What fuels and supports the rigid binary logic of sadomasochistic sexual relations is a fundamental rejection of linguistic loss. To hide the presence of castration and nongendered desire, perverse sexists need to impose a rigid binary logic of structured difference.

12. I do not want to give the impression that I am blaming the victim here or arguing that one simply has to stop enjoying subjection in order to be free; rather, I am exploring the psychological forces that allow subjects to accept states of oppression.

13. In Sidney's *Astrophil and Stella*, one finds a constant eroticization of religious subjection: "I swear, my heart such one shall show to thee / That shrines in flesh so true a deity, / That, virtue, thou thy self shalt be in love" (4.12–14). In order to reconcile the opposition between his sensual will and his spiritual wit, this poet transforms his relationship with God into a sadomasochistic erotic experience. I believe that we can locate the birth of our own modern sense of subjectivity in this early modern conception of religious devotion. This type of subject is one whose subjectivity is defined by his or her acceptance of the power of a dominating Other (the Church, the Monarch, the Father). In other terms, subjectivity is born out of subjection.

14. From a psychoanalytic perspective, we can affirm that the subject of the unconscious never fully accepts the "imprinting" of culture by the Other.

15. What links linguistic castration and same-sex desire together for the subject is the way that both of these forces repressed into the unconscious. The threat of losing control to language is also attached in homophobic discourses to the fear of losing one's gendered identity through same-sex desires.

16. In *Male Subjectivity at the Margins*, Kaja Silverman argues that the dominant fiction that holds our society together is the equation of the penis with the phallus (15). This ideological equation allows for the derivation of sexual difference and the mediating role of the father in the resolution of the Oedipus complex (28). Furthermore, the fictional relationship between the penis and the phallus accounts for the ways that men (the penis) become controllers of (law) and social reality (33–34).

17. In order to work against this form of cynical prejudice, we must first explore the ways that the social structure shapes unconscious desires and the ways that unconscious desires help to determine social structures.

18. I want to stress the idea that the repression of same-sex desire and linguistic castration forces subjects to accept a fictional form of social discourse.

19. Lacan's stress on the Name-of-the-Father in the imposition of the dominant symbolic order connects the need for an articulate form of language with the power of patriarchal heterosexual control.

20. Greenblatt argues that Shakespeare himself can be identified with this colonial master of letters (24) and he cites Terence Hawkes in order to clarify this relationship between colonialism and writing: "The dramatist is metaphorically a colonialist. His art penetrates new areas of experience, his language expands the boundaries of our culture, and makes the new terri-

tory over in its own image" (24). Of course these acts of linguistic and cultural colonialism are founded on an ethnocentric disregard for the native's home culture and language. Furthermore, we can posit that one way that a writer makes the new world knowable is by playing on his or her own culture's deepest stereotypes, anxieties, and prejudices.

21. According to Luce Irigaray, feminine subjectivity, sexuality, and language are derived from this stress on the fluidity:

> Now if we examine the properties of fluids, we note that this "real" may well include, and in large measure, a physical reality that continues to resist adequate symbolization and/or signifies the powerlessness of logic to incorporate in its writing the characteristic features of nature. (10)

In the binary logic of this passage, Irigaray insists that femininity, fluids, the Real, and nature resist the logic of symbolization and reason.

Irigaray affirms that feminine discourse and existence must be thought of in other terms than in the mechanics of solids. She posits that femininity is "continuous, compressible, dilatable, viscous, conductible, diffusible. . . . That it is unending, potent, and impotent owing to its resistance to the countable . . . it is already diffuse 'in itself,' which disconcerts any attempt at static identification" (11). The resistance of the feminine for Irigaray is thus a resistance that is due to the viscous and flowing nature of feminine existence. But is this existence defined by the purely biological categories of sexual secretion and lactation or is Irigaray pointing to a nonbiological notion of fluidity?

It would seem that, in fact, Irigaray bases her notion of feminine fluids not on an extended biological metaphor, but rather on an analysis of feminine discourse. "And yet that woman-thing speaks. But not 'like,' 'the same,' not 'identical with itself' nor to any x, etc. Not a 'subject,' unless transformed by phallocratism. It speaks 'fluid'" (11). From this perspective, the flow of feminine discourse is due to the fluctuating and contradictory quality of a speech that has to mime the words of the Other, yet constitutes its presence in-between the lines and outside of them.

22. This feminization of the ship and storm has already been presented in *Othello*, where Desdemona declares: "That I did love the Moor to live with him / My downright violence and storm of fortunes / May trumpet to the world" (1.3.248–50). Later on in the play, Iago will pun on Desdemona's claim that her love is both a storm and trumpet by calling her a strumpet (prostitute).

23. Rubinstein points out that Shakespeare's usage of the terms monster and beast relates to the early modern conception of sodomy as a form of sex-

uality that threatens the distinctions among classes, religions, races, species (fish and man), and forms of sexuality (164).

24. Shakespeare's ingenious depiction of the bisexual and bilingual colonial native shows how Caliban represents the materialization of the colonialist's unconscious desire. Freud's theory of universal bisexuality posits that all subjects desire both sexes in their unconscious. Linked to this initial form of bisexuality, we also find a primary form of language that works by combining linguistic opposites together. In order for the dominant social order to maintain control, it must repress both bisexuality and bilingualism.

25. Mario Digangi posits that the homoerotic aspects of master and slave relations in the early modern period show how one of the only ways that a male servant could gain power over his master was through erotic manipulation (10).

26. In *Totem and Taboo*, Freud describes his theory of the primal horde:

> One day the brothers who had been driven out came together, killed and devoured their father and so made an end of the patriarchal horde. United, they had the courage to and succeeded in doing what would have been impossible for them individually. (141)

After this all-powerful primal father is killed, the sons become guilty and create the foundations for civilization:

> They revoked their deed by forbidding the killing of the totem, the substitute for the father; and they renounced its fruits by resigning their claim to the women who had now been set free. (143)

The subjects thus resolve their Oedipus complexes through the generation of a series of symbolic laws and identifications that will serve to regulate the desire of every subject.

27. After Ferdinand agrees to control his own lust and to keep his desire "chain'd below" until after the wedding, Ariel appears on the scene and asks Prospero "Do you love me master?" (4.1.47). Prospero responds: "Dearly, my delicate Ariel" (4.1.48). I would argue that this reemergence of homosexual desire represents a return of repressed libido that has been released through Ferdinand's acceptance of temporary celibacy.

28. Throughout *Totem and Taboo*, Freud clearly equates infantile sexuality, the unconscious, and primitive cultures.

29. Paul Brown posits that Gonzalo's political utopia is derived from Montaigne and "rehearse the standard formula by which the colonized is denigrated even as it appears to be simply the idle thoughts of a standard courtier" (56).

CHAPTER FIVE

1. One of the most powerful aspects of Shelley's work is the way that she links together the "masculine" activities of scientific discovery, colonial expansion, and literary creation.

2. For a detailed discussion of different feminist interpretations of *Frankenstein*, see Johanna Smith. Warren Montag has also read this text from a Marxist perspective.

3. In *The Ruling Passion: British Colonial Allegory and the Paradox of Homosexual Desire*, Christopher Lane sees homosexual desire as a force that threatens many national and colonial activities: "I am interested in a counterforce that shatters national allegory by introducing inassimilable elements of homosexual desire" (2). For my purposes, I am more concerned with the way that colonial projects are supported and fueled by the constant production and repression of same-sex desires.

4. I would suggest that Mary Shelley's incredible sensitivity to the problems of slavery and prejudice are in part connected to her feelings of enslavement to her own creative productions. In the Introduction to her novel, she declares that: "When I placed my head on my pillow, I did not sleep, nor could I be said to think. My imagination, unbidden, possessed and guided me" (22). Shelley thus presents herself as someone who cannot control the textual monster that she has created.

This Introduction also depicts the ways her husband Percy forced her to create a text so that he could judge and criticize her: "At this time he desired that I should write, not so much with the idea that I could produce any thing worthy of notice, but that he might himself judge how far I possessed the promise of better things hereafter" (20). Mary Shelley goes to great pains to point out here that her desire to write came from her husband and Lord Byron who constantly asked her each day if she had produced anything: "I felt that blank incapability of invention which is the greatest misery of authorship, when dull Nothing replies to our anxious invocations. Have you thought of a story? I was asked each morning" (22).

I believe that one of the reasons Mary Shelley became such an astute social critic was due to her awareness of being oppressed by male-dominated world, and in this sense she is herself the learned but rejected monster who, after all, is only searching for understanding and companionship.

5. One could respond to my interpretations of Walton's use of homoerotic language by arguing that I am simply projecting current understandings of same-sex relations onto a literary period that had a much different conception of same-sex friendships. Even if this argument is true it does not discount the ways that purely "Platonic" relations between men have always had to deal with the cultivation and repression of homosexual desire.

6. If Walton's quest to support the slave trade is indeed thrown off course by his homoerotic encounter with Victor, we do find a strong example of Lane's theory that same-sex desire can subvert colonial aspirations. However, it is unclear at the end of the novel what effect Walton's relationship with Victor will have on his imperial voyage.

7. In this passage, we find an early reference to race as as a source of interpersonal unity and as a distinguishing element between an out-group and an in-group. For a detailed history of this term, see Appiah.

8. To my knowledge, none of the filmic representations of this story have dealt with Walton's voyage nor Shelley's sustained discourse on slavery, racism, homosociality, and homosexuality.

9. My usage of homosociality is for the most part derived from Eve Sedgwick's *Between Men: English Literature and Male Homosocial Desire*. However, one of the major problems with Sedgwick's work is that she constantly places every psychosexual relationship within a triangular structure and thus ignores the role played by the fourth part of the structures that I have been articulating (21–27). Moreover, her usage of psychoanalytic theory tends to neglect the more subtle and interesting elements in Freud's theory. In particular, like many current theorists in Queer Theory and Gender Studies, Sedgwick develops a form of psychoanalytic criticism that functions without mentioning the role played by the unconscious. Without the presence of this disruptive internal force, there is very little possibility in positing a subjective agency that can resist the social circulation of power and erotic interest in the text that she examines. Sedgwick employs a structural model that is based on the early Lacan and Rene Girard's work on erotic triangles. These theories fail to take into account the role of the object (a) as a resistant element that prevents the smooth flowing of the dominant symbolic order.

10. Johanna Smith in the St. Martin's edition of *Frankenstein* argues that the females in this novel are constantly being represented as inferior beings, in terms of both class and intelligence, who need to be saved by the wealthy men in the text (281).

11. Freud argues that one of the conditions for certain male subjects to take a woman as a love-object is that they must be put in a position of saving their sexual Other: "The man is convinced that she is in need of him, that without him she would lose all moral control and rapidly sink to a lamentable level. He rescues her, therefore, by not giving her up" ("A Special Type" 234).

12. This aspect of rendering the female Other exotic and the male Other horrific is still at work in current mass media representations of foreign cultures and vacation destinations.

13. Johanna Smith stresses the idea that women in this novel, especially Elizabeth, function as objects that are exchanged between men in an economic and erotic way (283). For more on this theory of the circulation of

women as objects of exchange, see Gayle Rubin's groundbreaking text "The Traffic in Women: Notes Toward a Political Economy of Sex."

14. My stress on the relationship between racial and sexual idealization points to the need to combine gender studies and postcolonial studies within a psychoanalytic cultural criticism. Without this combination, many feminist interpretations are rendered incomplete and unsatisfying.

15. Freud's theory of the conditions of the love-object is extremely helpful in explaining the structure of Victor's desire. According to Freud, the typical male-subject only desires a woman who: (1) other men desire (232), (2) has a lower moral or class standing (233), (3) is a substitute for the man's mother, and (4) needs to be rescued.

16. In "On Narcissism," Freud argues that men look for narcissistic women to be their love-objects in order to recapture their own narcissism that they have previously lost (80–81).

17. One of the shortcomings of this brilliant insight by Freud is that it does not consider the way that this structure would effect a woman. In many ways, Mary Shelley's text allows us to complement and complete Freud's theory of the relationship between homosociality and homosexuality.

18. Victor's intense feelings of subjection and linguistic castration can be directly related to Mary Shelley's claim that she could not control the objects of her creation: "My imagination, unbidden, possessed and guided me . . . I opened my mind in terror. The idea so possessed my mind, that a thrill of fear ran through me" (22–23).

19. Victor's submission to the discourse of science should be connected to the growing dominance of a symbolic form of capitalism that submits all natural things and relations to an economic and mathematical calculation.

20. One of my arguments throughout this work has been that this psychological form of slavery that Victor and other subjects experience helps to allow for the justification of the institution of slavery. Moreover, by enslaving other subjects, the masochistic subject can escape from his or her own feelings of alienation and loss.

21. In "Lesbian Panic in Mary Shelley's *Frankenstein*," Fran Michel argues that Victor's homophobic panic can be associated with Mary Shelley's own panic in front of possible homoerotic relations between women (238). Michel posits that the monster is a representation of a female subject who is rejected from her society because of her appearance. The monster's desire to have a female partner is thus equated with a request for a lesbian relationship. According to this reading, it is this fear of lesbian desire that pushes Victor to refuse the monster's request: "And if this creature is like a woman here, he is specifically like a woman denied a female object of desire" (243).

Most of Michel's proof for this theory of lesbian panic in *Frankenstein* is derived from biographical information concerning Mary Shelley's mother and the books that she was reading. While I do not attempt this type of analysis in my work, I do believe that Michel's interpretation does serve to reinforce my stress on homophobia in this work.

22. This opposition between homosexual desire and heterosexual marriage is a constant theme in the homophobic discourses of Western culture. For a discussion of this opposition, see Michel 247–250.

23. For an analysis of the relationship between Mary Shelley and her family, see Shelley 3–18.

24. Mary's mother died ten days after giving birth to her and two of Mary's own children died in infancy (Shelley 9–10).

25. Warren Montag's Marxist reading of *Frankenstein* becomes blocked by its simple equation of the monster with the working class (303). While the monster may be a symbol of oppressed people, I do not think that his oppression is limited to an economic relationship.

26. One of the problems with Shelley's analysis of racism, classism, and sexism is that she tends to equate all forms of oppression. One of the goals of my work is to show how these different forms of prejudice are both different and related.

27. Like the other men in this novel, Felix attempts to save the woman that he loves. In Felix's case, this act of rescuing the female love-object also entails a desire to save her from her debased ethnic status.

28. These notions of alienation and separation are derived from Lacan's account of the psychoanalytic process (*Four Concepts* 203–43).

29. By connecting the monster's sexual desire to an internalized form of prejudice, Shelley depicts how diverse forms of oppression are accepted by subjects through their erotic attachments.

30. Many critics (Sedgwick, Rubin, Johanna Smith) have effectively tied homosociality to homophobia, misogyny, and nationalism; however, these same critics have often failed to take into account the role that racism plays in these structures.

31. The fact that most critics see Victor's relationship with the monster as a heterosexual one points to the heterosexism of many forms of literary criticism.

CHAPTER SIX

1. For an extended discussion of homosexual panic, see Sedgwick 83–96.

2. In his reading of Conrad's *Heart of Darkness*, Mark Bracher argues that most criticisms of this text have failed to take into account the diverse forms of desire, identification, fantasy, and sexual pleasure (jouissance) that

affect the readers of the novella (141). Bracher posits that many historicist and formalist interpretations tend to view textuality and ideology only in terms of knowledge and discourse, and thus they are unable to clarify the diverse modes of interpellation that occur between a text and a reader (140). Furthermore, he explores the ways that critics and other readers get locked into a mirroring relationship with the text that they are trying to analyze, and therefore they tend to repeat and reproduce the diverse forms of prejudice and oppression that they are trying to condemn (142).

One of the central elements that readers of Conrad's novella tend to reproduce is the call for the renunciation of diverse forms of sexual enjoyment (142). In Bracher's view, readers and critics are motivated by the text to sacrifice their own desires and sexual pleasures in order to identify with Kurtz's quest for complete knowledge and narcissistic closure (144). On the level of imaginary identification and homosocial ethnocentrism, critics become locked into an obsessional form of prejudice that is centered on the rhetorical use of irony and other distancing techniques: "Irony is the ultimate trope of ego-mastery, a favorite obsessional strategy for remaining free of all limitations or encumbrances" (145). In this type of ironic discourse, all experiences are contained through a play of knowledge that acknowledges its own failures, yet does this acknowledging on a purely intellectual level.

One can ague that in many forms of criticism, the egos of the reader and the critic are able to maintain a sense of mastery through this structure of discourse that rejects all unconscious drives and fantasies by judging everything in relation to a preestablished knowledge. Bracher uses this theory of obsessional irony in order to argue that Hillis Miller's reading of *Heart of Darkness:*

> allows readers to achieve a tacit final pronouncement of rejection in relation to their own unconscious drives and fantasies precisely while congratulating themselves on their open-minded, undogmatic attitude and their ability to resist closure because of the fact that they have refrained from any final pronouncement concerning the manifest content of the text. (145–46)

The key aspect to this obsessional form of literary criticism is the use of a discourse that separates affect from intellect, knowledge from desire, and textuality from political reality. The result of all of these divisions is an emergence of a profound sense of doubt that is one of the strongest symptoms of any obsessional discourse.

For Bracher, this cultivation of doubt and undecideability undercuts the possibility of critical and political activism. Furthermore, it is this obsessional type of knowledge that tends to dominate in what Lacan calls the discourse of the university. I now want to build on Bracher's argument by emphasizing the way that the cultural rejection of same-sex desire helps to determine the structure of both Conrad's text and different obsessional critical reading strategies.

3. Christopher Lane reads Conrad's *Victory* as a homosexual allegory that challenges the homosocial underpinnings of colonial exploration (99–125).

4. Young-Bruehl's description of the obsessional form of discourse and subjectivity is very helpful in understanding some of the psychological dynamics that structure many types of literary criticism and other modes of academic research. The old saying that "those who don't do—teach" displays this connection between passivity and the university discourse. Many academics work for tenure as a form of protection against any destabilizing forces that can threaten them and place them in a passive position. This fear of passivity may result in a constant need to anticipate, in an obsessional and intellectual way, any form of sexual and cultural difference.

5. We shall see how anal eroticism also establishes an erotic zone around a hole that threatens both bodily closure and narcissistic unity.

6. In *Totem and Taboo* Freud argues that the obsessional subject is plagued by doubt because he or she isattracted to what he or she rejects (28). This radical form of obsessional ambivalence is derived from the subject's early anal erotism and the later social condemnation of this form of sexual desire.

7. For more on this structure of obsessional circularity, see Samuels, *Between* 84–92.

8. For an extended discussion of Lacan's theory of the university discourse, see Bracher 54–59.

9. Bracher's theory of academic discourse helps us to link together the discourse of the university with the discourse of the obsessional: "a preconstituted knowledge remains the goal of such an education; hence, the student remains subordinated to a system of knowledge" (56). This submission to a preconstituted knowledge allows the obsessional subject the ability to anticipate his or her encounter with the Other.

10. Lacan does not equate the discourse of the university with the discourse of the obsessional. However, I believe that we can make this equivalence if we realize that the obsessional subject modifies the discourse of the university by transforming the object (a) into a narcissistic object of textual and bodily unity.

11. One of the difficulties in discussing Conrad's text is the multiple levels of narration. At the beginning of the story, we have a third-person narrator who narrates Marlow's story about his own experiences that have already

passed. This distancing technique is another key element to the obsessional discourse. As Lacan has argued, the obsessional is always elsewhere and always thinking about something else. By keeping a distance from his or her own experience, the obsessional subject wards off all threats of affective loss and castration.

12. As Freud and Young-Bruehl argue, this combination of passivity, disgust, and the fear of penetration all center around the subject's early experiences in trying to control his or her body in the process of toilet training.

13. Due to the fact that this notion of the bisexual primal scene of sodomy reverses many of the heterosexual paradigms of space and temporality, it is continuously being repressed and blocked from representation. However, we know from Freud's theory of the return of the repressed that nothing can be completely negated psychologically, and therefore we can expect an unconscious return of the repressed primal scene. The obsessional symptoms of doubt and brooding are indicative of this repression of the sexual knowledge regarding the bisexual primal scene.

14. Silverman stresses the multiple levels of identification and desire that can be derived from the fundamental fantasy and primal scene. "The primal scene fantasy opens onto both the positive heterosexual and the negative or homosexual versions of the Oedipus Complex . . . it promotes, in other words, desire for the father and identification with the mother, as well as desire for the mother and identification with the father" (165). Since the primal scene occurs for the subject before the recognition of sexual difference, Silverman posits that the initial forms of identification are fundamentally bisexual. In fact, she hints that the child participates in his parents' secret copulation as a third party who unconsciously would like to be penetrated by the father from behind while he also penetrates the mother. In this structure, the child presents, "the desire to be sodomized by the 'father' while occupying the place of the 'mother,' and the desire to sodomize him while he is penetrating the 'mother'" (173). Silverman combines both of these cross-gendered forms of desire under the rubric of "sodomitical identification" (174).

15. This passive masochistic position, of the one who looks but cannot act, dominates in many forms of academic discourse.

16. Johanna Smith argues that women are often placed in the position in this novel of being the ones who believe in the masculine colonial project (Conrad 177). Marlow's aunt and Kurtz's intended are portrayed as naive subjects who support their men no matter what. This sexist opposition between active, knowing men and passive, believing women is undermined by the masochistic passivity of Marlow and the narrator.

17. For an extended analysis of the relationship between the discourse of the university and the discourse of the master, see Bracher 58–59.

18. In many ways, our present postmodern culture is determined by this obsessional form of discourse where the signifying chains of the capitalist mass media are placed in the position of dominance. In this structure, there seems to be no masters and no one who can control the universalizing forces of the global economy and the spread of popular culture.

19. Bracher argues that most forms of cultural criticism function through this discourse of the University where "a preconstituted knowledge remains the goal" (56). In other terms, this obsessional form of discourse is based on the acceptance of a preestablished system of knowledge and understanding. The origins of this knowledge are no longer questioned; rather, the university subject is motivated to apply the tools and signifiers that have been previously developed by the discourse of the Master. One reason for this subject's acceptance of the preestablished forms of knowledge is that they offer a form of safety and predictability. Obsessional subjects use knowledge as a form of narcissistic anticipation that help them to avoid encountering their own subjective and bodily lacks.

20. Lane relates the presence of holes in Conrad's *Victory* to a state of abjection and disgust that a male subject feels toward his own desire (123).

21. Young-Bruehl posits that a key element to obsessional forms of prejudice is this dominance of ideas that the subject cannot control (211).

22. Marlow's superficial form of racism relates to the postmodern stress on the mass-mediated representation of the Other. As subject of a television culture, we are constantly watching images of cultural Others from a safe distance.

23. This period of toilet training and the mastery of the body represents one of the central ways that society controls subjects by introducing the factors of shame, disgust, and fear in relation to the anus.

24. Freud explains this transformation of faeces into money in the anal economy: "It is possible that the contrast between the most precious substance [gold, money] known to men and the most worthless, which they reject as waste matter (refuse), has led to this specific identification of gold with faeces" ("Character and Anal Eroticism" 214). This combination of extremes is based on Freud's notion that in the unconscious, and in the primary forms of language, all oppositions are collapsed.

25. There can be no one fixed point of interpellation in a text; rather, I am arguing that there are multiple points of identification that the reader is called to take on.

26. This passage also stresses the obsessional need of the writer to get the reader to see what he or she sees and thus form a bonding relation on the level of a shared vision.

27. Recent debates concerning the maintenance of a literary cannon are shaped by this desire to use literature as a source of individual and collective narcissism.

28. Smith connects imperialism to an act of rape of women and natives, but like most other critics she does not consider the possibility of a homosexual form of penetration and abuse (169–170).

29. For a detailed discussion concerning the debate over the racism of Conrad's novel, see Brantlinger.

30. In reading a text for clues to a repressed form of sexuality, we must take into special account the multiple meanings of words and phrases. For as Freud and Lacan have shown, the discourse of the unconscious presents itself through wordplay and the figurative aspects of metaphor and metonymy.

31. It is difficult to say whether Conrad really exposes this mechanism of displacement on purpose or whether this revelation results from an unconscious awareness of the processes that produce prejudice.

32. Conrad's stress on the "manly" reader calls into question the relationship between gender and reading. In this text, it appears that women are only treated as passive objects that are read by men and who are not given the opportunity to engage in the activity of critical reception.

33. In her discussion of obsessional agitators, Young-Bruehl posits that these types of prejudiced subjects "prefer radio . . . they are disembodied voices, and thus—in a delusional way—free of their bodies" (213). This pure voice of the obsessional is presented in Conrad's text through Kurtz's character.

34. Smith posits that Marlow needs to silence women because he equates them with the wildness of the jungle and the native population (174).

CHAPTER SEVEN

1. These connections between class and race allow us to see how slavery can be considered to be the repressed truth of American culture. For the slave economy was not just a simple extension of amoral capitalism; rather, slavery represents the coming together of patriarchy, racist hierarchies, and economic individualism. In other words, to explain the possibility and effects of slavery in American culture, we have to examine the ways that racism, sexism, and capitalism work together.

2. In a postmodern system, all relationships and representations are determined by universal symbolic discourses that undercut the intentionality of the individual subject. This new form of discourse is based on the universal spread of capitalism and the mass media. Slavoj Žižek has posited that in response to this universality of capitalism, there is a constant desire for subjects and nations to affirm their particular modes of enjoyment and identity

(*Awry* 162). The postmodern outbreak of ethnic nationalism can thus be tied to the capitalistic effacement of all forms of ethnic difference.

Žižek also connects the spread of postmodern capitalism to the dominance of the democratic theory of subjectivity:

> The subject of democracy is not a human person, "man" in all the richness of his needs, interests and beliefs. The subject of democracy, like the subject of psychoanalysis, is none other than the Cartesian subject in all its abstractions, the empty punctuality we reach after subtracting all its particular contents. (163)

By defining each subject in democracy without regard to their race, sex, religion, wealth, and social status, the democratic subject becomes nothing but an empty universal that has been voided of all particularities. In democracy, everyone is supposed to be equal in front of the law; yet, this equality serves to efface subjective and ethnic differences. In fact, Žižek argues that the democratic subject is equivalent to Lacan's notion of the barred subject (S) who has been effaced and transcended by the symbolic realm of law and language (163).

Faced with this democratic and capitalistic erasure of subjectivity and ethnic difference, the postmodern subject seeks out a pathological form of identity and difference:

> The national Cause is ultimately the way subjects of a given nation organize their collective enjoyment through national myths. What is at stake in ethnic tensions is always the possession of the national Thing: the "other" wants to steal our enjoyment (by ruining our "way of life") and/or it has access to some secret, perverse enjoyment. (165)

On a national level, subjects seek to undermine the postmodern loss of identity and difference by holding onto to national myths and particular forms of enjoyment. In this structure, the encounter with other cultures, races, and sexualities, is determined by a hysterical projection of repressed sexuality (the other has a secret access to a perverse form of enjoyment) or through the obsessional fear that the Other has invaded our body and nation and is now stealing our inner enjoyment.

Žižek adds that this pathological aspect of sexual enjoyment is the actual core and center of postmodern democracy and capitalism (166). Our ethnic and subjective enjoyments represent the surplus value that is extracted from the capitalist principles of equivalent exchange. In other terms, every fair deal or exchange is motivated out of the desire to get something extra from the Other. Moreover, this notion of surplus value is tied to every subject's particular fantasy or myth:

Fantasy is the absolutely particular way everyone of us structures his/her "impossible" relation to the traumatic Thing. It is the way every one of us, by means of an imaginary scenario, dissolves and/or conceals the fundamental impasse of the inconsistent big Other, the symbolic order. (167)

Žižek's notion of fantasy is equivalent here to Althusser's conception of ideology. Just as ideology serves to translate "real" economic relations into imaginary relations, fantasy serves to hide the conflicts and contradictions of the symbolic orders of democracy and capitalism by creating imaginary scenarios of reconciliation and pathological enjoyment.

3. In order to analyze the ways that a young girl can grow to hate her own race and existence, Morrison begins her novel by writing and rewriting the Dick and Jane educational primer (5–6). This text that celebrates the white nuclear family is spread throughout the novel in the same way that the ideology that equates whiteness to family unity is spread throughout our society. This initial primer shows how our educational system participates in the production of heterosexual, capitalistic, and ethnocentric desires.

4. One cannot overlook the importance of advertisements in the shaping of postmodern forms of subjectivity and sexuality. As Slavoj Žižek has pointed out, the postmodern subject is not told to repress his or her's sexuality and desire; rather, society now tells subjects that they must enjoy themselves in a certain way (*Metastases* 16–26).

5. Throughout the novel, the girls attempt to relate social events to natural occurrences: "We thought, at the time, that it was because Pecola was having her father's baby that the marigolds did not grow" (7). In other words, the lack of the growth of these virginal-golden flowers is tied to a scene of rape and incest that determines the "primal scene" of this novel. Morrison continues by introducing a double metaphor of blackness into the text: "We had dropped our seeds in our little plot of black dirt just as Pecola's father had dropped his seeds in his own plot of black dirt" (9). The obvious analogy that is set up in this sentence is between the planting of seeds into black dirt and a father's planting of his semen into his daughter. The insidious nature of this metaphorical expression is that it equates an evil act of incest with a innocent act of planting a flower. However, we know from the first paragraph that this type of metaphorical thinking is misguided and relates to the magical and melancholic thinking that pervades the youthful narrator and her sister.

I will argue that Morrison is here pointing to the pernicious effect of naturalized metaphors, at the same time that she highlights the way that no one can escape from their grip. In other words, even if we all know that there is very little connection between human actions and nature's reactions, we cannot stop using these metaphors because they are so central to the very way we think. What is also highlighted by these opening paragraphs is the way that certain racist metaphors are internalized by the people that they hurt the most. For it is clear that the narrator is equating her own dark body to a plot of dirt that others plant there seeds into, just as she mourns the loss of the celebrated marigolds.

6. Like the psychotic subject who rejects the symbolic only to have it return in the real through hallucinated perceptions, Baudry posits that movies confuse representations and real sensory experiences by collapsing temporal and spacial differences.

7. The characters that the black subjects in Morrison's novel idealize are always white people like Shirley Temple and Jean Harlow. Claudia resists this idealization of Shirley Temple:

> I couldn't join them in their adoration because I hated Shirley. Not because she was cute, but because she danced with Bojangles, who was my friend, my uncle, my daddy, and who ought to have been soft-shoeing it and chuckling with me. Instead he was enjoying, sharing, giving a lovely dance thing with one of those little white girls whose socks never slid under their heels. (19)

Once again, Claudia's dislike of this poplar culture idol is derived from her desire not to be white.

8. Throughout Morrison's novel, homosocial female relations are constantly circulated in the discourses of rumors, storytelling, and gossip.

9. The placement of the Breedloves in a storefront window functions like the television talk shows that put minorities on the air so they can confess all of their darkest sins and traumas. In this way, they become a public display of hatred and capital failure.

10. Currently, the African-American "welfare mother" often plays this role of the symbol of all of America's democratic failures.

11. Like Frantz Fanon, Morrison shows the importance of the imaginary aspects of racism and subjectivity. The white man's refusal to look at the black girl creates a situation where the imaginary mirror of self-reflection is undermined and the subject is left with a sense of self-negation.

12. This demarcation between the imaginary and the symbolic orders is not always easy to determine. In postmodernism, there is a constant reshaping of the imaginary by the symbolic forces of consumer capitalism.

13. In this postmodern world of destabilized identities, the fixation on race as a static visual object may cause an increase in this form of racism. In other terms, racial and sexual difference may provide for a desired form of static identity.

14. Pecola's desire to get rid of her own eyes is connected to her realization that other people do not like the way that she looks. In her delusional

state, she thus confuses her appearance (her look) with the look of the Other (193–204).

15. In her encounter with the white shop owner, it is the Other who first destroys the foundations of her subjectivity. In other terms, the collapse of her imaginary world is derived from an external force.

16. For an extended discussion of Freud's and Lacan's theories of psychosis and foreclosure see, Samuels 30–43.

17. In postmodern consumer culture, the name-of-the-father becomes transformed by the ethnocentric economic order. The foreclosure of this symbolic element can thus be connected to a rejection of economic castration.

18. The horror of real homelessness and excessive modes of enjoyment serve to police the activities of subjects in our current economic order.

19. In this structure, obsessional discourses represent a middle class attempt to escape from the lower-class psychotic state of sexual enjoyment and economic foreclosure.

20. Morrison's description of the middle-class subjects who have internalized racism in an obsessional way are structured by the same forces that produce obsessional anti-Semitism. For more on this connection, see Young-Bruehl 210–19.

21. This link between the unconscious equation of blackness to excrement allows us to see how negrophobia can replace or heighten homophobia. In both structures, we find the same fears of anal penetration and excessive sexuality.

22. In this structure, blackness becomes equated with the obsessional subject's repulsion and attraction to excrement.

23. As I have previously pointed out, Young-Bruehl argues that in racism, one finds a hysterical projection of unwanted desires onto a debased out-group. In this structure, the hysterical racist often shows a horror of interracial marriages, a fear of falling into a lower class, and an exaggerated fear of crime (219–30). I would like to stress that this form of prejudice is central to the psychology of the upper class. Young-Bruehl points to this connection between class and psychopathology when she writes:

Hysterical characters feel themselves to be more refined and less sexual than the people against whom their prejudices are directed. And it is always crucial to them that their others be lower, which means designated as coarse ones, the more sexual ones. (222)

In this structure, the lower class subjects play the role of expressing the upper classes' own rejected desires and fears. This form of hysterical racism is thus founded on the strict differences that are generated between different socioeconomic groups. As in Bahktin's theories of the grotesque and the carnivalesque, the "low" in this model becomes the symbol of the lower class and the lower parts of the body.

Young-Bruehl also relates sexual location to class location in the following passage:

> The object of hysterical character's prejudices are—in one way or another, literally or symbolically—domestics . . . Prejudiced hysterical characters find it necessary to have servants—and these come from the lower classes or from groups that have been acquired as slaves or servants, or, in colonial contexts. (222)

This theory helps us to see the psychosexual foundations of class-based forms of racism. For the hysterical master, the Other is both an object of control and of displaced sexual desire. In Morrison's text, it is Soaphead Church who best represents the internalization of this hysterical form of racism.

24. For a detailed description of the discourse of the hysteric, see Bracher 65–68.

25. As Bracher argues, the discourse of the hysteric displays the subject's alienation that results from being subjected to the dominant realm of language (66). In the case of a subject that is born into a racially divided social system, the alienation in language is doubled by the alienation in a dominant ethnic or racial order.

26. In the context of Soaphead's family, Morrison adds that this forced form of white noble identity is coupled with a hysterical desire to transgress the law through privilege: "That they were corrupt in public and private practice, both lecherous and lascivious, was considered their noble right, and thoroughly enjoyed by most of the less gifted population" (168). As in Young-Bruehl's discussion of the upper-class hysterical racist, Soaphead's father and his siblings all partake in the sexual enjoyment of the lower classes while maintaining a sense of social and racial superiority.

27. In many perverse sexual relationships, there is an intense desire for each subject to play the role of either the aggressive actor (sadist) or passive receiver (masochist). This strict binary logic is often performed by the role-playing of different symbolic social stereotypes. One dresses up like a cop, a nun, or a fascist, in order to clearly indicate what side of the binary opposition one is performing. The clearest example of this is in transvestite practices where one takes on a gender position by exaggerating certain stereotypical roles. While some critics have argued that this type of gender performance is liberating because it shows the constructed nature of all gender formations, I have been arguing that it is often oppressive because it unconsciously reiterates rigid social definitions of identity.

28. Freud posits that one of the reasons why perverse subjects have to posit and then transgress the law of the Other is that perversion represents an attempt to move beyond the neurotic sense of shame, guilt, and morality (*Three Essays* 109).

29. For the study of prejudices, this theory of the fetishism implies that in the perverse formations of racism and sexism, what has to be revealed is the denial of castration and the unconscious fantasy that disavows the differences between genders and races. In other words, the criticism of racist and sexist statements made by perverse subjects may only serve to increase their prejudices if the unconscious core of sameness is not first attacked. For perverse subjects have split their symbolic knowledge off from their unconscious fixation on sexual and racial sameness, and this means that educational attempts will not succeed if they are not directed toward the subject's unconscious.

30. Like many other perverse social scientists, Soaphead believes that "to name an evil was to neutralize if not annihilate it" (164). This form of overcoming sin is based in part on the misrecognition of the psychotherapeutic process. Soaphead believes that if he can "religiously" name his unconscious desires, they will simply go away. This of course is not the case, and his religious depiction of his debased needs only serves to strengthen their hold over his weak ego: "He believed that since decay, vice filth, and disorder were pervasive, they must be in the Nature of Things. Evil existed because God had created it" (172). This reasoning is very similar to the Marquis de Sade who argued that his perverse desires were merely following Nature's evil plan. For more on this connection between Sade and Lacan's concept of perversion, see *Kant avec Sade.*

31. Lacan stresses the idea that in perversion, the sadist is only the instrument of the Other's will ("Kant avec Sade" 773).

32. The light on Cholly's behind gives this whole scene the sense that it is part of a movie or a forced form of popular culture that demonizes black sexuality.

33. I am using this term "over-come" in order to stress the sexual enjoyment (coming) that the perverse subject derives from transcending the will of the Other.

34. For this perverse masculine African-American subject, the failure to attain any standard of white beauty results in a desire to repeat the white male's subjection of his disempowered Other. Cholly's repetition of the scene of castration is thus reworked through a racial order that idealized whiteness and debases blackness. Due to the emasculation of black men and the abuse of black women during the periods of slavery and segregation, we can posit that this model is both historical and psychosexual. In Cholly's case,

since he feels that he cannot overcome the power of his white oppressors, he displaces his anger and humiliation onto his hopeless daughter and his crippled wife.

35. I do not want to give the impression that I am blaming the victim in my discussions of internalized racism; rather, I want to articulate some of the psychoanalytic causes for the internalization and the maintenance of states of oppression.

36. From clinical experience we know that in perverse scenarios, abstract symbolic codes and contracts are materialized through the different role-playing of the participants. Thus, a sadist will materialize the presence of abstract symbolic law by wearing a police uniform and donning handcuffs, just as the masochistic subject will prove their submission by wearing a dog collar and chains. Mrs. Breedlove does not dress up in this way, but she does gain a sense of self and grandeur by being beaten up by her husband in a ritualized fashion.

37. For a detailed discussion of the discourse of the master, see Bracher 59–65.

CHAPTER EIGHT

1. In this chapter, I will not be developing an exhaustive interpretation of Morrison's text; rather, I will concentrate on the possible effects and strategies of her writing about prejudice.

2. Throughout this chapter, I will use the term "real" to indicate a state of existence that resists all forms of symbolization.

3. Žižek also discusses some of the negative forces that hold a community together through his theory of the perverse superego: "Explicit, public rules do not suffice, so they have to be supplemented by a clandestine 'unwritten' codes" (55). These unwritten codes often take the form of socially accepted acts of violence (i.e., gay bashing, lynching, hazing).

4. Debates concerning welfare mothers, inner-city crime, Ebonics, and affirmative action are often based on this double fear of excessive sexuality and linguistic loss that is projected onto African-Americans.

5. In *Playing in the Dark,* Morrison argues that in American literature and culture, African-Americans have played the role of defining the dominant group's sense of freedom, individuality, isolation, and mastery (5).

6. For an excellent discussion of the relation between the Holocaust and different theories of language and history, see LaCapra.

7. As I have been arguing, postmodernism can be tied to this inability of any master signifier to ground the endless proliferation of knowledge and technology.

8. One reason the trauma of slavery did not produce the same post-modern reaction that the Holocaust did is the fact that slavery has only recently been seen as a calling into question of the dominant Eurocentric order of subjectivity and representation.

9. In his introduction to *The New Historicist Reader,* H. Aram Veeser delineates three major aspects of New Historicism:

> 1. The idea that ideology positions readers as subjects—black middle-class post-colonial lesbians, working-class second-generation Italian-American heterosexual marxist—called a virtual halt to the practice of speaking as if for a common humanity; 2. Foucault's Knowledge/Power fusion gave intellectuals confidence that their knowledge had power, but the power source—housed in oppressive institutions—clamped down on their subversive desires to promote cultural change; 3. Dialogism, also acknowledged that conflict defines social interactions. (2–3)

The decentering of the dominant white male subject, the relation between power and discourse, and the stress on dialogism are all central aspects of African-American literature.

10. Valerie Smith has examined this question of the relation between representation and experience. She stresses the fact that our histories are always representational and narrative, yet she does not want to lose the possibility of presenting real bodies and real facts (343). I would like to argue that Morrison is able to effectively negotiate this binary opposition between real experience and symbolic representations by constantly reminding the reader of the limits of all forms of representation at the same time that she stresses both the materiality of language and the sensuality of memory.

11. The materiality and sensuality of Morrison's language can be located in her stress on the aural aspects of words and her constant attempt to show the material presence of forms of representation. For example, the scars on Sethe's back become a material mode of writing that other characters try to read.

12. For an extended analysis of the limits and possibilities of slave narratives and histories, see the Introduction to Charles Davis and Henry Louis Gates, Jr., *The Slave's Narrative* (i–xxxiii).

13. For a discussion of the problematics of narration in relation to slave narratives, see Spillers 25–61.

14. Lacan also defines the real as that which always returns to the same place (*Seminar II* 238).

15. In his introduction to *Slavery and the Literary Imagination*, Arnold Rampersad argues that slavery, "is the American heart of darkness, the historic national sin that no holy water will ever wash away, the stony fact that

denies many claims about the purpose of the historic American experiment"
(vii–vii). I would add to this argument the idea that if the postmodern period
is in part defined by the importation and the domination of the "American
way of life," this also entails that the buried history of slavery has been ex-
ported to other industrialized nations that may not have participated directly in the slave trade.

   16. For a similar account of the relationship between slavery and writing on the body, see Goodman 313–30.

   17. The call for a communal reading of *Beloved* has recently been made
by April Lindsky 191–216.

   18. Robert Broad argues that St. Paul's statement in the Bible represents
a rewriting of the prophet Hosea's speech in the old testament (194).
Furthermore, Broad shows how Hosea's story is indeed relevant to
Morrison's narration, by citing the following passage from the Hebrew
Bible:

> And the numbers of the sons of Israel will be like the sand on the
> seashore, which cannot be measured or counted. In the place
> where they were told, "You are no people of mine," they will be
> called, "The sons of the living God" . . . To your brother say,
> "People-of-mine," to your sister, "Beloved." (Hosea 3:1–3)

I believe that this reference to the inability of counting the number of the
sons of Israel can be related to Morrison's statement concerning the "Sixty
Million or More." The "More" here is an indication of the limits of all
forms of representation and Morrison's desire to go beyond traditional
forms of language to speak about her people.

   Broad adds that: "What Hosea presents here is nothing less than a vision of cultural renaissance, the climatic moment of a people's reclaiming its
greatness, reclaiming itself" (194). I would like to broaden Broad's interpretation by arguing that Morrison is asking all Americans, not only African-
Americans, to claim the greatness of the people lost in the Middle Passage.

   19. As we have seen in *The Bluest Eye,* cultural narcissism and the idealization of the Beloved most often entails a celebration of whiteness and
debasement of other ethnicities and races.

   20. Morrison's text functions by inverting the psychocultural structures
of desire and prejudice that I have been analyzing throughout this work.

   21. Freud develops his theories of psychotic projection and animism in
Totem and Taboo, where he argues that in both of these instances, "internal
perceptions of emotional and intellectual processes can be projected out-
ward in the same way as sense perceptions" (64). In the case of animism, this
form of projection entails the confusion between inner evil impulses toward
a recently deceased person and the intentions of demons:

> The fact that demons are always regarded as the spirits of those who have died recently shows better than anything the influence of mourning on the origin of the belief in demons . . . a dearly loved relative at the moment of his death changes into a demon, from whom his survivors can expect nothing but hostility and against whose evil desires they must protect themselves. (65)

This description of the spiritual return of the lost love-object, can be easily applied to Morrison's use of the figure of beloved, who certainly does harbor evil desires.

22. In his first seminar, Lacan argues that the real is itself most prevalent in the form of a hallucination; "The real, or that which is perceived as such, is what resists symbolization absolutely. In the end, doesn't the feeling of the real reach its high point in the pressing manifestation of an unreal, hallucinatory reality" (66–67). From this perspective, one could argue that by presenting Beloved in the form of a hallucination, Morrison is able to provide a real "pressing manifestation" of the sixty million or more who died in the Middle Passage.

23. Iyunolu Osagie has argued that there are different forms of psychoanalysis and that only a community-oriented form of analysis is appropriate for a reading of a text like *Beloved.*

24. In her book *Bearing the Dead,* Esther Schor argues that our current psychological culture has lost the ability to mourn loss on a communal level: "Whereas a psychological account interprets mourning as a discourse between the living and the (imagined) dead, a cultural account interprets mourning as a discourse among the living" (3).

25. For a critique of the white, male-dominated structure of Modernism, see Linda Hutcheon 23–29 and Marshall 181.

26. I will posit that the poststructuralist critique and deconstruction of the unitary subject can be seen as the first stage to the development of a multicultural form of discourse. In other words, before the repressed and rejected voices of Other cultures and minority groups could emerge, the repressing and dominant white, male subject had to be called into question.

27. Lacan's theory of the barred subject is presented in *The Four Fundamental Concepts of Psychoanalysis,* 141–42, 209.

28. Lacan insists that this placement of the unconscious in a position of subjective blindness rules out the possibility of any form of self-analysis. In order for subjects to read their own unconscious, they must enter into a dialectic with someone else.

29. Some people may say that this lack of stability and grounding in postmodern writing serves to upset any attempt at taking a political or ethical stance. I would like to counter this claim by arguing that the diffusion of

power and the instability of meaning and subjectivity are historical facts that cannot be denied, and in fact, they help to open up a space for other voices that have been traditionally oppressed and repressed. In other words, the destruction of the unitary self is the first step in the construction and affirmation of the multiplicity of the Other.

31. By forcing readers to accept their own sense of linguistic castration, Morrison undermines many of the academic attempts to use literature in order to displace subjective and social problems into the distant realm of another culture or people.

32. Valerie Smith also reads Morrison's repeated phrase, "This is not a story to pass on," as an ironic and doubled reference to both the forgetting and the remembering of slavery (353).

33. We can read the repeated address of 124 Bluestone as an indication of the 3 that is missing between the 2 and the 4. This 3 indicates a form of Oedipal resolution that degenders the role of the intervening third party.

Works Cited

Appiah, Kwame Anthony. "Racisms." *Anatomy of Racism*. Ed. David Theo Goldberg. Minneapolis: U of Minnesota P, 1990. 3–17.

Bakhtin, Mikhail. *Problems in Dostoyevsky's Poetics*. Trans. Carol Emerson. Minneapolis: Minnesota UP, 1984.

———. *Rabelais and His World*. Trans. Helene Iswolsky. Bloomington: Indiana UP, 1984.

Barry, Peter. *Beginning Theory: An Introduction to Literary and Cultural Theory*. New York: Manchester UP, 1995.

Barthelemy, Anthony. *Black Race, Maligned Race*. Baton Rouge: Louisiana State UP, 1987.

Baudry, Jean-Louis. "The Apparatus: Metaphysical Approaches to the Impression of Reality in Cinema." *Narrative, Apparatus, Ideology*. Ed. Phil Rosen. New York: Columbia UP, 1986. 299–318.

Bell, Bernard. "Introduction: Clarence Major's Double Consciousness as a Black Postmodernist Artist." *African American Review* 28.1 (1994): 5–9.

Bhabha, Homi. *The Location of Culture*. New York: Routledge, 1994.

Bloom, Harold, ed. *Modern Critical Interpretations: William Shakespeare's Sonnets*. New York: Chelsea House, 1987.

Booth, Stephen. *Shakespeare's Sonnets*. New Haven: Yale UP, 1977.

Bracher, Mark. *Lacan, Discourse, and Social Change: A Psychoanalytic Cultural Criticism*. Ithaca: Cornell UP, 1993.

Brantlinger, Patrick. "*Heart of Darkness*: Anti-Imperialism, Racism, or Impressionism." *Case Studies in Contemporary Criticism: Heart of Darkness*. Ed. Ross C Murfin. New York: St. Martin's, 1996. 277–98.

Broad, Robert. "Giving Blood to the Scraps: History, Haints, and Hosea in *Beloved*." *African American Review* 28.2 (1994): 189–96.

Brown, Paul. "'This Thing of Darkness I Acknowledge Mine': *The Tempest* and the Discourse of Colonialism." *Political Shakespeare: Essays in Cultural Materialism*. Ed. Jonathan Dollimore and Alan Sinfield. Ithaca: Cornell UP, 1994. 48–71.

Cohen, Thomas. *Anti-Mimeses from Plato to Hitchcock*. Cambridge: Cambridge University, 1994.

Collings, David. "The Monster and the Imaginary Mother: A Lacanian Reading of *Frankenstein*." *Case Studies in Contemporary Criticism: Frankenstein*. New York: St. Martin's, 1995. 245–58.

Conrad, Joseph. *Case Studies in Contemporary Criticism: Heart of Darkness*. Ed. Ross C. Murfin. New York: St. Martin's, 1996.

Davis, Charles T., and Henry Louis Gates, Jr., eds. *The Slave's Narrative*. New York: Oxford UP, 1985.

Dean, Tim. "Bodies that Mutter: Rhetoric and Sexuality." *PRE/TEXT* 15.1–2 (1994): 81–117.

Derrida, J., *Margins of Philosophy*. Trans. Alan Bass. Chicago: U of Chicago P, 1982.

———. *Writing and Difference*. Trans. Alan Bass. Chicago: U of Chicago P, 1978.

Digangi, Mario. "Asses and Wits: The Homoerotics of Mastery in Satiric Comedy." *English Literary Renaissance* 25 (1995): 179–208.

Doane, Mary Ann. *Femmes Fatales: Feminism, Film Theory, Psychoanalysis*. New York: Routledge, 1991.

Dollimore, Jonathan. *Sexual Dissidence: Augustine to Wilde Freud to Foucault*. New York: Oxford UP, 1991.

Dollimore, Jonathan and Alan Sinfield, eds. *Political Shakespeare: Essays in Cultural Materialism*. Ithaca: Cornell UP, 1994.

Douglass, Frederick. *Narrative of the Life of Frederick Douglass, An American Slave*. New York: Viking Penguin, 1982.

Drakakis, John, ed. *Alternative Shakespeares*. New York: Methuen, 1985.

Du Bois, W. E. B. *The Souls of Black Folk*. Greenwich: Fawcett Publications, 1961.

Edelman, Lee. "Seeing Things: Representation, the Scene of Surveillance, and the Spectacle of Gay Male Sex." *inside/out: Lesbian Theories, Gay Theories*. Ed. Diana Fuss. New York: Routledge, 1991. 93–118.

Fanon, Frantz. *Black Skin, White Masks*. Trans. Charles Lam Markmann. New York: Grove, 1967.

Fineman, Joel. *Shakespeare's Perjured Eye: The Invention of Poetic Subjectivity in the Sonnets*. Berkeley: U of California P, 1986.

———. "The Sound of O in *Othello*: The Real of the Tragedy of Desire." *The Subjectivity Effect in Western Literature*. Cambridge: MIT Press, 1991. 143–64.

Foucault, Michel. *History of Sexuality: Volume I*. Trans. Robert Hurley. New York: Pantheon, 1978.

Freud, Sigmund. "A Child Is Being Beaten." *Freud: On Psychopathology*. New York: Penguin, 1987.

————. *Beyond the Pleasure Principle*. New York: W. W. Norton, 1961.

————. "Character and Anal Erotism." *Freud: On Sexuality* New York: Penguin, 1977. 205–16.

————. *Civilization and its Discontents*. *Freud: Civilization, Society and Religion*. New York: Penguin, 1985.

————. *The Ego and the Id*. New York: W. W. Norton, 1960.

————. "Fetishism." *Freud: On Sexuality*. New York: Penguin, 1977. 345–58.

————. *Group Psychology and the Analysis of the Ego*. New York: W. W. Norton, 1959.

————. "Instincts and Their Vicissitudes." *General Psychological Theory*. New York: Collier, 1963. 83-103.

————. *The Interpretation of Dreams*. New York: Avon, 1965.

————. "Mourning and Melancholia." *General Psychological Theory*. New York: Collier Books, 1963.

————. "Negation." *General Psychological Theory*. New York: Collier Books, 1963.

————. "Notes Upon a Case of Obsessional Neurosis." *Three Case Histories*. New York: Collier, 1963. 15–102.

————. "On Narcissism: An Introduction." *General Psychological Theory*. New York: Collier, 1963. 56–82.

————. "On the Transformation of Instinct as Exemplified in Anal Erotism." *Freud: On Sexuality*. New York: Penguin, 1977. 293–303.

————. "On the Universal Tendency to Debasement in the Sphere of Love." *Freud: On Sexuality*. New York: Penguin Books, 1977. 243–60.

————. "Psychoanalytic Notes Upon an Autobiographical Account of a Case of Paranoia (Dementia Paranoides)." *Three Case Histories*. New York: Collier, 1963.

————. "Some Psychical Consequences of the Anatomical Differences Between the Sexes." *Freud: On Sexuality*. New York: Penguin, 1977. 323–44.

————. "A Special Type of Choice of Object Made by Men." *Freud: On Sexuality*. New York: Penguin, 1977. 227–42.

————. *Three Essays on the Theory of Sexuality*. New York: Basic Books, 1962.

————. *Totem and Taboo*. New York: Collier, 1963.

Gilroy, Paul. "One Nation under a Groove: The Cultural Politics of 'Race' and Racism in Britain." *Anatomy of Racism*. Ed. David Theo Goldberg. Minneapolis: U of Minnesota P, 1990. 263–82.

Goldberg, Jonathan. *Sodometries: Renaissance Texts, Modern Sexualities*. Stanford: Stanford UP, 1992.

Goodman, Anne E. "I Made the Ink: (Literary) Production and

Reproduction in Dessa Rose and *Beloved.*" *Feminist Studies* 16.2 (1990): 313–30.

Greenblatt, Stephen. *Learning to Curse: Essays in Early Modern Culture.* New York: Routledge Press, 1992.

———. *Renaissance Self-Fashioning.* Chicago: U of Chicago P, 1980.

Greene, Gayle. "'This That You Call Love': Sexual and Social Tragedy in *Othello.*" *Shakespeare and Gender.* Ed. Deborah Barker and Ivo Kamps. New York: Verso, 1995. 47–62.

Hall, Kim. *Things of Darkness: Economies of Race and Gender in Early Modern England.* Ithaca: Cornell UP, 1995.

Henderson, Mae. "Toni Morrison's *Beloved:* Re-membering the Body as Historical Text." *Comparative American Identities: Race, Sex, and Nationality in the Modern Text.* Ed. Hortense Spillers. New York: Routledge, 1991.

Holton, Robert. "Sexuality and Social Hierarchy in Sidney and Rochester." *Mosaic* 24 (1991): 47–65.

Hutcheon, Linda. *The Politics of Postmodernism.* New York: Routledge, 1989.

Jacobs, Harriet. *Incidents in the Life of a Slave Girl.* Cambridge: Harvard UP, 1987.

Kellner, Doug. *Postmodernism/Jameson/ Critique.* Washington: Maisonneuve, 1989.

Lacan, Jacques. *Ecrits.* Paris: Editions du Seuil, 1966.

———. *Ecrits: A Selection.* Trans. Alan Sheridan. New York: W. W. Norton, 1977.

———. "Kant Avec Sade." *Ecrits.* Paris: Editions du Seuil, 1966. 765–90.

———. *Seminar I: Freud's Papers on Technique.* Trans. John Forrester. Ed. Jacques-Alain Miller. New York: W. W. Norton, 1988.

———. *Seminar II: The Ego in Freud's Theory and in the Technique of Psychoanalysis.* Trans. Sylvana Tomaselli. Ed. Jacques-Alain Miller. New York: W. W. Norton, 1988.

———. *Seminar VII: The Ethics of Psychoanalysis.* Trans. Denis Porter. Ed. Jacques-Alain Miller. New York: W. W. Norton, 1988.

———. *Seminar XI: The Four Fundamental Concepts of Psychoanalysis.* Trans. Alan Sheridan. Ed. Jacques-Alain Miller. New York: W. W. Norton, 1977.

LaCapra, Dominick. *Representing the Holocaust: History, Theory, Trauma.* Ithaca: Cornell UP, 1994.

Lane, Christopher. *The Ruling Passion: British Colonial Allegory and the Paradox of Homosexual Desire.* Durham: Duke UP, 1995.

Mannoni, Octave. *Prospero and Caliban: The Psychology of Colonization.* New York: Praeger, 1964.

Marshall, Brenda. *Teaching the Postmodern: Fiction and Theory.* New York: Routledge, 1992.

McCulloch, Jock. *Black Soul White Artifact: Fanon's Clinical Psychology and Social Theory.* Cambridge: Cambridge UP, 1983.

McLaren, Peter. "Multiculturalism and the Post-Modern Critique: Toward a Pedagogy of Resistance and Transformation." *Between Borders: Pedagogy and the Politics of Cultural Studies.* Eds. Henry Giroux and Peter McLaren. New York: Routledge, 1994. 192–224.

Michel, Fran. "Lesbian Panic and Mary Shelley's *Frankenstein.*" *GLQ: A Journal of Gay and Lesbian Studies* 2:3 (1995): 237–52.

Montag, Warren. "'The Workshop of Filthy Creation': A Marxist Reading of *Frankenstein. Studies in Contemporary Criticism: Frankenstein.* New York: St. Martin's, 1995. 300–11.

Morrison, Toni. *The Bluest Eye.* New York: Penguin, 1970.

———. *Beloved.* New York: Penguin, 1988.

———. "Black Matter(s)." *Grand Street* 10:4 (1991): 205–25.

———. *Playing in the Dark: Whiteness and the Literary Imagination.* New York: Vintage, 1992.

———. "Unspeakable Things Unspoken: The Afro-American Presence in American Literature." *Michigan Quarterly Review* 28 (Winter 1989): 1–34.

Newman, Karen. "'And Wash the Ethiope White': Femininity and the Monstrous in *Othello.*" *Fashioning Femininity and the English Renaissance.* Chicago: U. of Chicago P, 1991.

Nicholson, Linda, ed. *Feminism/Postmodernism.* New York: Routledge, 1989.

Osagie, Iyunolu. "Is Morrison Also Among the Prophets?: " 'Psychoanalytic' " Strategies in *Beloved.*" *African American Review* 28.3 (1994): 423–40.

Pequigney, Joseph. *Such Is My Love: A Study of Shakespeare's Sonnets.* Chicago: U of Chicago P, 1985.

Rampersad, Arnold. *Slavery and the Literary Imagination.* Baltimore: Johns Hopkins UP, 1989.

Rubin, Gayle. "The Traffic in Women: Notes Toward a Political Economy of Sex." *Toward an Anthropology of Women.* Ed. Rayna Reiter. New York: Monthly Review, 1975. 157–210.

Rubinstein, Frankie. *A Dictionary of Shakespeare's Puns and Their Significance.* New York: St. Martin's, 1989.

Samuels, Robert. *Between Philosophy and Psychoanalysis: Lacan's Reconstruction of Freud.* New York: Routledge, 1993.

Schor, Esther. *Bearing the Dead.* Princeton: Princeton UP, 1994.

Sedgwick, Eve Kosofsky. *Between Men: English Literature and Male Homosocial desire.*

Shakespeare, William. *Othello.* Ed. David Horne. New Haven: Yale UP, 1955.

———. *The Tempest.* Ed. David Horne. New Haven: Yale UP, 1955.

Shelley, Mary. *Studies in Contemporary Criticism: Frankenstein.* Ed. Johanna M. Smith. New York: St. Martin's, 1995.

Sidney, Philip. *Astrophil and Stella.* New York: Anchor Books, 1967.

Silverman, Kaja. *The Acoustic Mirror: The Female Voice in Psychoanalysis and Cinema.* Bloomington: Indiana UP, 1988.

———. *Male Subjectivity at the Margins.* New York: Routledge, 1992.

———. *The Threshold of the Visible World.* New York: Routledge, 1996.

Singh, Jyotsna Singh. "Othello's Identity, Postcolonial Theory, and Contemporary African Rewritings of Othello." *Women, "Race," and Writing in the Early Modern Period.* Eds. Margo Hendricks and Patricia Parker. New York: Routledge, 1994. 287–99.

Smith, Bruce. *Homosexual Desire in Shakespeare's England.* Chicago: U of Chicago P, 1991.

Smith, Johanna. "'Cooped Up': Feminine Domesticity in *Frankenstein.*" *Studies in Contemporary Criticism: Frankenstein.* Ed. Johanna M. Smith. New York: St. Martin's, 1995. 270–85.

———. "'Too Beautiful Together': Ideologies of Gender and Empire in *Heart of Darkness.*" *Case Studies in Contemporary Criticism: Heart of Darkness.* Ed. Ross C. Murfin. New York: St. Martin's, 1996. 169–84.

Smith, Valerie. "'Circling the Subject': History and Narrative in *Beloved.*" *Toni Morrison: Critical Perspectives Past and Present.* Eds. Henry Louis Gates, Jr. and K. A. Appiah. New York: Amistad, 1993. 342–55.

Spillers, Hortense. "Changing the Letter: The Yokes, The Jokes of Discourse, or, Mrs. Stowe, Mr. Reed." *Slavery and the Literary Imagination.* Eds. Deborah E. McDowell and Arnold Rampersad. Baltimore: Johns Hopkins UP, 1989. 25–61.

Stallybrass, Peter. "Patriarchal Territories: The Body Enclosed." *Rewriting the Renaissance: The Discourse of Sexual Difference in Early Modern Europe.* Eds. Margaret Ferguson, Maureen Quillligan, and Nancy Vickers. Chicago: U of Chicago P, 1988.

Taylor-Gutherie, Danille (ed.). *Conversations with Toni Morrison.* Jackson: UP of Mississippi, 1994.

Traub, Valerie. *Desire and Anxiety: Circulations of Sexuality in Shakespearean Drama.* New York: Routledge, 1992.

Turner, Victor. *Dramas, Fields, Metaphors.* Ithaca: Cornell UP, 1974.

Veeser, H. Aram. *The New Historicist Reader.* New York: Routledge, 1994.

Williams, Sherley Anne. *Dessa Rose.* New York: Berkeley, 1986.

Wyatt, Jean. "Giving Body to the Word: The Maternal Symbolic in Toni Morrison's *Beloved*." *PMLA* 108:3 (1983): 474–88.

Young-Bruehl, Elisabeth. *The Anatomy of Prejudice*. Cambridge: Harvard UP, 1996.

Žižek, Slavoj. *Looking Awry*. Cambridge: MIT P, 1992.

———. *The Metastases of Enjoyment: Six Essays on Woman and Causality*. New York: Verso, 1994.

———. *The Sublime Object of Ideology*. New York: Verso, 1989.

———. *Tarrying with the Negative: Kant, Hegel, and the Critique of Ideology*. Durham: Duke UP, 1993.

Index